PRAISE FOR *TAPS*

"A classic, luxuriant Southern novel." —*New York*

"Filled with gritty, offbeat characters, the book is a sweet, magnolia-scented farewell from a man who embraced life." —*Town & Country*

"The best things in *Taps* are the backgrounds: long summer evenings with children playing out late, a winter ice storm with automobiles sliding and colliding like dodge-'em cars at a carnival . . . Morris's passion to convey the South's character and its past is evident and at times moving . . . *Taps* recounts a Mississippi place and time—the 1950s—with steady soulfulness." —*New York Times Book Review*

"An engaging and thoughtful novel set in the fictional town of Fisk's Landing . . . Willie Morris's language rings with poetry and meaning . . . *Taps* is just one more good reason why Willie Morris will be so deeply missed." —*Southern Living*

"The chief pleasure of *Taps* is his beautiful, melancholy way with language, a kind of minor key wistfulness that sings and sighs and elicits ineffable, sad, yet sweet feelings." —*Arkansas Democrat-Gazette*

"If William Faulkner and Flannery O'Connor are the twin deities of contemporary Southern literature, Willie Morris, who died in 1999, was surely a ministering angel . . . There is a sad beauty to this novel that readers jaded by the dissonance and complexity of contemporary life will find appealing." —*Richmond Times-Dispatch*

"Outstanding." —Kaye Gibbons

"Willie Morris's last book may be his truest . . . A very knowing look at small-town life in the 1950s." —David Halberstam

"By turns poignant, funny, heartwarming and suspenseful . . . this is a tale of young love, intrigue, jealousy, treachery and violence . . . A deeply affecting swan song by one of America's most beloved writers." —*Publishers Weekly* (starred review)

"*Taps* is a touching, beautiful story, told as only a master can tell it, with enduring passion and warmth." —Winston Groom

TAPS

Willie Morris

A N O V E L

A Mariner Book
Houghton Mifflin Company
BOSTON · NEW YORK

First Mariner Books edition 2002

Copyright © 2001 by
JoAnne Prichard Morris and David Rae Morris
ALL RIGHTS RESERVED

Visit our Web site: www.houghtonmifflinbooks.com.

Library of Congress Cataloging-in-Publication Data
Morris, Willie.
Taps : a novel / Willie Morris.
p.   cm.
ISBN 0-618-09859-3
ISBN 0-618-21902-1 (pbk)
1. Korean War, 1950–1953 — Participation, American — Fiction.
2. Delta (Miss.: Region) — Fiction. 3. Teenage boys — Fiction.
4. Mississippi — Fiction. I. Title.
PS3563.08745 T36 2001
813'.54 — dc21   00-068250

Printed in the United States of America

Book design by Robert Overholtzer

QUM 10 9 8 7 6 5 4 3 2 1

"The Sewanee Hymn" © The University of the South,
Sewanee, Tennessee

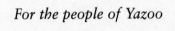

For the people of Yazoo

TAPS

1

WE WERE flatland people, each of us in this little long-ago tale: Luke and Amanda and Durley, Georgia and Arch and myself, Potter and Godbold and all the others. The hills came sweeping down from their hardwood forests and challenged the flatness, mingling with it in querulous juxtaposition. But it was the flatland, I see now, that really shaped us — the violence of its extremes, the tumult of its elements, its memory.

I knew the place better then than I did my own heart — every bend in the road and the cracks in every sidewalk. It was not in my soul then, only in my pores, yet as familiar to me as water or grass or sunlight. The town was poor one year and rich the next, and everything pertained to the land — labor and usury, mortgage and debt. We lived and died by nature, Anglos and Africans bound together in the whims of the timeless clouds. Our people played seven-card stud against God.

It was one of those years when everything seemed to happen, and sometimes all at once.

Luke Cartwright became for me a harbinger of death in that year. He was in his middle thirties but looked older. He was tall, slender, and taut. His dark brown hair fell aslant on an ample forehead, his translucent blue eyes often filled with mirth.

His handsome features were bronzed even in the winter; he seemed to belong outdoors. He moved about everywhere in a slow, tentative amble, not so much a suggestion of our regional lassitude, I would learn, as an inquisitive caution as to what might lie ahead. His expression in repose was more often than not that of a hunter squinting out from the brush.

I had known him only slightly beforehand, and that from the small-town salutations. I knew he was a bachelor, and that he had grown up on a farm. After high school he had attended the state university for two years, where he played basketball, and made good grades, he would later tell me, except for a D in chemistry under a professor with dubious credentials called Cyanide Thompson. He wanted to graduate, but the farm was in trouble, and when his father died, he went to work in the hardware store on the main street. Luke had enlisted in the army on December 8, 1941. He was a rifleman in an infantry company in North Africa, then landed with the invasion at Normandy. He was promoted to platoon sergeant and fought across France. At the Battle of the Bulge he won the Silver Star. Later, leading a point platoon a few miles east of the Rhine, he was shot in the foot by a sniper. When he returned home, he became a partner in the hardware store. He was made an officer in the hometown American Legion, and I would see him occasionally at public functions wearing his blue cap with the braided gold letters: "Paul Hamill Post No. 12, Fisk's Landing."

It was an ambient evening in early summer when Luke first came by my house. My mother was at a bridge tournament at the country club and would be late, and I was relishing the solitude from her injunctions. Our house was the most modest one on the boulevard, the longest and most imposing thoroughfare of the town, which was lined with the honored domiciles of an earlier day, the gabled and cupolaed and porticoed and ginger-breaded houses of old substantial families in cotton and merchandising and banking and the law, the sweeping porches half-hidden by flourishing magnolias and hickories and gums and chestnuts and weeping willows. There were three Gothic revivals along the boulevard and a grand and lofty Italianate with an oval driveway, all built in that era of confident prosperity when this was the richest cotton county in the state and, for all one knows, the world: black people were bought to raise more cotton to buy more blacks to raise more cotton — the divine decree, the curse upon the unfortunate son of Noah.

I was barefoot in the dew-wet grass. I wore a long-tailed, short-sleeved shirt and department-store khakis so common in that distant time. Earlier it had rained, and the trees arched in shadowy silhouettes, darkly green now before the coming of the heat, dripping with moisture in the cooling breeze. Fireflies were everywhere, embraced by the sibilant dark. The hills began only a hundred yards from the house, and the whole earth sang with crickets and other nocturnal things. Soon the DDT truck came by spraying for the season's first mosquitoes, known and acknowledged as the largest and most aggressive in Christendom, or so we believed.

At first I was looking for frogs in the grass. Then I turned to a private exercise of my own: standing on the sidewalk about thirty feet from the concrete steps leading onto the porch of the house, I threw a golf ball, aiming for the bottom step. If the ball hit the bottom one it was a strike; if it hit the second it was a ball; if it hit the third or fourth I had to catch it on the fly before it got past a certain crack in the sidewalk. Otherwise it would be a single, double, triple, or home run, depending on how far it traveled. I threw one ball so hard it landed on the lawn of the forbidding Victorian across the boulevard; this naturally was a home run.

The chimes from the courthouse clock sounded eight, echoing down the deserted street. I lay down on the moist lawn and gazed into the skies, absorbing the improvisations of the insects all around, and thought about my girlfriend, Georgia. My dog ambled from around the house and sat next to me. "Look at all the stars coming out, Dusty." He lay with his head on my lap. After a while he rose and examined a frog near the sidewalk. When the frog croaked, Dusty jumped back; he had learned a long time ago to leave the frogs alone. He was a golden retriever. My father had gotten him for me from Memphis six years before, when he was a bright-eyed puppy who chewed shoes and clothes and once consumed the entire sports section of the Memphis *Commercial Appeal.* I did not know this then, but a boy or a man makes an unspoken pact with himself when he gets a dog. A good, intelligent, deep-feeling dog will give him a few years of fine comradeship, and when they part, the man fulfills the pact with his own feelings of sorrow and loss. But back then nothing was further from my mind; Dusty bent down and looked at me, nuzzling me with his nose, then indolently disappeared into the darkness among the shadows and crickets and owls.

I heard the wheeze of a motor at the front curb. I looked up and saw Luke Cartwright stepping out of his red pickup truck with its high, rectangular cabin and a black cat sprawled on his dashboard. I stood to greet him. He was in khaki trousers and a metallic blue sports shirt that glowed under the streetlamp.

"Taking a snooze, weren't you?" From a few feet away a frog jumped in an arc and landed with a whish. "Ain't you a little old to be barefoot in your front yard in the middle of the night? How old *are* you, anyway?"

Sixteen, almost.

"That's old enough."

I had never thought of it that way, if indeed I had considered it at all. Does the only child — the solitary *son* of a widowed and indomitable mother fraught with an inordinate propensity for intrusion — dwell on age? Especially when the mother teaches *tap dancing?* Or survival, perhaps, although I would not have used the word then — or *escape* or *improvisation* or even *loneliness.* Old enough for what?

"Can we sit down and talk?"

I led him to the front steps, and we sat down. There was, from inside the house, an uncommon silence, and on the street the mosquito truck drifted by again, shushing arcs of poisonous mist against the deepening night.

"I hear you play the trumpet in the band. And you're good."

Only pretty good, I replied.

"Who else is good?"

Arch Kidd, I said, he was very good. He was the best. He practiced all the time.

"Anybody else?"

"No." The others were younger, and learning. In fact, they were terrible.

I was beginning to perceive in this puzzling interrogation something unusual, if not ominous. Luke sat mysteriously silent for a while, then leaned over and spit on the grass. When I later grew to know him, about as well as I would ever know anyone, I would recognize this as an act of reverence.

"Can you play 'Taps'?"

"Yes, but it's hard. On the trumpet you play it with the first valve down," I said, "in B-flat. That means you have to hit the high F." Arch Kidd always got the high F right. Arch had the lips for it. I could have told him also that the human face was not designed to play the trumpet. At that time, it was impossible for me to articulate that brass, especially trumpets, are instruments of life in their sound, while reeds are fragile and elusive and deathlike. Could anyone image a clarinet on "Taps"? It is *wood* that makes the sound of the clarinet; *flesh* makes the sound of the trumpet. Pondering these unspoken secrets as I sat next to this perplexing inquisitor, I noticed that I had been moving the index finger of my right hand up and down from instinct, as if I were about to push the first valve.

"I need to talk to Arch too," Luke said. "Let's go inside and phone him."

Arch was not home. He had gone to the coast on vacation.

"Oh, *shit*!" It was an intonation of despair, so loud and precipitate that it would have shocked the widowed neighbors.

"There will be a military funeral tomorrow afternoon," Luke said, "up in the town cemetery." They were sending the town's first dead soldier back from Korea, a boy named Oscar Goodloe. I vaguely remembered him — a squat, resolute, red-faced young man from the hills, a ponderous lineman on the high school team of a few years before.

They needed two trumpets to play "Taps" in the cemetery, one by the gravesite, one in the distance to play it again as an echo. "We'll have to get by with one this time. You'll play at the grave."

I felt dry-mouthed and giddy, breathless with doubt. The thought of trying to hit the high note at a grave surrounded by mourners looking straight at me was an unpleasant prospect, and dangerous. I had a fear of being watched too closely, and of being laughed at. And all the while that body in the coffin.

"Can't you get somebody else?"

"What are you, *scared*?"

"You don't even know me," I replied petulantly.

"I'm trusting you anyway. You're it."

"I'll have to oil my trumpet."

"Then *oil* the damned thing." Wear a dark suit, he said. And a white shirt and tie. And regular shoes. No saddle oxfords, no sneakers. Be at the grave at 2:30, just before the procession, and be *at attention* when the hearse and the people arrive. He explained to me the precise place in the old section. Just look for the Ricks Funeral Home tent.

In later years, I wondered: Why did I do it? It happened so swiftly and simply, less a decision than an acquiescing. And the night itself was so soft and private and inviolate. I could have said no — or lied, saying that I could not hit the notes. Was I, a solitary boy, more lonesome than scared? Did I consent that night out of loneliness? Or was there something more?

"Play slow," Luke said. "And proud."

"How do I play *proud*?"

"You'll find out."

He got up and stretched, then looked lazily into the night-time sky. "Oscar Goodloe!" he said. "I knew he wouldn't last."

I walked along behind him to his truck. Far up the boulevard a freight rumbled through town, its whistle disembodied against the drowsing facades.

Luke leaned against his truck. Then, almost tenderly, he said to me: "See you tomorrow. This won't be the last one. Where the hell is *Korea*? Do *you* know anything about it?" He opened the door and waved farewell. With a rattle of gears he disappeared down the street, with only the question lingering behind him.

We had heard about Korea. How could we not? Radio broadcasts told about the Yaks and Stormoviks and T-34s, Syngman Rhee and Trygve Lie and Harry S. (for nothing) Truman and Douglas MacArthur and the 38th parallel and the bloody battles for a few feet of mountaintop and "Let every man stand or die" and the "Pax Americana" and the "New American Imperium" and "No more Munichs." We listened to the alien freakish names of places we could not fathom: Osau, Pusan, Chukminyung, Yongdok, Inchon, Desperation Corner, Frozen Chosen, the bloody Naktong, the black waters of the Yalu, and Bloody Ridge, Heartbreak Ridge, Bunker Hill, the Punchbowl. We had to look them up in the atlas at school to find out where they were. But what was going on there?

This war was not like World War II when you were nine years old and exchanged gum cards of the latest heroes like Colin Kelly and Colonel Rickenbacker and followed the maps of the battles in the Memphis *Commercial Appeal* and went to the war movies and saw the Pathé news and knew whom to hate — crazy, frothing Hitler, who ruled from the French coast to the Turkish steppes and gassed and burned little innocent naked children and probably even enjoyed it, and fat, degenerate Goering and clubfooted, satanic Goebbels and banal, murderous Himmler, and baldheaded and loudmouthed Mussolini, whom his own people sooner or later hanged upside down, and the Nipponese and the Day of Infamy and the Death March on Bataan and the rape of our nurses while their fingernails were pried off and their ears ripped out, and our prisoners being starved. And we knew whom to admire, too — the valiant English who had defended their land for a thousand years and the London children wearing gas masks, the Free French, the Russians at Leningrad, the noble, all-suffering Chinese. *Life* magazine published a list: among all towns of its size in the nation, my town, Fisk's Landing, had sent the fourth most men to that war, and as children we roamed about in an effort to help their cause, collecting kitchen drippings, scrap metals, and coat hangers, empty toothpaste tubes, old rubber, and the silver paper inside cigarette packages. But now with this war in Korea there was nothing to hold on to.

The entire National Guard unit of our town had been called. It was part of the Dixie Division, the grand old Thirty-first, the same local unit that had been summoned as the Germans overran France in '40; when called, they went. They had been activated several weeks ago, and we all knew they would be dispatched to the fighting as soon as possible. So the small faraway land grew more palpable to us by day, and the Stars and Stripes from that other, more comprehensible holocaust were washed and ironed and brought out again to stand before the houses and storefronts. The younger brothers of veterans of the last war were fighting this one. Fisk's Landing was there, as it had always been.

The local National Guard was an array of the provincial Anglo-Saxon amalgam, interspersed with Lebanese and Jews and Italians and even a few Greeks and Poles. Hill and flatland boys were equally represented, with some of the World War II men.

Yet everything reflected the social and geographic divide. As with the high school football teams, where the prematurely aging hill boys were the tackles, guards, and centers, and the boys from town the ends and backs, so, too, with few exceptions, such as Lieutenant Billy Permenter, the hills provided the ranks and the flatland the officers. The hill-country boys from the small hardscrabble farms had enlisted in the late forties to draw their $30 monthly pay and to preen about on the main street or in front of the Elks Lodge or Crenshaw's or the Rebel Theater or the courthouse on Saturday nights.

It was an unprepossessing main street, with the patina of the uncertain cotton economy, of sthe dubious elements and the debt, a raw little thoroughfare ending precipitously at the bend of the murky river where an entrepreneur named Fisk had established his landing years before the Civil War. But on Saturday nights in the milling interracial cosmos with drunks everywhere and summer bugs swarming in violent clusters about the streetlights, the guard boys from the unrepentant backcountry, with their starched khakis and their angular girls in pale calicoes, added an element of theater that I have not to this day forgotten. I remember, too, their names, from the blood source of our nation's sturdiest defenders: Strong, Biggers, Steptoe, Puckett, and Chisholm, Boone, Wingo, Pounds, and Rance, Jetter, Huskey, Glass, Bull, and Scuttles.

"Hey, Hardy!" one of them would shout. "Let's go drink beer at Crenshaw's."

"Too many niggers in there." They would stare across the street at the very Negroes themselves sniffing out the night for its possibilities.

"Then let's get the gals and go up on the Peak."

"Now you talkin'."

They would lounge about on the crowded Saturday street corners, filling the air with their riotous hosannas. They were as spare as hardtack. They would have been with Stonewall in the Valley.

Guard meetings were held every other week. Arch, Georgia, and I would sometimes ride by the fetid old armory built by the WPA and observe the guardsmen lying in the crabgrass looking into the sky or cracking pecans with their knuckles or polishing their obsolete carbines or playing kick the can around the derelict baseball diamond in the rear. The officers and sergeants were brisk and professional, often conferring among themselves in tense little huddles, but when they gave orders to the cadres in the ranks, these were less the standard commands than indigenous cajolery.

"Come on, boys. Up! Up!"

"Too hot."

"*I'll* make it hot. Come on, now, fellas."

"Give me a minute, sir. I got a stiff leg."

"Don't you want to get home early today?"

"Hell, why didn't you *say* so?" And they would rise and stretch and brush the grass off their fatigues and snap into formless activity. Only Lieutenant Durley Godbold could handle them, it seemed, and mostly through fear.

Then the message came down from Washington. They were given one month's notice. Arch and I drove out in Arch's Plymouth the day they departed. The officers had asked our band director, Mr. Percival, to muster an ensemble of brass, reeds, and drums for the formal farewell. We gathered in the shade of a tall pecan. Georgia was standing with us at the edge of the shade; her flute gleamed like magic in the reflected sun. It was a cold, windy forenoon under amorphous skies. Jeeps and transport trucks marked with the solitary white stars had appeared from nowhere; wives and children and parents and girlfriends and dogs crowded about the vehicles. *"Let's get them gooks!"* This led to exuberant shouting and rebel yells — then suddenly it was very quiet. The guardsmen formed in ranks and came to attention. Two young men held the American and state flags, which flapped strenuously in the wind.

From under our pecan I gazed down the lines. We knew many of these boys. A few of them were seniors in high school. One officer, Lieutenant Tommy Ross Morgan, and two sergeants there were members of our church. Several were from a nearby junior college that gave athletes one-half scholarships and put them in the guard to pay the other half. The tableau before us was touched with a troubled, bittersweet sadness.

The officers had asked us to play "Dixie." For the Dixie Division, they said. And then "The Star-Spangled Banner." The director waved his baton. The flags snapped so that the sound of them echoed off the gray facade of the armory.

When it was finished, Arch and I, trumpets in hand, went over to the trucks. Luke Cartwright and several of the older American Legionnaires, Sarge Jennings, Son Graham, Roach Weems, and the others, were shaking hands with the troops. An air of enigma and bafflement seemed to accompany these proceedings of departure, as if some people felt that the hapless foot soldier was no longer needed.

"We're federal property now," Luke Cartwright's cousin Lieutenant Billy Permenter was saying to them. He was a compact young man with thinning red hair and ears like ovals, who had taught us seventh-grade science and math. I recalled him during recesses disappearing behind the oaks at the farthest edge of the grounds for a secret chew of tobacco. When he saw Arch and me, he shook our hands. "Hold down the school," he said dramatically.

On the steps of the armory I saw Lieutenant Durley Godbold with his wife, Amanda, who taught piano lessons at the high school. At first he was laughing, but soon his expression soured to surliness and venom, so out of character with the prevailing mood of sad farewell that I stared at them for a moment, hypnotized, until he saw me looking and stared back. I moved away in embarrassment.

In the crowd we saw Lank Hemphill, our older classmate, a

wizened, ageless boy whose khakis sagged on his bone-thin frame. I remembered him from as early as the second grade, when he lacked the money for the cafeteria lunches. He and the other relief children would come into school from the hills barefoot in the warm weather; sometimes they brought small jars of home-canned goods to swap for lunches. I wanted to invite them to my house after school and give them something to eat. "We can't have *them* in the house," my mother said. Of all the Ruston Hill children, a hard, inseparable cadre, Lank was the most gentle. They were as profane as their impenitent earth, but I never once heard him swear. Across the nearly unfathomable chasm, he was the one who seemed to want most to be our friend. As a child he sometimes walked the three miles into the town to play with Arch and Georgia and me in the alleyways, the backyards, the empty fairgrounds, the cotton gin. He kept falling back in school, and by junior high had so receded that he finally found himself in our class. "I can't go back down no more," he would say. "I guess I'll go on up with you, just one step at a time." In front of the armory on this day, he was the most dispirited figure I had ever seen, as spindly as a straw, a sulky scarecrow who at that moment could not have alarmed a sparrow or a chipmunk, much less a fanatic, armed-to-the-teeth Oriental. We stood uneasily in the tumultuous scene.

"I don't want to go," he said. "Why ain't you comin' with me?"

We promised to write him letters — the whole class.

"Where *to*? I don't even know where I'm goin'."

They departed that day for Fort Jackson in South Carolina, where they were broken up into other units. Then, we later learned, across to the West Coast, and then Japan. After that, to the obscure little peninsula of Korea, and we lost touch for a while.

Lieutenant Billy Permenter wrote his cousin Luke Cartwright from aboard the *General D. I. Sulton* after they had shipped out from Camp Stoneman in California to Japan:

We sailed down river, around Alcatraz, under the Golden Gate Bridge and out to sea. We watched the bridge just as long as we could. We wondered if we would ever see it again. It took 5 days to get to Hawaii. They gave the boys a 12 hour pass to Honolulu, and when they came back to the ship some had Hawaiian shirts, some had sailor shirts and some sailors had army shirts. They had lea's around their neck and most were drunk. We watched Hawaii as long as possible, too. When it went down the horizon, we said "Well the hell with it. It's all over now." We laid out on the deck, wrote letters, etc., but it was boring. It took 9 days to get to here. Flying fish would jump out of the water and sail about 10 feet before diving back in. Some time we would see porposes, in schools, going along side the ship. When we crossed I'nt Date Line, one day was Wed., the next Fri. We never did figure out what happened to Thurs. Some morning I would walk out on the deck look around and think "This looks like the same place we was at yesterday." Somebody wd. say "There's land about 5 miles." And we would say where. He would say "straight down." Wise guy from Chicago.

A letter came one day addressed to the class from Lank Hemphill:

This worse I ever seen. Worse I ever got in to. This *terrabel*. I dont want get up in the morning. Peeple blowed up. Best buddie Michagan shot in head on potrol late nite. ~~Japs~~ N. *Korans* outnumber U.S. 2 degree! *Snow*. How football team? Cant sleep so much nois. *PLEAS* write me!

We wrote Lank a group letter, telling him about the football team, the new cheerleaders, the weather, the cotton crop.

When Luke Cartwright left my house that night, I went inside to my bedroom. The walls were strewn with Southeastern Conference football pennants. In a bookcase was my collection of things: defused World War II hand grenades and the insignias of various fighting divisions, a row of empty snuff cans, a football signed by Y. A. Tittle, a stack of *National Geographics*, a Clyde Beatty Circus poster, and my accumulation of old creamy bottles gleaned from country stores: Sloan's N & B Liniment, Dr W. B. Caldwell's Syrup Pepsin, vintage Dr Peppers and Coca-Colas, California Fig Syrup Company Calipic, Uncle Tom's Gin. I paused before this childhood treasure. Then I warily took the trumpet from its case.

It was a silver-colored instrument that my mother had bought secondhand from Mr. Percival three years before for $28. That was when Arch and I started taking lessons from him, after the beginners' band practices; he was a peculiar man, hot-tempered and as emaciated as a bird, with a wife even more fragile and wispy, but he knew music, a brass man who could play the trumpet, trombone, bass, and French horn with grave and equal facility. I held the trumpet in my lap, touching its surfaces: "*Fawcett Fine Instrument Co., Saint Louis Mo.*" From the dresser I brought out the polish and the valve oil, also purchased from Mr. Percival, and reluctantly went to work. Dusty sat on the bed and watched.

In minutes the trumpet was shining and the valves were in order. I inserted the quartz mouthpiece and blew the old spit out of the spit valve. Then I got the mute and put it in for my practice. It was now 10:00 at night. It would have been ironic to awaken the neighbors with "Taps." First I went up and down the scale to warm up. The moment I began, my dog jumped from the bed and left the room; the trumpet always hurt his ears. Next I ran through the high school fight song, which had been purloined years before from "Hail, Michigan." My lips were soft. I had not practiced since school turned out the month before. Now I tried "Taps" several times. The muted sounds filled the room.

I kept wobbling on the high note. I tried several times and got no better. That was when I knew I was afraid.

I rose early the next morning to the sounds of the roosters from across the alley in the Quarters. Still half-asleep, I recalled my agreement of the night before. Soon I could hear the jarring staccato clicks of the tap dancing up front. I loathed those sharp, unceasing clicks. One of my last memories of my father was his saying to me: "Those little brats are driving me crazy." A year before he died, he had exacted a commitment from her that she would never try to teach *me,* and this was a covenant I blessed more and more with each day, more valuable by any yield than the Magna Charta or the Bill of Rights.

My mother had gone to ballet school in New Orleans before she married my father, and when they settled into the house in Fisk's Landing, the first thing she did was install a special floor in the dining room. Her pupils were the daughters of the planters and merchants, and more than a few of them came twice a week with their piercing raps and squeals from outlying towns as far as Lutherville and Monroe City.

I suppose I should have felt sorry for my mother for having to tolerate her graceless wonders five or six hours every day, but since her students always won ribbons and medals in the state competition, she was respected by those in the demonstration arts and took that estimation as her due.

I made toast for myself in the kitchen and fed my dog. The noises from the dining room reverberated through the house. They put me in a brackish frame for the task that awaited me.

In my bedroom I pulled my navy blue suit out of the closet.

"What are you doing?" My mother was suddenly standing in the doorway to my bedroom.

She wore the loose gray cotton shorts and bright red smock she preferred for her lessons. She was lithesome and slender from the dance regimen; her dark abundant hair was streaked with silver. She had serious hazel eyes, and a plump face, which more often than not was obscurely troubled.

I told her about the funeral that afternoon.

She reached in the closet and brought out a blue tie. "Here, wear this. You need a haircut. Why didn't you get a haircut last week? Look at you!" I promised to get one that morning.

"Be nice to those people now. People are going to be looking at you."

In the lexicon of discourse, her favorite phrases were: "What will people around here think?" This was often followed by "We've got to live with them" and "Be popular!" If the citizens of the town had voted in a plebiscite to nationalize the Illinois Central Railroad or to communize the cotton farms, she would have endorsed the plan and I believe would have even condoned the abolition of the Episcopal Church if such a resolution was carried by a respectable local plurality.

"Are your shoes shined?" She looked down at my feet. "No, they're *not* shined."

I would get them shined, I said.

"Have you practiced your trumpet? What time's the funeral? You cannot be late."

In seconds she would bring out the hairbrush and start in on my hair. My hands began to sweat. Mercifully, however, her next pupil was at the front door. The doorbell jangled behind her.

"Go get a haircut. Have you returned the library books?" In a flutter of apprehensions known to me since earliest memory, she departed down the hallway.

In hindsight I recognize that my life through its modest years had been a chronicle of dire compromises and capitulations. An axiom of my childhood was that it was easier to acquiesce in hysterical solicitude and to protect in at least some private apartness what was barely mine, at least as best I could. One day when I was a child, after a volley of imperatives, I saw her browsing through the clothes in her closet. I tiptoed to the door and locked it from the outside. There was not a sound for the longest time except for the turning of the handle. Then:

"Swayze?"

I stood there triumphant.

"Swayze!"

I withdrew into the backyard. From time to time I would return to the house.

"Let me out this minute!" There was loud banging on the closet door.

"Let me *out*!"

I went to my room and listened to the radio, the one my father had bought years before, the big boxy console shaped like a cathedral arch. I must have heard three or four afternoon serials. For a while the banging ceased, then frantically resumed.

"Swayze . . ." Finally: *"Please?"*

She had been in there over two hours. I might have kept her there forever, but guilt intervened. What if she *suffocated*? Again I tiptoed to the closet and silently turned the key. I made it out of there quickly, down the back steps, across the alley, and into Independence Quarters, where I loitered almost until dark. Then I walked down the boulevard to Arch Kidd's house and persuaded him to come home with me for supper. There was no pointed retribution, merely an icy silence. She served us mayonnaise and ketchup sandwiches with a stricken glare. Even Arch was intimidated and felt he had been used.

After a time she retaliated. She had decided, she told me, that I would sleep every night with my hair in curlers so that I could get a pompadour.

My mother's ceaseless agitations seemed to well from a nearly bottomless source. She led an anxious life riven with gloom. How I envied my contemporaries with big families, their rough and boisterous fathers and giggling, voluptuous mothers, their clamorous activities! I saw myself, fatherless and brotherless and vulnerable, lonely and alone, as a mere handy and fortuitous victim. How could I have comprehended then that she must have seen herself a fallen patrician, that her inmost spirit resided in the noblest hierarchies who possessed the wit to come down from the Upper South and found and organize the state and belong to its burgeoning aristocracy, or whatever passed then for aristocracy — a territorial governor, a Mexican War colonel, a great-uncle who taught history at Sewanee (and on our sideboard a silver chalice granted him at graduation there in '08), a warrior and Whig politician — and who gave it its very place names, and lost everything except perhaps their pride, and drifted in their dispossessed spirit into the modern century in bitter loss and penury? Surely that was an old story. And that she feared she had married beneath her? And that her marriage was bereft of love? And that in her troubled soul the son was only an artifact of failed and embittered unfulfillment?

Simple survival was at stake, and it was mine. This knowledge was as instinctual as my own breathing. Self-pity would be subjugation, and so, too, would guilty transgression. I was only a boy. It would take a steel and linear volition. Survival would involve surreptitious withdrawals, tactical surrenders, agile advances, swift movements along the flanks, and a lot of solitude. Luke and Amanda and Georgia would be my silent allies, but that was in the future.

Selective memory is a human trait, and memory itself, I have learned, is the corrector of existence. Was I really a prisoner of my own childhood? When my father died suddenly, I was ten years old. I got things mixed up. I missed him and wondered where he was. Could I have kept him here? He is a dim figure for me now, dwelling mostly in shadows, yet sometimes the brief remembrances of him, images long buried and forgotten, well up so vividly that I am startled by them. He was a tall man, I believe, of gentle countenance. I see him on the front lawn of a distant summer, wetting the grass with a green garden hose. Or in the kitchen reading the *Commercial Appeal*. Or throwing a baseball with me in a mottled spring twilight. Or showing me how to bathe the new puppy, Dusty, with flea soap under the backyard elm. Several times he took me to his office, where he kept books for a wholesale firm, and there was a secret, musty smell and sounds from the main street below and long ledgers bearing minuscule tallies and gadgets, the best of them a large black typewriter on a scarred oaken desk, and I would stand behind him and watch as he typed something on it, laboriously and with two fingers. And somehow from the obscure darkness words come to me.

"Leave him alone, Ella. Let him grow."

After he died, I thought myself immured by distress and uncertainty, and that this was true only of me among God's creatures. I worried about everything. I could not sleep. I never wanted to leave the house. I had no one to tell these things to.

"What's the matter with *you?*" Arch Kidd would ask.

"I don't know."

Or my mother: "What in heaven's name is wrong with you?"

"I don't know." And I didn't.

It was summertime. I started getting scared around dusk. Scared of what? I felt a sense of betrayal, precocious and terrible, but of who or what had betrayed me I lacked the faintest notion. I believed God was mocking me. I thought people were always looking at me from behind and laughing at me. I shivered under the sheets at night even in the warmest weather. Some nights to get away from my mother I went into the backyard and tried to sleep under the shrubs. Loneliness lurked in every shadow. I was the most worthless of impedimenta and miserable in the very tributaries of my soul; I cried to myself, feeling an angst of such intense sorrow that to this day the remembered pain comes back to me as a beastly predator. In this sunless labyrinth of desperation I sprouted warts on the back of my hand and developed an itchy rash on my neck, and sometimes I went into the bathroom and threw up. This is no "sensitive boy" story of indulgent, silly, unearned unhappiness. My nameless anomie was as true and genuine as anything I ever knew. I began to sense smells as never before, was bombarded by sights, sounds, feelings. If we are indeed shaped, as some say, by our tenth year, was I rebelling against life itself?

These inner distresses coincided with the great polio scare of that summer. Several children went down with it. Five of them died. People's descriptions of the iron lung made me shudder. We were warned against swimming and advised to stay indoors, all lights turned out, on the hottest afternoons. What kinds of germs were these? Did they float in the air? Bathe in the water? I feared I was catching polio.

"Nothing wrong with him," the doctor said. "Just growing pains." But he prescribed a new kind of pill, anyway, which made it worse.

When modern medicine did not help, my mother concluded that my problem was bumbling incompetence and mediocrity: "I'm sick and tired of this," she said. "You can't do *anything*." I believed her. Once when I wet the bed, she hung the sheets from the window for all to see. At first I had nobody on earth to turn to, nobody at all, except Dusty. He was always there, asleep next to me on the bed or staring affectionately down at me, rousing me in the mornings with his moist, cool tongue on my nose or cheeks, luring me from my cruel childhood insomnia into the light of day. Through all of time there have been boys and their dogs, and they belong together, and always will.

One torpid afternoon after the polio fright had diminished I was walking with Dusty down the streets of the town. I paused before the Catholic church. The side windows were open. I went to one of them and peered inside. It was scary: the dark shadowy interior, the icons, the strange odor of incense. Dusty stood there sniffing at it. A large Lebanese woman named Mrs. Monsour was lighting a candle. Then she knelt before a statue.

> Hail Mary, full of Grace,
> The Lord is with Thee.
> Blessed art Thou amongst women,
> And Blessed is the fruit of Thy womb, Jesus.

I watched as the woman crossed herself. Suddenly, outside a side door nearby, I saw a shadowy outline. A figure appeared before me. It was Father Cosgrove, the Irishman. He wore a black robe with a rope about his waist. He looked down at me inquiringly.

"Are you religious, Swayze?"

"Yes, sir."

"You're Episcopalian, aren't you?"

"Yes, sir."

"Are you all right? Is anything wrong?"

"No, sir."

"Want to come inside and look around? You're welcome to. You'll have to leave your dog."

We had better be going, I said.

"God be with you, my son."

Ecumenical as I was in my discontent, I began spending time with an old black preacher in the Quarters. He lived in a tidy frame dwelling across the back alley, passing the long summer afternoons in the parsimonious shade of a chinaberry tree in his front yard. His hair was pure white like bristly cotton, and he fanned himself with a Centennial Burial Association fan and swatted at flies with a big homemade fly swatter and kept a timeworn Bible in his lap at all times. While Dusty romped with the skinny dogs in the yard, I would sit on the grass as the preacher's constituents dropped by for succor and counsel about debt, illness, infidelity, grief, the human distresses. A woman brought a sick infant, coal black and shriveled, with crusted mucus around its nose, and the preacher put his hand on its head while he and the woman prayed together. Another woman in a starched white apron and polka-dot bandanna who worked in one of the large boulevard homes untied a handkerchief and handed him three wrinkled dollar bills for the building fund — the roof on the church still leaked, he told his people, and they also needed a new floor — and he said,

"Bless you, holy sister," and they prayed also. He read me the whole of Genesis in one afternoon's sitting, then dipped into various other books.

How could the Lord make the whole world in six days? I asked.

"He was a fast worker, sugar, and he had it planned out real good before he started."

How did Noah get two of everything onto his ark?

"Well, honey, it was a *big* ol' ark — 'bout as big as this whole town put together. Noah had room to spare."

We sat there in the drowsy heat among the buzzing flies. "You got sad eyes, little boy. Is you sad as you looks?"

I was pretty sad.

"Then take sweet Jesus on this day by the hand."

Where was he so I could take his hand?

"Right there next to you on the grass. You just ain't seen him yet."

We were of a long line of Anglicans, but I had never given it much thought. It was merely the church I happened to be born into. The local congregation was so venerable that the Fisk's Landing cemetery had originally belonged to it, but the cemetery outgrew itself and had been turned over to the town more than a century ago. The old settled families educated at the state university, a Harvard Tidwell, two Princeton Turnbulls, the Sewanee Culpeppers, and a University of Virginia Barnwell really controlled our church, as they always had, not only as an institution of religion, but as an unattenuated stronghold on the culture. It was the only church in the town actually made of *wood*, built in the 1850s — the others were of post–World War I brick and concrete — an ivy-strewn structure of indigenous oak and with pine floors so that it smelled of the real true earth.

Almost by rote I started walking to the chapel in the dying

afternoons, when my fears sprang out. It was just down the boulevard; I could be alone there, all by myself, with Dusty waiting on the lawn outside. I loved its quiet, secure beauty, its cool, dark privacy, the hand-wrought chandelier from an old monastery, the graceful beams, the richly carved chancel and pulpit and altar designed decades before by a black sexton who himself was buried from the church, the old family names on the stained glass, the undulating light and shadow from the west sun reflecting the elegiac lines of the glass on its pews.

God be with you, the Catholic father had said. Dear Lord, I prayed, help me. Don't let me die before I get this taken care of. As the weeks went by, I grew to need that church, the way it took the terror, but not the mystery, out of everything, and when life burst forth in a flood, it was there — not the emphatic young vicar and his earnest sermonologies, but the *feeling* of it, the Nicene Creed in all its strange wonder and affirmation, its deep ritual, its pomp and display, its anthems and thanksgivings and communions and litanies and prayers, comforts against oblivion, they were. Whoever wrote that Book of Common Prayer was *smart*. Soon after that I became an acolyte, wore the red robe with silver buttons, lit the candles in the dark bronze candelabra, walked in the processions carrying the flag of the church one Sunday, of the state the next.

I did not envy my contemporaries of the fiery denominations with their insipid pieties and their domineering, whiny-voiced preachers and their everlasting regimen of fear and retribution and fire, the sere dreariness of the Sundays, the dull religiosity that could deaden everything, make it all fit a mold, take the fun and wonder out of it. They *proscribed*. Three or four times I attended the Baptist church with other children I knew. The preachers actually shouted, raved in torment, one with saliva trickling down his angry lips. How mad and silly they were, how grim and ill-spirited! Who were these strange, crazed, threadbare men? I found it curious that at age ten we were consigned to Hell if we failed to get our lives straight. We did not even know what life *was*, and here we were already being relegated to doom, right here in Fisk's Landing itself. "They don't have any question marks," the lapsed Methodist Luke Cartwright would say in later days. "Ain't life itself a question mark?"

There were no ready answers. Bad days. Good days. It was hard at age ten. I needed nothing in those dim times if not the Merciful and Benevolent Presence, His tender lingering pervasive solicitude.

And when the anguish slowly lifted like a veil, a door of childhood slowly opening onto the outside world, I started listening secretly to people, and looking at them without much plan, perhaps to see how *they* dealt with things. Yet thinking back now, I believe I must have developed a sort of tremulous inner compulsion for complex and troublesome situations, an almost Jesuitical introspectiveness at the difficult crossings, and a strange secret urge toward persecution and, yes, paranoia.

Dusty and I left the house two hours before the funeral. I wanted to compose myself. I was only a few feet down the front walk when she dashed out the front door brandishing the hairbrush. Why hadn't I slipped out the back? She ran up behind me and began brushing my hair.

"Stand still!" She had wetted the brush with water, and drops of it slid down my nose and face.

This was not an unusual sight in the neighborhood. In the mornings during school, as I would start to leave, she would rush behind me to comb my hair and look me over. Once she actually hid behind a bush and leapt out at me with the hairbrush. People driving by in cars would turn and stare.

"That's better. Now, straighten the tie. Button your coat. Be nice to everybody. Look them in the eye and shake their hands and call them by their *names*. And play 'Taps' perfectly!"

I struggled to break away. She stood on the corner until I was out of sight.

The cemetery was a few blocks removed, at the westernmost edge of the hills, both remote from the town and an integral part of it, in proximity with its serene daily experience. I was carrying my trumpet in its black leather case; Dusty trailed along behind me. It was a warm day of intermittent sun and shadow, and as I walked down the familiar streets with their blazing daylilies and perfumed jasmine and the crape myrtles offering their tentative pinks, and black men with bandannas clipping the hedges and mowing the lawns, my starched dress shirt prickled at my neck and I began to sweat.

We reached the cemetery. It was situated in one of the loveliest glades of the town, at the precise locale where the deep wooded hills tossed downward to the flatness. The June sun reflected on the gray stones stretching away on the grassy slopes, and the elms and oaks and cedars and magnolias were great figures of green in the quiet of this early afternoon. Everywhere on the trees and shrubs and the wrought-iron fences enclosing the oldest plots were the verdant tangles of wisteria and honeysuckle vines. I looked up the slope rising gently to the east of the front gate and saw the dark blue canopy with "Ricks Funeral Home" in stark white lettering.

Except for one man mowing the grass at the salient of a hill, no one was about. I called to Dusty and began walking between the stones toward the tent.

It was a displeasing scene — the tawdry green artificial grass mat covering the tall mound of dirt, the empty straight-backed chairs in ghostly rows with paper funeral home fans already placed on each, and then the sudden open grave, yawning before me like the apparition of one's bleakest dreams. The mechanical device that would lower the coffin into that grim hole was already in place. So was the temporary marker at the head: *PFC Oscar Goodloe, US Army.* Only the disarming sight of

Dusty sniffing about that lurking aperture in the earth and then hiking his leg on one of the tent poles relieved the austerity.

It was still an hour and a half before the ceremony. I bent down before a water hydrant, only a few feet from Mr. Pelham Fortenberry, 1868–1940, and washed my face. Dusty came up and licked at the water. We walked around. My father had brought me to this ground when I was a child. "Let's get away from the damned house," he would say, and we would drift among the graves for a long time until twilight came. Once we arrived upon the new grave of Arch Kidd's grandmother, the first funeral I had ever attended. I remember asking him if she had a telephone down there so someone could let her out when she wanted to leave.

"No," he replied. "She can't get out."

I loved the different shapes and sizes of the stones, the smells of the rich, surging earth. Years later, the great urban cemeteries of the east would always fill me with horror, the mile after mile of crowded tombstones that no one ever seemed to visit, as if one could *find* anyone there even if he wished to. And the suburban cemeteries of those later years with their manicured lawns and bronze plaques embedded in the ground seemed permeated with affluence and artifice.

When we were children we came here by ourselves for picnics and games on the mossy benches scattered here and there where people came to ponder and pray. Like brainless gazelles we would take off and run and leap over the graves. All around us on the darkened stones were the same names as the people our age we knew, giving to this very environment a supple ironic ambiance: *Georgia Haynes Applewhite, 1884–1938 . . . Archibald T. Kidd, 1874–1933 . . . Pauline Zamma Bailey, 1880–1929.* We watched the funerals from afar in the hushed awe. Bordering the oldest section of all, with crumbling crypts marble green with moss, was an area of deep ravines ensnarled in kudzu, and beyond this the bayou, which brought the water from the hills to the river.

The cemetery had separable divisions, I had learned long before, invisible yet implicitly recognized — Anglo-Saxon, Catholic, Jewish, African. As I wandered about uneasily before that first "Taps," absorbing again the ethnic amalgam, I came across stones as familiar to me as comrades, strangely calming on this day. Under an oak I saw the solitary obelisk around which four people had been buried a century ago, and the words near the top: *The Dead.* I went past General Featherstone, aide-de-camp to General Pershing in World War I, whose funeral in 1928 was said to be the grandest in the history of the county, with the words of Pershing himself on the stone: "Duty was always his guide." And a stone with a cross on top of the venerable Father Burke of St. Mary's Church, the first white man I ever saw shake hands with a black man and surely the first ecclesiastic I ever witnessed drinking a beer in public, who, like old elephants and Eskimos when their time comes, had wandered several years before into the back garden of his church with a Bible and sat down under a shade tree and died. And the Revolutionary soldier named Dan Perkins who had fought for a Virginia regiment, and the stone figure of the child "Our Charlie" embracing a big dog not unlike Dusty, and Old Man Montgomery, buried with his three wives, and the undertaker who shot the newspaper editor and came back and climbed into one of his own coffins and shot himself through the head, and the yellow fever victims of 1878 and the French nuns and priests who fell nursing them, and the 207 Civil War dead said to be buried in a mass grave, and the dear four-year-old Amy whose stone was topped by an angel with a broken arm and in the rains she seemed to cry.

And then the Jewish enclave with Hebrew words and Stars of David on the Wises and Schaeffers and Finks and Hirsches and Gollobs and Levines, and beyond that the black section, which encompassed a whole field all to itself, yet mingling here and there in fateful little pockets with Aryan and Catholic and Jew. Farther up this slope, someone was raising tomatoes and cabbages right next to the moldering stones. Nearby, I sighted the crypt with two adjoining sepulchers, one of them dark and empty: the occupied one containing a black man, the vacant one planned for his white friend, but when his time came, his family ignored his wishes.

I was now in a bosky circle of oaks and elms. It was one of the highest points in the old section, and, spreading out beneath me, as far as the eye could see, was the town of Fisk's Landing: the courthouse with its dark green cupola, where at this very moment the clock was striking two; the main street and the bend in the river; the red-brick rectangle of the grammar school; and beyond that to the north the grand boulevard, where I could barely make out the front lawn of my own house. Behind me from this spot, on a succession of even more abrupt hills, was the cemetery's new section, which had only recently been opened, treeless except for a few young mimosas scattered here and there, divided from the old part by a precipitous ravine as if some tangible and purposeful landmark were required to sequester the generations. New tombstones, dazzlingly white in the brightening sunshine, had begun to dot this freshly landscaped ground, and from the distance I could see the boxwood hedges enclosing the high granite stone where a mother came with sheets and quilts to sleep every night by the grave of her daughter, recently lost to leukemia.

Far down the hill there was activity around the Ricks Funeral Home canopy. A pair of cars had just driven up. I was at least two hundred yards away, and I hastened now in that direction. When I got about fifty yards from the gravesite, I ordered Dusty to sit. We were under a cedar and next to the tombstone with the broken-armed angel. "You *stay*. Stay!"

Luke Cartwright was waiting by the grave. He looked smart in a dark gray suit and his blue and gold American Legion cap.

"Where you been? We've only got fifteen minutes. I'm glad you left the dog up there."

A black man was puttering about the grave. Tall and agile, with graying hair about the temples, he was slightly stooped at the shoulders, and in his dark suit and tie carried an air of faintly proprietary bemusement. Did I hear him whistling as he worked?

He was testing the mechanical lowering device. Then he pulled the artificial grass more tightly around the mound of earth. He went to the Ricks van and brought out a half dozen more chairs, which he punctiliously arranged in a back row among the others.

"This is Woodrow from the funeral home," Luke said.

"We buried your daddy," the man said, as if he had known me all along. "Valentine's Day, either forty-three or forty-four."

Forty-three.

"Forty-*three*. Buried him with the Poindexters in Poindexter. Your mama's people, I believe."

"You stand here," Luke said, taking me by the arm and leading me to a spot a few feet from the canopy. "You play right after they fire the shots. There's a big crowd today."

I unsnapped the case and brought out my trumpet. I licked the mouthpiece and inserted it, then hid the case behind a nearby tombstone. I shook the trumpet and flicked the spit valve, then started up and down the scale just as I had the night before.

"Hey, that sounds *good*!" Luke said.

"Don't it?" Woodrow said.

Suddenly a red sedan of undistinguished aspect and numerous serious dents sped through the front gate and came to a halt at a distance from us. The occupants got out. From the trunk they withdrew their rifles. Then they came our way. I recognized them. They were the Legionnaires from World War I, all in their late fifties and sixties. They too wore suits and ties and blue and gold caps. Some of their suits were wrinkled and shiny.

"They're on their way," one of them said. "Maybe three or four minutes." They assembled in a haphazard semicircle near the canopy and began trying the bolts on their rifles.

I took a deep breath; my palms were clammy. I gazed up the way and saw Dusty sitting obediently next to the mutilated angel. Several aged people from Blackberry Hill had gathered in the road above to watch. I took the mouthpiece from the trumpet and buzzed it with my lips.

"Don't *worry*," Luke said.

"Here they come!" Woodrow said.

On the road leading into the gate I saw the long obsidian hearse, Potter Ricks at the wheel, its motor a nearly soundless purr as it led the procession of vehicles into the cemetery, rounded the turn, and approached us. The Legionnaires formed a row.

"*Hey!*" One of them was whispering to me.

"Hey! Straighten up!" Holding the trumpet in my right hand, I too brought myself to attention.

I often look back on that first of our burials, and even now I remember the sight of the hearse and the agitation in my midriff and my silent, febrile admonition: Arch, where are you when I need you?

Some things come back in memory as in a dream. Psychiatry reminds us that dreams tell us who we are. I myself have long since discovered that many of the moments of life — of grief or ecstasy or sorrow — are dreamlike in their unfolding, at once starker and more fragile than reality itself. Yet I was struck too by the horrified feeling, a kind of weird paramnesia, curious and startling and inexplicable, that somehow I had experienced this scene, this event, before, but where, and what *was* this illusion? The rest of that afternoon is blurred and attenuated like that, rising as in a reverie, a nebulous hint of things to come: the silver-toned gray coffin draped in the Stars and Stripes, Potter Ricks leading the mourners to the funeral home chairs, the pomp and display of the military service, the preacher's recitations, the family's tears. *"Ready . . . aim . . . fire!"* The Legionnaires lifted their volleys high across the summer hills, and the echoes boomed along the farthest horizon, and rolled back to us again among the windless trees.

Is it surprising that my high F was unsure?

The official escort sent by the army, wearing his dress uniform, folded the flag and presented it in a case to the mother, whispering to her that he represented the president of the United States. As the minister led the mourners in the Lord's Prayer, the apparatus lowering the coffin made a slow, grisly creak. In moments the crowd had dispersed, disappearing around the bend back into town. Two little black boys, who must have been watching from a hidden place, appeared from nowhere; gleaning and gathering like squirrels, they swooped up the empty brass casements from the rifle shells. At that moment I saw the gravediggers for the first time, two black men in sweaty khakis and a gray-faced white man in stained work clothes, as they walked languidly toward us from their own secret station. The white man, I knew, was the sexton, Chase Bowie, who had overseen this graveyard since the days of Potter Ricks's father, drove a black prewar pickup truck with "City of Fisk's Landing" in white enamel lettering on both its doors and half a dozen shovels and a wheelbarrow rattling in the back, and lived alone on a screened-in houseboat on the river. Everyone knew of the ten-year-old boy beaten to death by his parents in St. Louis in '39 and how the parents had driven fortuitously all the way here with the boy in the trunk and dug a hole in the cemetery late at night and left him there and how Chase Bowie had discovered the uncertain grave and bought the boy a suit of clothes and a coffin and marker and given him a Christian burial, and then answered all who inquired, "Maybe someday I'll meet the boy in heaven and God will say, 'Well done, good and faithful servant.'"

Now Chase Bowie joined Luke, Potter Ricks, and Woodrow near the hearse. As they inspected the scene, Mr. Bowie turned slightly sideways and spit out a thin stream of tobacco, performing the act so esoterically and avoiding the nearest tombstone by at least three feet, that one had to be looking straight at him even to have noticed.

"A nice service," he said.

"I think so too," Potter Ricks said.

I climbed up to the angel to get my dog, and when I returned the artificial grass had been removed and the workers were already shoveling dirt into the grave. Potter Ricks and Woodrow were carrying the chairs back to the van. The Cadillac hearse was still parked nearby, and the Legionnaires were standing at their car. They were casually holding their rifles, and I noticed they were passing around a pint bottle; they were laughing — a boisterous laughter of release. It impressed me that the trappings of grief were being so quickly discarded.

The gravediggers went about their work in silence, grunting now and then as they shoveled. Luke Cartwright looked thoughtful as he observed this ritual.

"Say, you did fine. Really fine," he said.

I messed up the high note, I said.

"Well, just a little bit. But you'll get better."

The chairs had all been removed now, and Potter Ricks bustled pointedly in our direction, pausing once or twice to give instructions. He shed his coat, which he carefully draped over a tall, immaculate tombstone; he was wearing brilliant green suspenders. He wiped his brow with a matching green handkerchief.

He was of medium height, in his late forties, with ponderous horn-rimmed glasses supported by an auspicious nose. His hair was long and silver, and at the crown of his head was a prominent bald pate like a cleric's tonsure, crimson now from the sun. He had an expansive paunch, which he rubbed now and again in nervous habitude, and he moved about in his errands at a slight list, like a ship in distress. I had seen him everywhere in the town — at funerals, of course, and at churches, coffee shops, ball games. It was a funeral-going society in those days, and for that reason if no other he was a ubiquitous presence. He read occasionally in the Episcopal services, and always in a high, impatient voice, as if he were expecting more than the Scriptures themselves had to offer or he had seen too much of mutilated ruin and decay to permit mere words to convey the solaces.

He was unmarried and childless, I knew, and more often than not was alone, or was with Woodrow, in those places where Woodrow was allowed to go. I had often seen just the two of them riding about in the black hearse.

An observant boy in the small town of that long-ago American era could learn much by just listening and watching, and could privately appropriate merely in the course of events more knowledge of an adult person than that person might have of himself; the whole village context was as interesting as a radio show, or a Hollywood one, and did not cost a cent. The ornately polite and elaborate society of that old small town rewarded the child for keen observation and encouraged him to listen — a society of extremes with secrets not easily honored. I understood something about Potter Ricks that I could not readily articulate.

In the months ahead, as I grew to know Potter Ricks, I would discover him to be a fount of lore, very shrewd and intelligent and funny, not unlike Luke, but more self-conscious, having a monkish and ascetic kind of sagacity in the midst of his dismal craft. If the mortician's trade is by design a gregarious one, then perhaps he was an incongruity. He seemed to mix easily when he had to, in the professional sense at least, but I would soon feel in him when he was at leisure a diffident unease and inadequacy, a bottomless dissatisfaction. He seemed anything but lonely in this moment of denouement in the cemetery.

"Luke, they gave me the message at the church. The fighting last week — Pine and Osbey were wounded. They've been moved to Tokyo. Marshall in the head, Hardy in the chest. Also, I think we can expect two more in a couple of weeks. Scuttles and Puckett."

The dirt plopped in the grave. Woodrow had opened the hood of the hearse and was looking inside.

"Pine and Osbey," Luke repeated.

"That's right."

"That's the Thirty-fifth. Where were they?"

Potter Ricks reached in the pocket of his shirt, brought out a wrinkled piece of paper, and squinted at it through his glasses.

"Wonju," he said.

2

P EOPLE FIND it difficult to believe that in those days we
started driving when we were thirteen or fourteen, or
even younger, greeting such a notion with resentment,
and, one suspects, envy. But the old blue Studebaker that my father had bought before he died was a reality of my existence,
and the use of it was my birthright. It rested in my driveway on
the boulevard and was really mine. One of my memories is of
being propped in my father's lap behind the steering wheel,
guiding the car; I believe I was eight. Cars were our comfort,
our means of breaking away into the vistas. They were not lux-
uries, but *necessities,* our mode of liberation. Georgia had a
car; so did Arch. On this warm, cloudy forenoon of wind and
drizzling rain, Arch arrived at my house in his white and black
Plymouth with dual exhausts, as he frequently did, to drive us
around. I shut the front door and departed from the squeals
and gyrations of the tap dancers.

Arch had come back with his family the night before, and I
was relieved to see him. I climbed in front, and we departed
down the boulevard. We were meeting Georgia, who also had
just returned to town from Memphis with her parents.

When I told him about Luke Cartwright and the military
burial, he reacted with his usual impervious scowl. He had the
car radio on, and it was surely not fortuitous that the report

from the war interrupted the dance music as I was talking: *Chinese Communist hordes attacking on horse and foot to the sounds of bugle calls cut up Americans and South Koreans at Unson yesterday in an Indian-style massacre . . .*

"Luke will have to tell the bosses," Arch said. Even well-off boys like Arch worked in the summers, if fitfully. He and I sacked groceries at the Jitney Jungle on the main street on Mondays, Wednesdays, and Fridays at 50 cents an hour.

"I'd rather play echo," he added, and I was not surprised. My descriptions of the grieving mourners, the accumulated dirt under the ersatz grass, my clammy hands, the starched and prickly dress shirt, the sickly, oversweet smell of the flowers, and the way all the people stared straight at me had had an effect on him.

I played at the grave last Tuesday, I said. It was only fair that it would be his turn next.

"We'll flip," he said.

That was the day we formed our agreement, as earnest and sacrosanct a compact as I would ever make. The winner of the toss would get echo. We could have chosen to take turns, I suppose, but there was something fitting, of a piece with the setting, in the arrangement. Also, we sprang from a province of gamblers. I believe it was as if we, Arch and I, in those later moments, would feel we had a choice in these matters, the divide between death and life, based on the flip of a coin. Is that why we would always call on a neutral party to make the flip, or was it that we did not trust each other? An echo, I would learn, was a kind of life in perpetuity, remote and immune, distant lingering notes from afar, sweetly voyeuristic, while the grave was, after all, the grave. Looking back, however, I do not think either of us knew that day how important the toss would be.

Arch's radio was playing one of the popular songs, "The Things We Did Last Summer." Little Baptist girls at vacation Bible school were gathered on the lawn of the Baptist church, which covered more than half a block, singing, "I'm a little Sunbeam shining every day . . ."

We drove past the town museum with its collection of old cannons, arrowheads, Confederate money, stuffed snakes, Indian skeletons, alligator skulls, a few Jefferson Davis letters, and a sword said to have been used at the Battle of Waterloo. Farther on was the motor court with its neat tiny white-framed bungalows never more than a quarter filled with tired, obscure, end-of-the-day transients en route down the state highway toward the capital city or New Orleans. Its weary green neon sign read: "Fisk's Landing Motor Court." My companion grasped the yellow knob on the steering wheel and with a deft whirl turned off the main street, then crossed the Illinois Central tracks by the abandoned depot. It was here, on a Sunday afternoon during the last war, that a POW train briefly stopped on its way into the flatland, and Arch and I mustered the courage to walk up to it and gaze at the Germans behind the barred windows, and they started talking to us in broken English in a friendly enough way. "I have boy like you," one of them said, and then they reached through the bars and handed each of us a can of Pet Milk, a rationed delicacy of that time, and in return we gave them some war bubble gum, and they waved at us as the train rumbled away, and all this was hugely confusing.

In the distance was the river. It was a very old river, they said, because of its elaborate twists and turns, and the way it was always winding away toward somewhere in a misty rain; with all its murky sidestreams it could be beautiful and serene, yet we knew it could be dangerous, too, and not to be trifled with, its odor now in the high season like good fresh mud, and on this day it was swollen from thunderstorms and filled with floating debris. We turned onto New Africa Road. The gravel lane approaching it was lined with shacks on stilts to escape the springtime floods. The smoke of overheated lard hung in the air. Patches of dull water still stood in the ditches and gullies. Half-clothed children sprawled on the porches. Old tires hung by ropes from the trees for swings. Rusty, broken-down washing machines and disembodied cars without doors or engines or windows or wheels, empty soft drink bottles, and a vast paraphernalia of defunct items filled the yards. Black women in flimsy cotton dresses walked toward the white precincts of town with baskets full of freshly washed clothes balanced on their heads; they carried their coins and dollar bills, I knew, in handkerchiefs tied tightly at both ends. Gray-haired men sat whittling wood in front of a beer joint called Lena's Lizard Den and another named Minotti's Club, which had an autographed picture of Mussolini on the wall until they took it down in December of '41, and the Chinese-owned grocery with its sign: "Hot Tamales 25¢ a Doz." We turned down the dirt road called Swamp Alley: Booga Bottom Store with its Shaystana's Beer Place, Maisie's Refreshment Co., Excelsior Pool Hall, Holy Ghost Revival Center, the Eastern Star, Sons and Daughters of the I Will Arise Society. Even at this hour younger men were staggering from the bootlegger's, carrying bottles of cheap wine. The whole milieu was as familiar to me as anything I had ever known, or would ever remember.

As we drove by the black school, called "Number Two," it began to rain harder. Long fingers of lightning flashed across the purple horizon out by the river, pulsing soundlessly above the darkened fields, and a bleak dampness rose from the gullies. Dusty sank low on the back seat to hide from the thunder, and Arch squinted hard through the windshield.

He was talking about the Gulf of Mexico, where you had to wade out a quarter of a mile to swim. "And they'll sell you beer in the honky-tonks even if you're twelve," he said. "Rich Yankees everywhere, for Chrissake. And girls in *bikinis*."

I had known him, as I had Georgia, as long as memory. He was an inch taller than I and six months older. In that time of short haircuts, his wavy black hair had the pompadour my mother wished of mine, which he kept in place with generous applications of greasy hair lotion, and he was constantly reaching into his pocket for a comb to keep the pompadour in the proper contour; and it glistened like polished teak; he called his greasy hair lotion "stinkum," and his pocket comb gleamed with the stuff, as if he had been dipping it all day into a vat of linseed oil. At sixteen he had already experimented unsuccessfully with a mustache; it looked *cheesy,* Georgia said. He suffered from sporadic pimples, and until recently had the nasty public habit of squeezing them dry with his fingers. It was Arch, not *Archie.* If people had liked him more, it would have been Archie, the diminutive then, as always, being a talisman of local affection, but they did not, although a number of the older students called him simply "Mullet."

He was a misanthrope by age ten. Although his mother and father were ardent Calvinists, even then he did not go to church, considering it a wasted effort. His father had acquired a great deal of real estate during the Depression and likewise owned a prosperous low-rate mercantile establishment on the main street that catered both to whites and to blacks and was indeed called the White and Black Store. His family lived in a sprawling Victorian manse on the boulevard with a large living room, where we often shot marbles on gray wintry afternoons, using chalk for the circles, a pool table in the basement, and a refrigerator crammed always to capacity with everything good, making the one in my own kitchen seem poor and bereft, and even an old pie safe with air holes, which was filled with pecan and lemon and sweet potato pies and fresh cornbread and biscuits. We once got in a fight that lasted four blocks up the boulevard. "He's no good," my mother had said twenty times if she had said it once. "No bloodlines. No *manners.*"

But in that time and that place there was obligation in the *modus vivendi,* and in the pubescent years Arch Kidd's precocious cynicism mellowed into what might pass for merely regional irascibilities, which even at that were not punitive, merely eccentric. To his credit he never denied his artifices and indeed seemed immensely proud of them. Certain human beings will go to any length to entertain themselves, and he distracted himself from lassitude in those days with flamboyant gambits and divertissements. For instance, one Halloween night he took a cow from a nearby pasture and led it into the school auditorium and left it there, and when Coach Asphalt Thomas came down the aisle in the dark to turn on the lights for the teachers to practice their faculty play, he bumped into the horns and nearly expired in a seizure. Later that semester, Arch secretly constructed several time bombs made of the most powerful firecrackers and planted them periodically in hidden crevices of the school building. For an entire week three of these bombs went off daily, at precisely 9:00 A.M., 11:00 A.M., and 2:00 P.M., rending the very air with their mighty detonations and prompting a frenzied inquisition by the school principal that led nowhere. In such ways did Arch Kidd taunt the deities and find his own way on this earth, a living embodiment if ever there was one of the childhood verse: "Run, run, as fast as you can. You can't catch me; I'm the gingerbread man."

Fey though he was in his caginess, he was still infinitely more of the world than I. He would drag-race anyone on the flat dirt roads slicing through the cotton fields. Away from home he smoked Camel cigarettes. Like the man who could resist anything but temptation, he claimed not to be superstitious, but he was consumed with archaic phobias and his dossier of demons was staggering: he confessed not to trust ice water because of the chemicals from the mosquito truck, believed old women in black dresses and dogs without tails were unlucky, and said that one in every ten black people was either a voodoo sorcerer or a juju mama.

Despite all this, or perhaps because of it, he belonged with a trumpet; it was his very métier. From the time he was a small boy watching the Christmas parades he liked the way a trumpet looked and sounded. In the fourth grade, he got a plastic four-valved Emenee trumpet, which you tooted into rather than buzzed, and carried it with him everywhere, driving half the borough to distraction with his ceaseless blowing. When he acquired the genuine instrument, he practiced every afternoon from the Arban Method book and the Schlossberg book — lots of études — so that the corridors of the school and his entire neighborhood rang with his frilly exercises and with difficult pieces like "Muskrat Ramble." He blew and blew, and the only true icon of his whole existence, as far as I knew, was the most popular trumpeter of that day, Harry James, whose records with their deft silken strains and titles like "You Made Me Love You" he hovered over at all hours and whom he referred to with the only deference of outright religiosity I ever heard from him: "Just listen! He's *hot*! He's *me*!" He had recently been named to the all-state band, and he also performed in the adult men's dance group called the Merry Makers, whose base was the Elks Lodge.

Back in the spring he and I had won a "Superior" in the state band contest in the capital city for a duet rendition of "The Flight of the Bumblebee." In the course of events, as all mystics comprehend, there can be a magic, defying all logic, which will seize a moment, something curious and indeed existential, undergirded by ancient mysteries — the eternal enigmas of the Old Testament, for instance — and this, of course, is the material of poets. On that afternoon, there was an artist's soul in the way Arch triple-tongued his part of that skittish tune. Afterward he told the judges that he thought we deserved an "Extra-Superior."

Except for the trumpet, which would one day earn him first chair in the state university band, he was satanically lazy, a veritable paradigm of sloth, and prided himself on never having made an A. When Mrs. Idella King assigned a book report, he read Classic Comics. He was ecumenical in his abhorrences, his assessment of human capacity being at best niggardly, and as if he were a victim of genetic misanthropy proudly confessed to hate and distrust just about everyone in varying degrees but himself. In a word, then, he was weird. Even today, all these years later, I cannot begin to fathom the poltergeist that inhabited the grottos in his head.

Merciless, mindless, and incorrigible as he was, being too a liar of Rabelaisian dimensions, Arch was my comrade out of convenience, I suppose, or perhaps just necessity. We came along at about the same time and in that particular place.

Whatever it was, I was glad to have another trumpet back in town.

At this moment he lit a cigarette and inhaled deeply. "I wish I'd started smoking three years ago," he said. "Think of all the pleasure I've missed." We were on the main street again. The rain had stopped for the moment, but the skies remained purple and implacable. On the minuscule lawn of the Ricks Funeral Home, the assistant, Woodrow, was clipping the hedges. Potter Ricks sat on the gallery reading a newspaper.

I suggested we see if they knew something.

Arch put out his cigarette and turned into the driveway. I had never been back there. The Cadillac hearse and an ambulance were parked in front of two macabre and ominous outbuildings, both tightly shuttered.

When Potter Ricks saw us, he set aside the newspaper, brushed his seersucker with his palm, and came out to greet us through the open windows of the car.

Was there any news?

"I'm afraid so." His glasses were cloudy from the unctuous humidity and his round face had a doleful expression. Behind his spectacles his eyes were as amorphous as mist. It was his *eyes* I always remembered — catlike but dim, if such a thing is possible. "Marshall Pine died. His family got the telegram last night. I've been out there this morning."

Were those the Pines on Burrows Road? Arch asked. And was his hand trembling as he lit another cigarette?

"The same ones. He was twenty-two. He worked at the lumber mill. He's got a wife and a boy eight months old."

I remembered him. He drove an old black Pontiac with whitewall tires and a Rebel flag and squirrel tail on the radio aerial. I once saw him very drunk in Son Graham's grocery store. He insisted that day on buying me a whole pack of chewing tobacco.

"It was pretty bad out there," Potter Ricks was saying in his high, querulous tone. "One of the doctors had to go out and give the mother some pills. The wife too. His older brother was killed in the Pacific, you know. Grady Pine. One of those little islands. Pelilieu, I think. In '44, as I recall. He's buried out there somewhere." As he told us this, a strand of his silver hair fell almost to his nose, and he swiftly brushed it into place with a finger again.

He seemed to want us to tarry, to talk with him for a while. "Of course, we don't know how long it will take to get him back. The Goodloe boy took almost three months. The Scuttles boy died over two months ago. Puckett too. We expect word from the army almost any time now."

Suddenly, from the rear of the funeral home emerged a startling apparition. A gaunt black man perhaps seventy years old was walking methodically up the driveway. His thin ebony hand was extended horizontally from his side and at intervals grazed the bricks of the building. He wore an immaculate blue suit and blue felt hat and matching tie. His eyes were glazed and dead. He seemed to float in the watery air.

"How are you today, Silas?" Potter Ricks said.

"I heard Woodrow clippin' out here." When he reached the front lawn he managed to turn without pause, as if from guileless intuition. In moments he and Woodrow were in conversation. Arch cranked the motor. As we departed, Potter,

Woodrow, and the disconcerting eyeless man withdrew inside from the reappearing gusts of rain. "Christ!" Arch said. "Was that a black ghost?"

Georgia was waiting on the porch of her porticoed house on the boulevard. She climbed into the back seat of the car, a tousled miracle in wet disarray. "Move over, Dusty!" She pinched me hard on the back of the neck. Then she shook her hair so vigorously that the moisture sprayed Arch and me on the front seat.

"I've been dying from boredom. Where are we going?"

In the summertime in those years that was the most suitable question of all. When you were not working at the Jitney, there was not especially much to do. You could see a show at the Rebel or the Rex, mainly for the air-conditioning, or visit the Coca-Cola Company to observe them putting the caps on the bottles, or lounge about the library, or go to the courthouse when court was in session and watch a trial. And to compound the malaise, many of our contemporaries were on vacation with their families: on the Gulf Coast, in the Ozarks, in Memphis or New Orleans, or even in St. Louis for the Cardinals ball games.

I suggested getting something for a picnic in the country.

"We'll ride around first," Arch, the captain of the vessel, said, consistent with his general inertia.

"Let's go to Lutherville," Georgia said.

"Too far in this rain," Arch said. And, withal, the resolution of all the world's ennui did indeed lie in "riding around," main street to country club, boulevard to cemetery, flatland to hills, then all over again, the rubric and imprimatur of the generation.

We were halfway down the boulevard. In the morning rain, the trees, which made a verdant tunnel there, were bent in deep, anguished contours, like falling curtains of green.

"Marshall Pine died, didn't he?" Georgia said. "He used to work for us."

I turned to look at her. The sight of her sitting there in her blue cotton dress with my dog's head in her lap touched me in that moment with a strange emotion of belonging, recent to me and imponderable.

I had known Georgia since the beginning. That was the way it was in Fisk's Landing. We had been together about as long as most people can be. She was three days younger than I. On school mornings she and Arch would be waiting for Dusty and me on her front steps. As we walked to the school, Dusty would always turn around in the same spot and go back home. Our great-grandfathers had been friends and political allies more than a century before. They were Whigs and Unionists and friends of Henry Clay himself and had both served in the state cabinet under a brave and irascible Unionist governor. She was tall and slender, dark-skinned for a light-haired girl, and she had thick blond eyebrows. A thin scar ran down the corner of her mouth, the result of her having stumbled into a wrought-iron fence when she was eleven.

Where does memory begin? She and I are sitting on the grass in her backyard in a summer's sun. We are taking turns with a hammer killing ants on a large stone and pretending they are Japanese soldiers. The rat-tat-tat of the hammer echoes down the alleyway and off the facades of her grandmother's house next door. We turn over the stone to stir up more ants. A hairy black spider with horrible legs suddenly crawls out toward us. With a horrendous shriek Georgia retreats on all fours and collapses on the warm grass, sprawled there with eyes rolling histrionically toward the sky. Somewhere in the mists there is the image of my father coming to the back lawn that day and taking us to the drugstore for ice cream cones.

Her maid Bermuda walks us into town for typhoid shots at

the county health office. Georgia refuses to go through with it, sitting in her chair and not budging, as stolid as a statue. The nurse could have been Cinderella's stepmother; she approaches us with the great needle. Georgia closes her eyes and shakes her head. Someone, perhaps I, had told her that the needle goes all the way through the arm, bone and all. *"Not today,"* she says. "Can we do it tomorrow?" But the deed is accomplished, and the reward is a war movie at the theater. Bermuda has to sit in the balcony, which people call the Buzzards' Roost, and Georgia and I sit crouched in the dark. Until age four I had thought the Metro-Goldwyn-Mayer lion lived under the stage and crawled out before every show to roar. In the fan-blown downstairs of the theater we watch wide-eyed as the Japanese torture and bayonet our starved soldiers and then our demure and frightened nurses, slapping them around, refusing them water, stringing them up to trees. Is this their revenge for the ants?

Walking home with the matching patches on our arms from the typhoid shots, Bermuda shepherding us, we avoid every crack in the sidewalk, jumping over them, chattering about the Japs.

She got mad at me in the seventh grade. We were going together to the junior high homecoming dance. All the other boys sent the girls mums, or corsages. She presented me with a boutonniere, but I had nothing for her. "You're cheap, Swayze," she said. "But I *know* you," I defended myself. "Oh, so that's it," she said. "You *know* me." She forgot the matter in minutes, but her mother would not speak to me for a long time.

Her father was a planter who drove in a pickup truck out from town to his cotton every dawn like a hired hand to coax the black workers to do what he said. As Georgia grew older, her mother terrorized her. Her name was Alice and she was a virago, with a big, malignant mouth on an otherwise handsome face. She and my own mother had a grave mutual respect for their family lineages, which gave them a haughty and prideful bond amid the generally unpolished bourgeois jousting for position, but beyond that as far as I could tell their relationship was fragmentary. Alice had been the ranking beauty queen at the state university in her day, and her elder daughter, Cassidy, had also won all the glittering trinkets before marrying a rich Kentucky lawyer and aspiring politician exactly twenty-four hours after her college graduation. So the mother demanded of the younger girl the requisite demeanor, the vacuous smiles, the docile compromises, the meretricious proprieties. Georgia was much too seditious to have much to do with that. "Let's swap mothers," she said to me one day, because she knew mine well. "At least I could learn tap dance." The subjugation of southern matriarchy was one of our serviceable bonds.

She never went out for the beauty contests in school, which was all but unprecedented among the pretty girls of the town. She was a good dancer, but the worst driver I ever knew, and sometimes she was clumsy. She had a strong, lithesome body and good calves and legs; more than once I suggested she should go out for basketball or track. She played a desultory flute in the band, and even refused a chance at drum majorette or cheerleader, a tripartite heresy. "I'm ugly and knock-kneed," she would say to me in those days. If you looked at her from behind, she really *was* a little knock-kneed, but on the eve of sixteen I began to notice the fine shape of her, her slender thighs and full hips, and the funny, bouncing way she moved about on her toes when she was in a good mood.

Back when we entered high school, she had started cursing profusely, and this budding profanity in her high, lilting accent was unaccountable to me, the maturing acolyte. She began stealing secretly from her parents' gin and bourbon supply and driving one of the family Buicks with a reckless disregard for herself and the commonweal. One evening when I was fourteen, I chanced upon a monumental scene. She and her mother were actually wrestling in their backyard, rolling madly about in the grass — two prehensile creatures of the night, calling each other names and trying to gouge out each other's eyes, her mother like a tigress who has just brought down an impala. When I embarrassedly separated them, they apologized sheepishly — not to each other but to me. One Saturday afternoon when her parents were out of town at a college ball game I went into her house and found her slumped morosely on the edge of her bed, surrounded by her vast collection of teddy bears and college football pennants, old Monopoly sets and photographs and childhood hair ribbons and little glass animals and porcelain birds. She was drunkenly smoking a cigarette. Then she began to get sick. I helped her into the bathroom, where she threw up, then led her back to the bed and rubbed her face with a wet towel.

"Just go away," she said, looking at me in sad distaste. "Just get out of here, jackass."

Something had obviously turned septic in her. She had always had a raw temper, but now she was given to ungovernable rages. When her sister, Cassidy, was home on a visit, they got in a terrible argument and Georgia threw a glass of milk at her. She once slapped Arch Kidd so hard in study hall that he claimed she knocked out a filling in his teeth. She discovered her parents' illustrated sex manuals in the back of a closet and read them cover to cover, then described to her older girlfriends the vivid aspects of sexual congress. She would go out drinking with these girls; they were a bad group. On weekend nights they would mix a villainous concoction that they called "Fisk's Juice" — gin, vodka, and five or six kinds of fruit juice, garnished with sliced lemons and limes and cherries — in a tin washtub and put it in the trunk of one of their cars and drive out to the remotest finger of Turtle Lake and smoke cigarettes, French-inhaling them the way the women did in the movies then, and drink and strip naked and splash around in the water.

Perhaps this was some odd rite of fertility, like the ones I read about in *National Geographic* concerning the hedonistic virgins of the Shiriantes rain forests. Arch claimed to have spied on them from down the way. An older boy said he found Georgia extremely drunk one night in the back seat of another girl's car and kissed her for ten minutes and fondled her breasts. This killed me, the thought of it. Her artless dementia touched a strange, hidden disquiet in me. Was it jealousy — or envy of her heedlessness?

At sixteen, for inexplicable reasons, she gradually calmed down. I could observe it happening before my eyes. To this day I am not sure what it was. Remorse? Fear? Desperation? Ancestry? "I won't call you a jackass again," she said. And she more or less lived up to that promise, though not fully.

She seethed with imperfections. Despite her tumultuous relationship with her mother, she was shamelessly, unregenerately spoiled. Her father was rich, but the preponderance of the fortune derived from her mother, who had inherited from her own parents' considerable property in the expanding capital city. Georgia carried a small mountain of $5 bills and was always buying the supplemental necessities for herself, mostly new gadgets, antique bric-a-brac, and expensive teddy bears. She always had two or three good cameras, and she liked to take photographs of fields and creeks and tree stumps and houses and people and dogs. She tried to buy things for other people, too.

"Let me get you that little radio," she would say to me.

No.

"You need that radio."

"No, I don't."

"Receiving is a form of giving," she said, in one of those sudden banal homilies that came to her every now and again.

"Please, no."

"Jackass." And the next day I found the radio gift-wrapped in red bunting on my front steps.

Her moods descended from heights of rosy hilarity to damp dungeons of melancholia. She thrived on extremes. She was given to half-contemptuous pouts and vague trails of indifference, though to her credit neither lasted very long. Away from her house she still smoked cigarettes, though not as much. She was a composite of polarities: sweet and mocking, innocent and cunning, careless and clever. Yet vanity was unknown to her, as was the meddling style of the other girls; gossip and idle prattle were not in her nature, and she lacked the nervous, overpreening self-consciousness of the others her age. She was funny. She thought about things. She listened to you and knew what you were talking about. She was warm and tactile; for as long as I could remember she liked to touch you when she talked with you, and her heart was proud and brave.

"I love my name." And she really did. "It's the only good thing my mama ever did for me." Sometimes, in Arch's backyard as we played our funny, lighthearted tandem trumpets, she would unashamedly sing a few words in a nebulous and quivery key: "Just an old sweet song keeps Georgia on my mind."

Spoiled, irreverent, unpredictable, she had, too, her insecurities. There was seven years' difference between her and Cassidy, the sorority president and beauty queen, and her mother never let Georgia forget her poised and unparalleled sibling. Georgia was rich and handsome, with all the advantages — still there had to be something in her at sixteen that secretly resented the arid beauties like our schoolmate Zamma Lou Bailey, middle-class, middle-of-the-road, Methodist, elaborately placid, thin-lipped, pliant, and coy, who mingled effortlessly with the other town students and secretly belittled the girls from the hills, and was naturally and inevitably rewarded with the titles Cheerleader, Most Popular, Homecoming Queen — groomed to speak in a certain way to prepare for Sorority Row at the state university, with an accent as distinctive as

Groton's or St. Paul's, yet next to impossible to replicate on paper, involving long accentuated vowels in the last words of sentences, like "Thank-*QUE!*" and which Georgia herself liked to mimic. And they did not care for her very much either.

I mentioned her absence of conceit, and of narcissism and vanity, but she liked clothes, and her mother bought them abundantly for her. As early as the fourth grade, when we were confirmed together in the church, kneeling next to each other at the altar as the bishop from the capital city rested his hands ceremoniously on her head, then mine, she fretted about whether her white French lace dress was all right on her. "Did I look okay?" As long as I knew her, this was her only concession to display, how she looked when she really dressed up. I never fully understood this, given especially her disdain for the usual niceties, but there was a hardy element of surprise in her. I would know her better than anyone, and then in her alternating temperaments of loyalty and rage and incertitude she would be someone I never understood at all, though I tried.

"I don't think anybody has any idea who anybody else is anyway," Luke said to me later in that year.

Much of the time her wardrobe was plain blouses and straight skirts or faded blue jeans worn tightly at her hips, but she also relished V-necked cashmeres and dresses from the capital city, and the previous year she had gone to the Christmas dance in her mother's white rabbit stole and the white pearls that had been her great-grandmother's. She seldom wore makeup, unlike most of the other girls who were heavily colored, but when she did, for a dance or some other special occasion, it was bare touches of rouge and lipstick, small deferences to the beauty she did not see in herself. Later that year, one night when she was dressing upstairs, I was the recipient of an improbable discourse from her mother, who informed me that Georgia wore an 8½ quad-A with a double-A heel, as if I knew the difference between that and a pair of basketball sneakers or football cleats. "It's an *aristocratic* foot," she explained. And she actually brought one out and showed it to me. "You see? Very thin. I wear the same ones. The stores here can't afford to carry a shoe like this. The Jews and Arch's daddy only carry shoes the Negroes and Ruston Hill girls can wear, and six-and-a-half Bs for the *Zamma Baileys*." She spit out the name as if she had just swallowed a jalapeño. "I have to go to Memphis to get shoes for Georgia." It was a lesson in genetics, and I have not forgotten it.

With all her failings, Georgia was never unkind to those her mother considered beneath her; she had a genuine intuitive responsiveness to blacks and poor whites like Lank Hemphill and a sympathy for the weak, reserving her scorn for the proper town girls with their varying pretensions. Several times I was with her in front of the little rural stores when she bought chewing tobacco and snuff and hard candy for the feeble old black men gathered there, and bantered affectionately with them, and they joined almost in chorus: "Thank you, Little Missy." There was an old blind man with a scraggly yellow dog, rather bleary-eyed himself, who shuffled along the main street on Saturdays. The dog had a tin can attached to his collar, and Georgia was always putting a handful of quarters in the can and bending down and petting the pathetic old dog, who looked at her tenderly and licked her hand and moved his ragged tail in benediction.

Why, I have often wondered over the passing years, did we come together, approach maturity together? I must have needed her softness, her emotion, her warmth, her loyalty, even the selfish part of her. But why *me,* unsure, too, and alone? She could have had any of the older boys. We were there in that time and circumstance, like Arch and me, but different by a very world. Perhaps it was simple — friendship and familiarity and family and the past and growing up — if things like that are simple. Maybe we were joined in the soul.

*   *   *

There was a morning two weeks before school let out. I had just won the high school spelling bee, a marathon that had already lasted three straight weekly assemblies, culminating in a lengthy *mano á mano* with a senior named Marion Whittington, an exercise that put everyone to sleep until, after nearly an hour, as we lobbed words back and forth as effortlessly as tennis balls on a dreamy summer's day, a subtle electricity seized the atmosphere of the auditorium, and all the bored boys and girls in the flush of creamy adolescence suddenly opened their eyes and stirred to life when Mrs. Idella King pronounced the word *sacrilegious*. Divine irony intervened when I defeated Marion Whittington, son of the Presbyterian pastor, on just such a word. I was surprised more than anyone by my prolonged triumph, as when on awakening from a particularly phantasmagoric dream, one drowsily tries to explain to himself where on earth all that came from.

When it was over, something astonishing and unforeseen occurred in the hallway. Georgia kissed me on the cheek and hugged me. That had never happened before. And right there in front of everybody! "You were so smart," she said, "and you looked nice," and she hugged me again.

Later that afternoon, after school was out, I took my dog into the backyard and gave him a flea bath. After lathering him profusely and washing him down with the garden hose, I left him outside to dry himself by rolling around in the grass. I was sitting in the kitchen with my mother, who wished to know if there was a *state* competition in spelling. Her anxious round face was heavy with trepidation.

"You wouldn't go far there," she said. "They're smarter in the big towns. You'd better get down to work on a lot more words."

There was a knock on the door, and it was Georgia.

"Hello, Mrs. Barksdale."

"Hello, Georgia. What are you doing here?"

Georgia rolled out her hand. "Look what I've got. I ran into Mrs. King and she told me to bring it by. She just got it engraved at the jewelry store."

It was a large round medal with my name on it.

"That's nice of you," my mother said. "Does he deserve it?"

"Of course he does."

"I don't know about that. He's so lazy I can't get him to do anything."

I swallowed a protest, knowing the odds against me.

"He doesn't care about himself. Doesn't care how he looks. He doesn't study his books." She punctuated this sobering disquisition with an unsatisfactory gesture to laughter, found it wanting, and lapsed again into the same lost gloomy hauteur.

"I tell you, Georgia, he's *lazy*." She had long ago convinced me of this putative truth. But an outlander, a student of the regional forms entering that modest kitchen in that instant, would likely have found this a most bizarre domestic burlesque, a study perhaps in mores.

"He's *not* lazy!" Georgia's stern and sudden admonishment surprised me as much as it did my mother, who glanced up at her with an expression so anguished and astounded that for the briefest moment I felt almost embarrassed for her. "Well," she said, and nervously began curling the back of her hair with her index finger, as she usually did when rendered speechless, "I don't know." And she glowered at the checkered linoleum.

Georgia remained standing. "I'm sorry," she said. "But you're just *wrong*." And then she surprised me again, for the third time that day. She actually began *laughing*. "Oh, I'm sorry!" And she giggled so hard that her cheeks grew rosy and her long blond hair fell onto her face. This swift levity, if that is what it was, brought Dusty in from the opened back door, water dripping behind him, to do a lavish, affectionate pirouette in front of Georgia. Even my mother giggled a little, but it was apparent her heart was not in it. Georgia apologized

once more, then said she had to be going. I walked with her
outside.

Georgia and I stood in front of the house. Under our great
walnut the sunshine made dappled shadows on the newly cut
grass. Bees and hummingbirds darted about in the air. A fresh
wind murmured lightly in the trees, and the lazy scent of late
springtime came gliding across the lawn.

"I don't know what made me do that," she said. "She's not
quite as bad as mine."

"She's driving me crazy," I confided, the words thick in my
throat.

"Maybe she *is* crazy. Better crazy than mean."

That very thought had begun to occur to me, as insidious as
a cancer, but I was wary of it, and afraid.

"Well, it's Friday. You want to do something?"

"Sure."

"Let's ride around."

Under the cobalt skies, people everywhere were out working
in their flower and vegetable gardens. In the park at the far end
of the boulevard little boys were playing softball and little girls
were jumping rope. The dogs were out in their normal abun-
dance, peregrinating the streets singly, or in pairs, or sometimes
in a formless and audacious mass. At the foot of the main
street, near the crooked bend in our river, a dozen or so people
were fishing with cane poles, and the sunlight flashed on the
water in sparkles like tiny stars. On the edges of the flat parts of
the town, acre upon acre of tender young cotton plants came
right up to the streets, and, just as in the neighborhoods of
the hills, the wilderness crept up to the very backyards of the
houses. Everything had a good flavor of the earth.

Mindlessly we drove toward a promontory in the hills a few
miles out, where our forestry class went on field trips, a succession of verdant slopes and salients and deep little valleys ending
at an eminence with a most transcendent view of the infinite

flatness. The sun was starting to go now, and the spring horizon was a poem, all golden and scarlet drifts and strands and light creamy wisps, and slowly below, the cicadas began their song. The dark land before us seemed to hum with its vast and prolific richness.

Georgia leaned out the window. "Just smell it," she said. "I don't want to leave."

I stopped the car.

For the longest time my vision of women — of girls — was timorous, expectant, inexpressibly delicious and foolish and sad, and in my lonely imagination touched ever so lovingly with a mysterious, barely understood promise and wonder. But what I was experiencing now was no fantasy. What on earth was happening? It was far too sudden, and not for a moment to be believed. I could feel my blood pumping like an engine. I was suddenly dry-mouthed and lightheaded, and I felt myself breathing very slowly. Please, Lord, I silently entreated the omniscient Anglican God, grant me the nerve.

In all of life there is so little rapture. Let it be cherished as we have it, I have learned, at whatever time, in whatever place, before it recedes from us and is gone forever. Suffering flows after it like an illness, floods the unknown contours of the heart, yet somehow we survive. And with survival come the memories, the sights and sounds and smells of the vanished days — the fresh scent of her hair, the touch of an old tune, the play of sunlight on a familiar lane.

I looked at Georgia, then she at me, with a tenderness I had never seen in her. There was a bright, knowing smile on her lips. I was more frightened than ever. "Oh," she whispered, when I moved close to her. "Oh — you want to kiss me?" It was as wicked as incest, and as innocent as a childish dream.

Arch and Georgia and I had driven to a tiny cotton hamlet two or three miles from town. All around us in the flat fields were the deserted shacks and churches fallen in upon themselves, overtaken by weed and bush and decay, slowly collapsing into the encroaching earth. We sat on the front stoop of a dejected little grocery next to what must have been the nation's tiniest post office, eating cheese and crackers. Dozens of black people, men, women, children, had been standing under a long tin-roofed tractor shed to escape the rain. Now, with hoes on their shoulders, they ambled across the gravel road into the young cotton, bent down en masse, and resumed their labors. Sometimes they called out to one another, or their sudden high laughter rose from the fields and lilted on into the boundless distance, but mostly they worked in silence, like ghosts in a landscape.

"That's our land," Georgia said. "Part of it anyway. We've got a lot of land. I wouldn't be surprised to see Daddy drive up." The bulk of his holdings were called Posey Mound Plantation, it too a miniature kingdom. And farther out toward the river there were three Indian mounds, which seemed always haunted in the fogs when we visited them as children.

Arch tossed Dusty a sliver of cheese. He ate it, glancing up for more.

"Is there anything that dog won't eat?" Arch asked.

Turnip greens and beets, I said.

The screen door to the store creaked open behind us, then noisily banged shut. A little black girl, barefoot and in a tattered green dress, stood impassively before us. "Here, little girl," Georgia said. She handed her a cracker and cheese. The girl took it and nibbled in silence.

"What's your name? Cat got your tongue, sweet little girl?"

"Carol Wanda Franklin."

Georgia reached into her purse for a 50-cent piece. The little girl held it in her palm and gazed down at it.

"Uh-uh," she said, and shook her head.

"Uh-*huh*," Georgia said.

The girl stood there briefly and uncertainly, then walked down the stairs and crossed the road into the fields.

"I feel sorry for them sometimes," Georgia said.

"Sorry for who?" Arch asked.

"For *them*." She gestured toward the fields.

"For Chrissake!" Arch said.

We went back to town and cruised around a little more in the summer indolence. Arch turned the Plymouth through the gate of the cemetery. I looked up the first hill to the site of the burial. That was where I played, I said.

The funeral home canopy had been removed. The mound of earth on the grave had been transformed by the rains to a muddy mess. The dirt that had been covered by the artificial grass ran with dark rivulets. The sprays of flowers so bright that day were now shriveled and sodden. The small rectangular sign with the name on it had fallen down, and lay aslant, a derelict artifact in the moist grass. This place of pomp and mourning, officiousness and curiosity, transient and melancholy beauty, seemed now to be sinking slowly back into the soil, lonesome and spectral under the petulant heavens.

The next day, after sacking groceries at the Jitney from dawn until 2:00 P.M., I left to meet Georgia at the Sears on the main street, where she wanted to buy a birthday present for her father. We had planned to go on to the courthouse to watch part of a murder trial taking place there. In front of the stores all along the street small flags were flapping in the warm early-afternoon's breeze. The whir of the ceiling fans from the sedate interiors could be heard out on the sidewalks. From more than a few of these establishments the sound of the baseball broadcast stirred the midafternoon stillness; the game today was from New York City, and one only had to stroll along the sidewalk to absorb the fragments of the action: the Yankees and the Tigers, and a pitching duel, Reynolds versus Newhauser. I went past the Earl Van Dorn, four floors and the tallest building in town, infirm and more frayed now than it was in its illustrious days, and the placid row of lawyers' offices in their old red-brick two-storied structures: Tidwell and Tidwell; Culpepper, Culpepper and Culpepper; Barnwell, Turnbull, and Hinds. An occasional bored merchant stood in his doorway fanning himself with a funeral home fan or swatting flies while gazing out at the sparse traffic on the street. I knew them all and, as my mother wished, I smiled at every one of them, looked them in the eye, and called them by their names, including the somber proprietor of the auto parts establishment, a prominent Baptist deacon named Brother Parkhearst. Georgia had told me that three times already that summer she had sighted Brother Park-hearst staring at her and the other high school girls lying in the sun by the swimming pool. From behind a high wooden fence he would be looking lasciviously down at them, only his head from the nose up visible at the top of the fence, not unlike the Kilroy-Was-Here drawings of the late big war.

The Sears store, too, was all but empty. Georgia was not yet there. I browsed among the counters, surveyed the harvest of the American bounty, this bonanza of latter-day riches in the poorest of its commonwealths: a cornucopia of textiles and synthetics and twills, appliances and devices of every size and description, gadgets and knickknacks and titillating appara-tuses: radios and record players and tape recorders, deep fryers and refrigerators and battery-charged carving knives and freez-ers and mixers and rotating blenders, toasters and vacuums and electric shavers.

I was attracted by flickering images from the rear of the store. I stood before a row of tiny television screens set in hefty maple cabinets, all turned on, the blurred, snowy images of a wrestling match brought in mysteriously from faraway Mem-phis on cumbersome mile-high antennas. Then the action switched to a baseball game, and "Muscles" Upton of the St.

Louis Browns was at bat in the manmade blizzard — my first glimpse of the new and horrific phenomenon, and on this day it transfixed me.

A clerk came and stood nearby. "They just got in yesterday," he said. "Ain't they somethin'?"

At that moment she appeared. I knew she had been swimming all morning at the country club. In her starched white dress and twine sandals she was as tanned and healthy as anyone who lived on this earth could ever be. Her soft golden blond–streaked hair shone under the fluorescent light, and when she delicately touched me, she smelled of the summertime: sunshine and talcum and grass and water. She paused before the ball game in the luminous snow; the ignominious Muscles Upton had struck out swinging. "We just ordered one from Memphis," she said. "Look at all this stuff! I want to buy one of everything." Among the interminable array of effects and equipment, it took her five minutes to choose the birthday gift, an electric waffle iron with two griddles.

Unlike any number of settlements in the region built around courthouse squares, Fisk's Landing had been laid out in the 1830s on nothing more protean than the pristine and serviceable Christian grid, and its courthouse sat on the final sloping corner before the flatness. The original one had been burned to the ground during a race riot in the 1870s, and the town was so dire and impoverished that it was not replaced for another decade or more. It came along in time to catch the flourishing Victoriana in all its quirk and eccentricity and disarray, flutes and cupolas and balconies and gables and careless frills and trim; it stood there an anomaly, an architectural capriccio, gaunt and intractable.

The courtroom itself was a muted, high-ceilinged old chamber with ornate chandeliers and long oak pews for seats and big brass spittoons and two tall and imposing outside balconies on each end. The spaciousness around the bench, the jury box, and the counsels' tables allowed the lawyers to move freely as they questioned the witnesses and contemplated them, an expression, perhaps, of an age when the law was leisurely and personal, if not especially just. It was not difficult to know when a particularly colorful or gruesome case came along, since most of the people talked about it — all you had to do was eavesdrop — and when we were younger, Georgia and Arch and I and two or three others would stealthily tiptoe into the gallery, barefoot sometimes, in the summers, hide ourselves in a corner, and absorb, awestruck, the imperishable litanies of rapine, deceit, and death, the brooding secrets of the adult universe. Even at that callow age, we must have felt the toxin cast upon us by mayhem and suffering — the incandescent voyeurism of the imperfect human heart.

Georgia and I climbed the stairs now and sat in the same niche in the gallery where we always had when we were younger. There were not many people in the courtroom today: it was a murder involving black people. The trial had begun early that morning. Sometimes such a case — one black person killing another — might not even come to trial, or when it did it would be disposed of quietly and efficiently, even in one sitting. But this one, we had heard, was different because of Mr. Leroy Godbold.

He had the largest plantation in the county. His land — called "Godbold" — was in the northern end about ten miles from the town and was traversed by the meandering river; and his house, an antebellum affair suggesting neglect more than the expected splendor, was situated at one of its most abrupt and sinewy turns. Much of his ground, some of the richest in the world, including the valleys of the Nile and the Ganges, had been the original Fisk holding, which Fisk himself had bought from the government in 1831 at $1.25 an acre and partially cleared of its sprawling hardwood forests, using Africans and Indian laborers. Even the rights to the virgin hickory Godbold could lease for $100,000 a year, and someday, in the far future — these perquisites would be worth more than the land itself.

One of Mr. Godbold's field hands had killed the owner's favorite yardboy, a "convict nigger," he called him, who had been leased to him long before from the state penal farm. Nearly split his face in two with an axe, people said. The field hand had run away and was finally apprehended one county to the east. Had he not left the plantation, it was known, the justice of the matter would have been meted out in the river bottoms or the woods. Normally a black person who murdered another black did not receive the death penalty. But Mr. Leroy Godbold wanted the field hand to get the portable electric chair, and Mr. Godbold usually got what he wanted.

It was a déjà vu of the simplest kind, sitting with Georgia there in the dark cool of the gallery as we always had, but the difference was palpable and vivid — I could *feel* her presence, her light, easy breathing, her talcumed scent, the new foreign pride in being there with her, and this was strange to me. The scene before us was familiar enough: the twelve white men in the jury box, the judge in his flowing robes, the lawyers at their mahogany tables, the gargantuan court reporter with the nose of an eagle and the waddle of a duck, the bored, paunchy deputies in their brown short-sleeved uniforms with .38 pistols on their hips. The defendant sat at one of the tables, a large ebony figure in khakis with an impassive face, gazing straight ahead at nothing.

"My daddy says he's bad," Georgia said, looking down at Mr. Godbold. "I don't know how his wife puts up with him." He was a tall, powerfully built man in his late fifties. His arms were folded casually against his chest, and he was wearing a disheveled light gray suit and white and black wingtip shoes. With his narrow, houndlike face and truculent little mustache, his sharp, knowing glances about the courtroom, his thin perpetual smile, he exuded an aura not so much of prestige as of veiled and privileged omniscience, of somber mystery and cunning, of a strapping feudal grandee in wrinkled summer seersucker. A hint of violence, casual yet imperious, hovered over him, and there were rumors, talk as vague as dust, of an assistant foreman who had vanished years before without a trace.

Leroy Godbold had few pretensions to the flatland aristocracy. The land had been in his family for only two generations (so that Georgia's mother considered them grossly parvenu), his people transplanted from the hills and most of their holdings accumulated in the nonflush times. He had once run for lieutenant governor and lost in the second primary by fewer than a thousand votes. He had helped establish the Dixiecrat Party and had been one of the principal benefactors of the Thurmond-Wright ticket of '48. He was often in the company of the governor of the state and an overnight guest at the mansion in the capital city, and was one of the governor's "Honorary Colonels." He would later help form the white Citizens' Council, which Luke Cartwright called the "KKK with a fancy mustache," but he seldom attended the more elegant parties, and he never deigned to "restore" the old house at the river's bend as the other planters had done with theirs. I had seen him once or twice at the country club and observed how unexpectedly charming he could be with women; yet he would never partake of the prolix recklessness of the playboy planters who drove the newest Cadillacs or Lincolns or sports cars to the Peabody or the Grand Lake Casino or Bourbon Street. Subterranean privilege and emolument and suzerainty and unchallengeable lordship of the alluvial acres were sufficient gratifications, or so it seemed. His maverick lack of interest in the accepted society and its garrulous caprice might have been less emphatic, the mothers of the town belles said, if he had had daughters. He had three sons, Parker, Porter, and Durley, who in differing ways were mirrors of the father. Durley, the eldest, was now an infantry lieutenant in the fighting. I had last seen him those many weeks before with his wife, Amanda, on the day the guard departed for the war in Korea.

As I looked down with Georgia from the gallery at the father with his hard, narrow face, I remembered the only moment when our lives had converged, the one time I had ever spoken to him. It was brief and unforgettable. He had a nephew two years older than I named Parker Jr., who lived in one of the houses on the boulevard. In the park one afternoon when I was twelve, his nephew's dog, a black and tan Doberman, beat up Dusty. He was a strong, sleek monster; Parker Jr.'s father called him "the fastest nigger-chaser in the county." Dusty fought back hard, but he was outweighed by at least fifty pounds, and at one moment the Doberman seized him by the neck so viciously that I feared for his life. In the presence of the unconcerned nephew, I kicked the Doberman in the loins; when he let go, Dusty escaped. "If your dog ever does that again," I shouted, "I'll kill him." Poor Dusty had to have fifteen stitches.

Two days later I was walking down the boulevard, my dog limping along behind me, when a long green Buick with mud on the hood and fenders pulled to the curb. Mr. Leroy Godbold was at the wheel alone, and he motioned stiffly to me with his arm.

"I hear you're going to kill Parker Jr.'s dog," he said through the open window of the sedan. He was smoking a cigarette, and he stared at me with his cold, immobile face. How did he know who I was?

I barely heard him, until he repeated what he had said.

But the Doberman had almost killed *my* dog.

"You're not going to kill Parker Jr.'s dog, are you?"

"No, sir. I wouldn't do that."

"Because it wouldn't be very wise. Ain't your mother that damned *tap*-dancing teacher?" Then he accelerated the car and was gone.

Sitting four years later in the gallery of the courtroom, I recalled the precipitate confrontation and its innuendo with shame: the shame I had felt in not defending myself, of my own sorry helplessness and vulnerability. In the days that followed, when Mr. Godbold and his progeny would enter our lives, Luke's and Amanda's and Georgia's and Arch's and mine, and in circumstances less ambiguous than a fight between dogs, I would reflect countless times on that glimpse we had of him in the courtroom, and my memory of him in the muddy sedan on the boulevard, and wonder if there were not some precursory admonition in the profound uneasiness, the mysterious presentiment, he touched in me that day. As he bantered with the sheriff's deputies during a short recess and conferred in whispers with the judge near the bench and leaned across the counsel's table to talk with the young prosecutor and paused to chat with the grotesquely rotund court recorder and gazed about the chamber with his thin, parsimonious smile, I perceived a man who would abrogate not merely the conventions, not merely the jurisprudence, but life too, if enough of something against him were riding on it. I would notice him more and more, mailing his letters to Durley at the post office, talking in terse, clipped phrases with the American Legionnaires about the war and the Communists, moving with royal fearlessness among the throngs of drunks at the lower end of the main street on Saturday nights.

The trial moved swiftly after the recess: the cantankerous mulatto woman from Godbold who called the field hand "a no-good nigger who ain't got the sense of a sow" and said that he once assaulted her in the bed of a rusty pickup, Mr. Godbold's cook who said he had stolen a $10 bill from her purse the previous Christmas, another who volunteered that the defendant had pulled a knife on him three or four times in the fields. And the summations by the defense lawyer and the glib and evangelical prosecutor and the judge's instructions and the jurors filing out and returning five minutes later with a sentence of death. And Mr. Leroy Godbold shaking their hands, ceremoniously, one by one.

3

"AT NIGHT the heart comes out," the poet from Wales wrote, "like a cat on the tiles." It was a mellifluous twilight, soft and shimmering pink — a midsummer's night, heavy-sweet with clover and tuberoses and the lingering honeysuckle. Georgia and Arch and I were going to a movie (we called it then a "show"), and to while away the time until they arrived I was sitting on the front steps watching cars go by and reflecting on Mr. Leroy Godbold in the courtroom. People would slow down and wave and shout *"Swayze!"* letting the word roll out long and liltingly as was the custom. A crew of older boys from the high school came by in a battered prewar Mercury convertible and gave me the finger. Mrs. Idella King, the high school English teacher, drove past, so myopic and of such wandering disposition that she was constantly running into things, a parked fire truck or the mosquito conveyance, and when I sighted one of the neighborhood boys bicycling several feet from her I closed my eyes, but she missed him. The tap dancing had shut down for the day, and my mother was across the street prattling with two skeletal spinster sisters in their eighties, who claimed they never married because all the available men were lost in that early war, the Civil War, though I always suspected other more obvious reasons.

The boulevard kids were already congregating down the way

to "play out," as it was called, in those sibilant evenings — run barefoot in the cool wet grass to the symphony of the crickets and cicadas, gather fireflies in jelly jars, scare one another in the delicious horrors of the shadows — just as we had done, especially around the looming old Darnell house ten doors down, hidden now in indolent crape myrtles and elms and a giant cucumber tree, where an ancient widow named Alabama Darnell, whom we hardly ever saw, dwelled alone with a nearly ancient mulatto named Isabella, a striking duenna. One night like this when we were little and Mars was close to the earth, we all kept gazing into the cloud-laden skies, up where people had said it would be. The clouds cleared, and there was Mars itself, and from our earthly nimbus we took turns looking at it through a cheap set of binoculars. Was anyone there at all? Did they play football on Mars?

Now the boulevard rang with the ineffable sounds of children at play. A group of six or seven black children came along the sidewalk pushing a worn-out tire; then scampering and chattering, they took the shortcut through our driveway and the line of pecan trees to Independence Quarters. From the house next door Mrs. Griffin was playing the piano; I could picture her wan and proud and thin in her heavy eyeglasses, poised at her keyboard in waxen gentility. Her repertoire consisted of Kern and Romberg. "Smoke Gets in Your Eyes" and "Ten Thousand Men" were her contributions to this fine summer solstice. From the beer place in the Quarters rose the resonant illicit laughter that always attended the gathering dusks, and then the sonorous cadences of "Sharecropper's Blues" and "Dust My Broom" blending shamelessly with "Indian Love Call" and "On the Road to Mandalay." Along the boulevard men in shirtsleeves were watering their lawns. Never mind the stout rains of three days before, or that the lawns themselves seemed lush enough now to outlast any summer. The gentle wheeze of two dozen hoses joined in with the pulsing life.

In that moment, as the children next door shrieked at some obscure horror, Luke Cartwright came to a halt at the front curb. I watched as he got out of his truck and came toward me with his slow, loping strides.

"It's me," he said, and sat down on the steps.

He wore khakis and tanned leather work boots with strands of wet Johnson grass stuck to them and a green work cap with the words "John Deere" on the front. His face was deep bronze from the sun, but his nose and ears and the backs of his hands were blistered red. He gently touched his nose, as if to ascertain whether there were any feeling left in it.

"I been working on the vegetables at the farm," he said.

He reached down and patted Dusty on the head. "How old's the dog?"

"Six and a half."

I would not have been surprised if he had replied, "That's old enough," as he had to me on our first encounter. But instead, he said, "I understand you and Georgia went to the trial today."

We saw the end, I said.

"Why did you go? Georgia shouldn't go. Maybe *you* ought to be there, but not her."

Well, we go sometimes.

"What was Old Man Godbold up to?"

I was tempted to describe everything I had seen from the gallery, the imperial presence of him, the jurors, the witnesses, the sheriff and his men, but merely told him that Mr. Godbold seemed interested in everything.

With this he bent down and picked a long blade of grass by the side of the steps, which he put between his lips. He looked across the boulevard toward my mother and the spinster siblings, who were conversing as animatedly as ever.

"I just bet he was."

We sat there for a while absorbing the sounds of the neighborhood. It was nearly dark now. Suddenly, as if the conductor of a philharmonic orchestra had brought down his baton with a bold emphatic flourish, every katydid in Fisk's Landing began to sing.

This odd man of truncated queries and unembarrassed silences and the quizzical, good-natured face never seemed in a hurry for anything. I suspected he would tell me why he came by when he felt like it. Only when I really grew to know him did I comprehend that for him words were too valuable to squander and that one might just as well use them forthrightly. Not that he could not talk when he was of the mood. As I would discover, he was occasionally given to sudden observations that may have had little to do with the subject at hand; this quirk led me to suspect that when he was alone he talked to himself the way I talked to my dog. "Sometimes it only takes about ten seconds to tell someone's a real ass," he might say, or "Weddings are harder than funerals," or "This town is five thousand swamp rats and five thousand hillbillies, and fifty Jews and eighty Episcopalians." His speech included bizarre rhetorical flourishes: "His crop is always good because he has 'ice cream land'" or "That farm's so poor a crow won't fly over it" or "She applied a tin bucket to his ears" or "The woman has snakes in her head" or "She's so ugly she'll kill young cotton." All this he delivered in a strong, throaty voice that was often so low you had to bend an ear to listen, and punctuated, sometimes surprisingly, by a funny, high-pitched, infectious giggle.

He habitually lapsed into the quintessential vernacular in his pronunciations. For instance, although he certainly knew better, it was every now and again not *once,* but *onct;* a baseball *inning* could be an *ending, chaperon* might be *chaferon,* and *business* became *bidness.* Serviceable *ain't*s and flamboyant double negatives and ill-matched verbs and subjects and dubious tenses and comical ellipses were more faithful and efficacious than the most refined of Latinates. Consistency in speech was never his goal, and he moved at will from the most backwoods dialect to the King's English.

Then there was the way he used the word *nigger,* a generic and earthy word to us in those unenlightened times; unlike most others who used the word, Luke delivered it so simply and naturally and bereft of meanness or hostility that with him the word itself somehow suggested a realistic and almost benign and even affectionate recognition of the hard fraternity of shared land and its people, our mutual heritage and fate.

On the surface, then, he was a simple and bucolic fellow, a creature of his spartan-hard heritage, a funny, grumpy, iconoclastic guy. But as it turned out, he was much more complicated than that. It took me a very long time to see that he was also an ironic man, full of surprises, and achingly American. Much as he loved the playfulness of life, more than almost any person I would ever know, he sensed the essential malevolence of things and aberrant behavior and people's limitations. He despised cruelty, but suffered buffoons. Do you have to know pain to know compassion? He would exchange intelligence with nearly anybody about anything, usually in a terse shorthand — the boll weevil, baseball, local history, veterinary medicine — an old-fashioned Jeffersonian if ever there was one.

He was always looking at things, clouds, trees, hills, grass, dogs, birds, people, as if they might vanish swiftly in a puff. He was half redneck and half coat-and-tie, half flatland and half hills, not four years at the aristocratic state university but two, handsome yet with the hard, callused hands of a yeoman, so that the very dichotomy of our land itself, its warring and contradictory imperatives, were who Luke was. One of his salvations, I would learn, was that he knew this about himself, and it must have amused him. More important, I think, all this had to do with pride and survival and remembrance and honor and right and wrong and the things that mattered. I would grow to love him very much.

"Well, we need you day after tomorrow," he finally said.

I asked who it was.

"Scuttles."

I paused as before to envision him.

"A good boy," he said. "Didn't talk much, as I recall. Didn't know much of nothing. Mortar got him."

My dog had left us to sprawl on the lawn and rub his back in the grass. He lay there with all four paws extended in the air, then got up to investigate some children in a tree next door. Mrs. Griffin was playing louder than ever, and was singing now to her own notes, and the two of us sat there for a moment listening to her. "Give me some men who are stouthearted men, and I'll soon give you ten thousand more."

Potter Ricks and Woodrow had met the coffin that afternoon at the railroad station in Monroe City, he said. "They shipped it all the way from Frisco to Brooklyn and then down here. All up and down the United States. You'd think they'd make it more *direct,* wouldn't you? Leave that to the army. I wouldn't be surprised if Scuttles had ended up in Mexico."

He was quiet, then said: "It's gettin' worse. You know that? Arch Kidd's back, ain't he? I thought I saw him yesterday."

I told him he would be along at any moment.

The funeral would be at 3:00 in the new section. "We'll do it right this time, echo too. Be there early like before. You can fill Arch in."

I already had.

"Good."

At this precise instant the black and white Plymouth came to a halt behind Luke's truck. Arch was at the wheel and Georgia next to him. Luke and I went out to greet them. He stopped at the window. "How are you on the high F?"

"The high F?" Arch asked. "On *what?*"

"On 'Taps.'"

"I'm great on the high F."

"See you day after tomorrow then," he said, and with a superfluous half wave departed.

I got in the car next to them. Arch negotiated the U-turn toward downtown, and I watched apprehensively as my mother disengaged herself from the spinsters and rushed to the curb. "Where are you going?" she shouted. "What time are you coming back? Be careful!"

Later that night the three of us lingered for a while on Georgia's lawn. In the sultry sky there was a glossy little moon, as thin as the tiniest saucer, but storm clouds were gathering again like snowbanks along the horizon, and a sudden flank of lightning illuminated the grove of oaks on the school grounds across the way. The mosquito truck was making its rounds, and the spray from it chased us onto the porch. Inside I could see Georgia's parents watching their new television. The flickering images cast a pallid glow on the shrubbery outside and on the tall white columns of the gallery.

As the three of us stood there, Arch reached in his pocket and brought out a quarter. He polished it dramatically on his sleeve. "Here," he said to her, "you flip it."

She held it in her fingers. "You call it," Arch said.

"Heads," I said, as she tossed it in the air and slapped it briskly on her forearm. "Heads," she said.

There was a small oblique rainfall, a warm summer rain as shy as tears, when Arch came to get me the next day. I had left the house early and was hiding in the bushes next to the Griffin residence to avoid my mother's hairbrush. I waited there amid the gnats and flies. When I saw the car, I burst from the shrubbery with my trumpet case in hand and hailed him down.

"What was *that* for?"

He was wearing a dark blue suit and matching tie, silver cufflinks and black shoes and socks. I, in salubrious contrast, wore blue jeans and a T-shirt and white athletic socks and crimson sneakers with "F. L. H. S." stenciled on them. I did not envy him his chafing wardrobe on such a day, and certainly not the sobering rite awaiting him at the gravesite. I was not nearly so nervous as the first time, when I was alone, but as we approached the cemetery I noted an irritable tenseness in Arch's silences and in the elusive drops of perspiration on his upper lip.

"Do you know how long to wait before the echo?" he asked.

About four or five seconds.

"Where exactly do I stand at this thing, for Chrissake?"

"I'll show you."

The tombstones in the old section were etched somberly against the inconstant rain, gray against gray, in the ponderous afternoon. We followed the road through the Catholic enclave in back, then crossed the precarious divide of dark slopes and ravines into the new section. There were not many graves in this recent addition. The Ricks Funeral Home canopy stood at that very spot where the clusters of new stones abruptly ended before the vaster emptiness beyond. The funeral home van and Luke Cartwright's truck had already arrived. We parked farther up the hill near a young mimosa tree and got out with our horns.

In this new setting the site and all its accoutrements were a replica of that first burial: the Ricks van, the forbidding aperture in the earth, the mechanical lowering device, the bright green artificial grass, the funeral home chairs. When Arch and I reached the grave he began investigating. As the rain tapped eerily on the roof of the canopy, he looked down into the gaping hole.

"Oh, *shit!*"

Luke in his blue and gold Legion cap and gray suit had been walking among the newest graves. Now he and I showed Arch where to stand. He took out a handkerchief and wiped the rain from his trumpet. After that he inserted the mouthpiece and started doing the scales. I took my own trumpet and ran up and down the scales also. This sudden cacophony, tuneless and perfunctory, drew the gravediggers hidden in a shroud of mimosas down the way to come out and watch, and the venerable sexton, Chase Bowie, too, walked over. Mr. Bowie looked especially thin and stooped on this day. He wore starched khakis and a broad straw hat pulled down almost to his eyes; raindrops dripped from the brim. His cheek bulged with a modest plug of tobacco. As he joined Luke and me, the two of them silently gazed out at the acres of green, empty ground.

"Lots of space here, Mr. Bowie," Luke said.

"Yes, sir. Big enough for the next two, I'd guess."

"Two *what*?"

"Generations." He gently spat.

"The economy ain't been good," Luke said with a sly glance. "How come you're *expanding*?"

"It comes in spurts. Not a one last week. Four put down out here the week before. But it's a pretty steady business."

Then, just as before, the ageless red sedan with the American Legionnaires sped up the hill in our direction. They climbed out in their customary flurry of activity, shouting salutations to Luke. They fetched their carbines from the trunk and stood there testing the bolts.

"I think I found you the spot," Luke said. "Come see what you think. They'll be here in a few minutes." As we left the gravesite, Arch was standing in sartorial display under the tent, his back to the grave, as dejected as I had ever seen him. "See you in a little while," I said. Where was his irascibility now?

We climbed the vacant slopes to a dense thicket of red oaks and hickories far above the grave; their broad, heavy branches deflected the rain.

"What do you think? They're not supposed to see you," Luke said.

It looked good to me.

"Here. Dry yourself off." He handed me a red bandanna. I

rubbed the moisture from my face, then from the trumpet. We stood there for a moment. Far below was the town again, under the dismal skies a glimmering diagram on its hills and flat places. Farther out still, the great flatness seemed a timeless sea in the mist.

"Pretty, ain't it?" he said. And he was gone.

It is easy to see why one would hope every time for echo. Two or three times that summer I even prayed, "Lord, grant me the toss." I wished the Book of Common Prayer had yet another perspicacious invocation: "For Those in Need of the Right Coin Flip." Standing all alone now, the rain swishing peacefully in the leaves, the trees like amiable guardians above me, I could almost hear the beating of my own heart. I had everything to myself, the giant sweep of the sky, the softly sloping earth, the whole green world.

I withdrew the mouthpiece from the trumpet and began buzzing into it. I emptied the spit valve again. And then I saw the funeral cortege coming up the road of the old section, mournful and slow, the hearse and the cars and the pickup trucks, weaving among the stones in serpentine dignity. As it gradually approached the canopy, Arch and the Legionnaires came to attention. The pallbearers brought out the flag-draped coffin and carried it to the grave, and Potter Ricks and the official army escort guided the family to the chairs. Then the others came up and encircled them. From my eminence I watched the service, a pantomime from where I was, a simple folk tableau with only the earth as the stage. Even the faint sounds of weeping wafted up to me, a nimble consonance from this distance, like the murmur of mourning doves at dusk, or the breathless flow of water in a summer's stream. Soon the Legionnaires fired their guns, and the sound boomed mightily across the woods. Then Arch began his notes, and they were firm and clear — until he missed the high F!

I waited for the notes to drift away, then put my lips to the mouthpiece and began. I got it right. And I felt for the first time the wonderful thrill of hearing the echo to one's *own* echo as it dissolves tenderly, reluctantly almost, into the distance, palpitating into the faraway hush.

I paused a few minutes for the mourners to disperse and then walked down the hill. The rain felt good on my face. The gravediggers were leaning on their shovels waiting for the last car to leave. Woodrow was folding the chairs. The smell of the flowers was cloyingly sweet as before, and Arch looked unwell. He had unbuttoned his collar and loosened his tie and was standing under the canopy as the gravediggers withdrew the fake grass and settled down to work. With the first thud of the dirt on the coffin Arch swiftly came out into the rain. Rarely had I seen him move so fast.

"The dead guy's mother drove me crazy," he whispered to me. "Could you *hear* her?"

As before, Potter Ricks was overseeing the tasks. "Good job, boys," he said to us as he came up to confer with the gravediggers. Arch, of course, did not say anything about the high note. I knew his pride had taken an irredeemable blow. If I had been the one, I would not have heard the end of it.

Luke found me in my backyard shooting baskets late the next afternoon. There would be a funeral the following day at 4:00 in a rural cemetery called Locust Grove. It was hard to find, Luke said. He had borrowed a station wagon, and he and the other Legionnaires would pick up Arch and me in front of my house at two. He promised to talk to our employer at the Jitney Jungle right away.

Arch and I worked that morning at the store. During a lull he motioned to me from the back. He was standing behind the meat counter next to Kinsey, a Negro boy two years our senior who played quarterback and ran and kicked for Number Two high school. He presided over the panoply of meat at the store, moving about on light nimble feet, which gave him a sort of gliding gait. Tall and fleet and sly, he had heavy-lidded eyes that read the slightest undue movement or unexpected nuance. His father was a carpenter, his mother a washerwoman, and there were ten siblings. Sometimes, during lapses in the commerce, Kinsey could be seen leaning on the counter studying hand-me-down textbooks from our school, as he was now.

"Here, Kinsey," Arch said, handing him a 50-cent piece.

I had been dreading this all day.

"What's this for?" Kinsey asked. He gazed at Arch obliquely, as if sensing some subtle betrayal. How could we have known then that in four years he would be the first-team running back for, of all places, the University of Illinois?

"We just want you to flip it."

"Tails," Arch said.

Kinsey looked briefly at each of us, tossed the coin high in the air, and slapped it into his open palm. It was tails.

The big thermometer in front of the bank registered 105 degrees that afternoon, making me yearn for the recent rains. On the thoroughfares of the town the asphalt seethed with black tar bubbles, the kind I tried to run my bicycle over when I was younger. On the drive out, the heat was so unbearable that my dress shirt became damp. The heavens were like hot brass, the sullen countryside soundless except for the wooden staccato of a pecker on a distant tree.

The narrow mazy road led past tangled woodland and gullies and ravines and patchy hills of cotton and corn and hay. The mindless kudzu sculptured the landscape, shrouding the hills and trees and telephone poles and vacant dwellings in crazy creeping green. One farmer claimed he once saw kudzu growing all over a lazy cow. The tiny crossroads hamlets with their "Jesus Saves!" and "Prepare for Thy God" signs and decrepit grocery stores — unpainted establishments covered with chewing tobacco and cigar and soft drink advertisements and hand-drawn "No Cussing" and "Do Not Spit on Floor" posters — languished in this wicked inferno, and the old men sat lifeless on the front steps and porches, too torpid even to glance at us as we sped by. We passed a pond dappled with cottonwood fluff and long stretches rampant with shortleaf pine and hardwood. The hilly countryside was dotted with tin-roofed dogtrot cabins, made of plank weatherboarding, and dusty yards full of chickens and dogs and clothes drying on fences and deteriorated houses resonant of the past and the people who once lived in them. Arch, sitting next to me on the back seat of the station wagon behind Luke and the Legionnaires, looked dauntlessly cool and smug in his thin khakis and short-sleeved cotton shirt and saddle oxfords, and he sat there uncharacteristically prim with his trumpet case on his lap.

I gazed at the backs of the veterans' weathered necks. Although they talked now and then to Luke or among themselves, they too seemed beaten and subdued by the elements. "Sarge" Jennings, as he was commonly known, had had to sell his farm for a pittance during the Depression and labored now behind the beer-and-soda counter at Crenshaw's Drug Store on the main street. Wash Rose was a used-car salesman. Cotton Ledbetter was a farmer who had once worked for Mr. Leroy Godbold. Roach Weems was a fireman. Fabian "Whiskey" Tubbs had the feed-and-seed store. Son Graham owned a small grocery on the fringes of the boulevard. They had been around so long, indeed, that they called the gravel road we were on a "rock road," and they all had stories, which more often than not they told.

Sarge Jennings won the Silver Star for valor in the First World War. This provost of pain and distress, of lantern jaw and burly rhythms, was one of the most perceptive observers among the Legionnaires, and I would come to know him well. With his epigrammatic and elemental speech, he had a poet's heart, although he would never have confessed to that.

He was a tall, full-stomached figure of oaken constitution, with a bulbous red nose, spindly legs, speculating almond-shaped eyes, a leathery face that sometimes seemed unexpectedly young after a few neat swallows of Jim Beam, a slow, weighty voice, and dark graying hair so abundant that he could not get his ceremonial Legion cap over all of it, and it poked out around the sides and looked comical even in the most sorrowful moments. The Sarge, like Arch and Luke, never went to any church and never wore a suit and tie except for burials. He was usually found at his station behind Crenshaw's long counters moving incessantly back and forth in brown boots and faded khakis and flowery multicolored shirts. He was a chain smoker of Chesterfields and judge of bourbon whiskey and a liberal fount of florid words, who knew the town as well as Potter Ricks or Luke did. He had single-handedly wiped out a German machine-gun nest and saved the lives of at least five of his comrades — New England boys — in the blasted Argonne earth, but he never talked about that.

Wash Rose had his thumb and index finger shattered in the wheat fields near the Marne. Cotton Ledbetter nearly died of a lung wound at Soissons. Roach Weems acquired his name, as the others would explain (which they did often and with embellishment when the bottles were passed), for scurrying like a roach in the western front muck and the shredded Somme wilderness when the cannonade came in. Small and wizened like an aging mouse, lips so thin that in dry weather they nearly disappeared, and bald to his ears, he was as tough and lean as a sliver of Johnson grass. He was wary of strangers, and, according to Sarge Jennings, had whipped men twice his size in crap-game fights, and probably could still, but he had mellowed a lot since '18. He sometimes said in his high-pitched voice, "I'm just *Roach*, Swayze."

The World War II men like Luke, who had chosen the Legion over the newer Veterans of Foreign Wars (Coach Asphalt

Thomas, for instance, had picked the V.F.W.), were gradually assuming the leadership of the town post, but the survivors of the earlier combat seemed united in a warm, heightened camaraderie, as if that might have been the last American war that men could talk about when they came home. They had three or four favorite gathering spots. One was the little rectangular-frame Legion Hut at the upper end of the main street across from the grammar school, where, in a province nominally dedicated to legal prohibition of the meaner spirits, they had their own privately stocked bar, for in this hard-drinking society the old veterans were the hardest of the hard, and there was a garishly lighted jukebox from the Depression era, and they brought their wives here for monthly parties.

Crenshaw's Drug Store with its sign in front, "Come in or we'll both starve," was another of the places the veterans liked to congregate. The appellation *drugstore* was the most facile of overtures, for it dealt in condoms, laxatives, talcums, aspirins, and the more indigenous of the patent cures but not much else. "The niggers come in when their nature's gettin' weak," Sarge Jennings said. This anomalous institution consisted of two lengthy counters facing each other and separated by a soiled grungy interior area perhaps six or eight feet wide. The white men sat at one of the counters drinking their beer or soft drinks; the black men sat at the other facing the whites. The stamped tin ceiling had once been shiny and bright, but over the years had turned sepia from the nicotine. The sawdust floor was usually littered with crawfish shells and watermelon rinds, and in addition to the hot dogs and Vienna sausages and rat cheese and crackers and regular sausages, Sarge Jennings dispensed an appetizer of ground hot peppers, ketchup, and white vinegar called "Bottled Hell," which he claimed encouraged the beer trade, and also the pungent Middle Eastern dish kibbi, since the store had once been owned by a Lebanese man named Skinny Hassan before the Crenshaws bought it in '46. A substantial hand-painted sign on the interior wall said, "We reserve the right to refuse service to anyone, colored or white," and a smaller one enigmatically declared, "Never Get Naked with Yankees," and another, "In God we trust, all others pay cash."

Another of the old veterans' favorite hangouts was Firehouse Number One, because Roach Weems was a fireman and always had a ball game on the radio, and, since it was adjacent to the jail, they could come out onto the lawn between poker hands and talk to the prisoners looking down from behind the barred windows upstairs. They also gathered at Son Graham's grocery next to his big unpainted house, the yard an indecipherable chaos of junk and outmoded equipment, with a narrow pathway leading through this uncommon debris to the cows and chickens and hogs in back. I had often come here as a boy to make childhood purchases, to be greeted effusively and by name, and to witness their raucous saturnalias. They kept their whiskey in a two-gallon jar marked "Vinegar," with other brands hidden behind the cornflakes, mayonnaise, and pickles. A great red rooster from Son Graham's backyard often perched high in the rafters. When I was eleven, one stormy September afternoon at the tail end of a hurricane that had risen from the gulf, I sat enthralled in these unseemly quarters as they talked of French women and the goings-on at World War I camps. One of them claimed to have known Alvin York and talked about "Alvin" as if they had been intimate companions. As the vinegar flowed, his tales about Sergeant York grew more and more inconsistent, conflicting with one another so direly that I began listening less for the facts and more for the contradictions. Then they broke into "Over There," and when they reached "the Yanks are coming," they were so loud and discordant that the rooster swooped down in a flurry of red feathers.

I recalled all these things as we bumped toward Locust Grove that afternoon, the Legionnaires as solemn and quiet as I had ever seen them.

The Locust Grove Baptist Church was more than a century

old even then: a tall inverted-V-shaped white exterior, high narrow windows with lime green shutters, a sloping whitewashed tin roof. The dust-mottled trees crept up to it on all sides and gave it the aspect of having been wrestled out of the hardwood forest itself, which, of course, it had been. Towering on a hill, it dominated the hard, unyielding countryside. The sign over its high arched doorway said: "I am the Eternal Truth that endures from generation to generation." We had forty-five minutes until the ceremony, and Arch and I went inside, under the high ceilings where it was cooler. I sat down in one of the ancient handmade pews and looked up at the simple stained-glass windows and the slave gallery with its separate railed entrance and tried, as I had on that first day among the stones of the town cemetery, to steady my churning anxiety.

Arch was smiling royally as he wandered about. I took out the mouthpiece of my trumpet and started buzzing into it.

The Legionnaires had sprawled in the shade of an oak at the entrance to the graveyard. A hand-painted sign nailed to a tree by the gate said: "No Tres. from Dusk to Dawn." Luke and Woodrow and two gravediggers from the area were sitting in funeral home chairs next to the open grave under the Ricks canopy. The tombstones were stained with years of soil, and the snarled underbrush encroached upon the graves.

"Whites and colored are buried all in here," Woodrow was telling Luke. "Back in that brush you won't find nothin' but slaves. I wish they'd clear it out. All around in here, just like in town, you dig into old iron coffins. You just bury on top or move 'em over. This soldier today," Woodrow said, "he'll be buried on top of a little baby, but he won't know the difference."

"In France, you know," Luke said, with a kind of grudging reluctance as if he did not want to tell, but did, "when they buried ours, they'd find bones all the time from World War I, unidentified bones."

"Bones is everywhere," Woodrow said, and shook his head. "I don't believe in ghosts, but they're there. The world's travelin' too fast. People don't listen no more to ghosts. *Bones everywhere*. Everywhere," the gravedigger repeated, and shook his head lugubriously too.

This was not exactly the kind of talk I needed. Wearing a dark suit and stiff shirt, I was beginning to feel a little weak in this stupefying atmosphere. I wandered away. A short-lived breeze tossed up a combination of dust and heat waves. A rabbit bounded out from behind a sassafras and scurried into the thicket. Wicked yellow jackets were everywhere and big buzzing horseflies, little swirling gnats, and black lizards with off-white stripes. This end of the county was cusp country for the Spanish moss, its northernmost locale, we were told in Coach Thomas's forestry class, and it hung from the older trees in iron gray pendants like silken threads.

At the edge of a flowering crape myrtle I came upon the grave of a little girl. Her name was Angel Sweeney, and she had lived from March 2, 1870, to June 25, 1876. This too was June 25. She had died on this very day! No other Sweeneys were buried around her, and there she was, in a far corner of that backwoods graveyard, so forlorn and alone and long forgotten that I suddenly felt a great melancholy sorrow for little Angel — almost as much for her as I did for myself.

"Let's get ready!" Luke shouted just then.

The Legionnaires congregated at the grave. Woodrow and the gravediggers retired to the rear lawn of the church. Luke went with Arch to inspect his post in a stand of trees fifty yards away. In minutes came the procession.

They were country farmers who knew mortgage and setback and tenancy and scraggly cotton. As I stood there at attention, they surrounded the grave — men, women, and children, in an earnest proprietary silence. A uniformed military man, the escort, was on crutches and labored up the hill with Potter Ricks;

all the toes on one foot had been blown off, we had been told, and I saw that one of his ears was gone. The father was tall and skinny, his face and knuckles sunburned, and his hair was plastered down with sweet-smelling tonic. There were two daughters, about ten and twelve. The mother was near collapse. The preacher spoke of heroism and sacrifice and the ways of God. Big tears kept rolling down the father's face, which otherwise was without expression, and the younger daughter suddenly shrieked: *"Jimmy! Jimmy! Where are you?"* The elder girl was convulsed with weeping, her torso racked in trembling spasms. She fell to her knees in front of her chair, and Potter Ricks tried to help her up. Throughout all this, the mother repeated: *"Why, why, why, why?"*

And then a terrible thing happened. As the preacher recited the Lord's Prayer, and the silvery coffin slowly descended into the dark maw of the grave, the mother stood full height and screamed, a wail of insane and awful anguish, strode the few steps to the grave, and threw herself down into it! Arms reached out for her, but she sprawled facedown halfway inside, her undergarments and naked thighs exposed, and fought madly as Potter Ricks and the father together lifted her out. After the guns were fired and I had played my equivocal notes and Arch his flawless response, the crippled escort presented the folded flag to the mother, who held him about the waist as he stood before her. The Legionnaires stacked their rifles and went to the family with great dignity and feeling, telling them that their son had died for his country and would always be remembered by everyone and that they were there representing the president of the United States, who could not make it to the funeral because he was so busy with the war. The father's tears stopped for a moment, and the mother swayed back limp into her chair. Then Luke came over and knelt in front of them, holding the mother's hand in his, and then the daughters' and father's, and whispered to them for a long time. When the moment came for the family to leave, in an imperceptible wave the crowd parted to let them through, and they walked to the funeral home car with a kind of doleful pride.

After they had finally disappeared in a veil of dust down the road, many of the others remained. There was a baffled rage among them that I had not seen before. *"Who's killin' our boys?"* one of them shouted. Another: *"What're we doin' over there?"* And another: *"Let's drop the A-bomb!"* They milled about for a while, as if the grave itself was their one magnetic touch with reality, and Luke and the Legionnaires went out and calmed them down, and slowly led them to their vehicles.

"That's the worst 'Taps' I ever heard, for Chrissake," Arch said to me when he came down out of the trees.

The graveyard was deserted now except for the usual retinue. Woodrow had the hood to the hearse open and was pouring water into the engine. Luke and Potter Ricks reclined listlessly in chairs. We sat down next to them. I was drenched with sweat, it was even dripping out of my ears and nose. When I had played my notes, there was so much moisture in my eyes that I had to close them to get through. Now I felt dehydration in the soul. I took off my coat and rolled up my sleeves.

Luke handed me his bandanna. "You look terrible."

"So do you." And he did. The skin around his eyes was deeply crinkled; his shoulders sagged wearily, and the sweat stains made half-moons around his armpits.

Plop. Plop. Plop. The gravediggers were at work behind us.

"It was bad," Luke said.

"It was bad," Potter assented.

"I guess we did all we could," Luke said.

"I've seen worse," Potter said.

"Worse?" I had to ask.

He was rubbing his glasses with his handkerchief. Exposed in the piercing sunlight, his eyes were pale and flaccid, like an old man's. "Double funerals. Triple funerals. Little children from car wrecks. Yes." He looked out ascetically across the stones, and suddenly there was such a swift, deadening pain in his features, an instant of dire and secret distress, as might have come with the sharp jab of a needle, that I was almost paralyzed by the sight. It vanished as quickly as it had come. Did he sense I had noticed? He briskly got up to talk with Woodrow at the hearse.

"Look at them," Luke said. "The old renegades deserve it." Down by our station wagon, near the church, the Legionnaires had propped their carbines against the fenders. They were in their shirtsleeves passing around a bottle, then another. Immediately after the burial they had been quiet, almost sullen, perhaps even a little angry. Now they were taking copious gulps and talking spiritedly among themselves. I was beginning to learn that they were not really clerks or storekeepers or car salesmen or farmers, but honorably retired warriors.

And on the long drive back to town in our station wagon, I acknowledged this more fully. Their bantering desultory talk as they shared the bottles of Four Roses and I. W. Harper helped take my thoughts from the grave, at least for a while. As we pulled away from the church, Wash Rose handed one of the bottles to Arch and me in the back seat with his three fingers. "Here, fellas," he said, "take a little swig — just don't tell your mamas." The raw acrid taste of my first whiskey caused me to shudder, and I stifled a gag. In seconds I could feel a mellow warmth to my toes.

I described our vehicle as a station wagon, but that is not precisely correct. It was an old Pontiac sedan welded to the backside of a station wagon, so that it was really a makeshift omnibus with five rows of seats. The welding on the outside resembled scabrous scar tissue. The owner of this unique vehicle was a crafty German merchant and loan shark named Herman von Schulte, or that is what he wished to be called (he was sometimes referred to as the "Kraut"), who had actually fought against these very Legionnaires in 1918 and then migrated through New Orleans to the town in the 1920s, for what reason it had never been ascertained. The black people regarded him as an enigma and thought him dangerous, and the Legion veterans treated him with a kind of buoyant and regal contumely. He was by any calculus the Silas Marner of Fisk's Landing. I had often observed this auslander with his soiled attire and obese midriff in the dual-countered drugstore trying to be friends with the old warriors who once were his foes or approaching them in his ceaseless perambulations up and down the main street with one of his feckless commercial propositions.

They ceaselessly taunted von Schulte about his aversion to the Jewish dry goods merchants whose establishments surrounded his, reminding him unmercifully that the town was blessed with a three-term Jewish mayor (vice president, too, of a mercantile store almost as large as Arch's father's and one of the owners of the wholesale grocery; and, for that matter, the owner of the cotton gin was Jewish, his grandfather having come up the river as the simplest and most peregrinating of peddlers, and when asked as an old man why he finally settled down permanently in Fisk's Landing was said to have replied that his horse died there, and then he started one of the most profitable junkyards in the whole of the flatland from there to Memphis).

In the name of honor, however, or whatever it was, the Legion men protected this garrulous and alien boulevardier from the more extreme of the home-front zealots during World War II, for after all he *was* technically an American citizen now, no matter how unlikely a one, and he had once even been a soldier as they had, although he *had* worn the kaiser's spiked helmet. But one suspects they told him, in the idiom, to watch his mouth. During that war he discovered he had a distant cousin in a German POW camp located farther north from us in the flatland, a corporal in the Afrika Korps, and when von Schulte visited him three or four times with cigarettes and candy, Sarge Jennings took it upon himself to go along, to make sure, he said, that they did not incarcerate the Kraut, too.

Still at this very moment, as the odd Siamese twin of a conveyance bounced and shifted on the gravel like a troubled ocean liner, Sarge Jennings was shouting: "The Kraut uses this to go get his *interest* payments from the piss-poor niggers. Charges forty percent and says he don't break even!" To which Roach Weems amended: "Even the niggers don't think he's white!" And Fabian Tubbs: "The Kraut wouldn't be caught dead at the funerals — he's scared we'll aim the guns at *him*!"

In the moment Fabian Tubbs shouted this, we came onto the asphalt county road with the little Holy Roller church at the side, and the sudden stillness after the jolting gravel, this and surely the reference to the funeral, cast a quick and uneasy silence upon our band. It was getting on to twilight, and restless glints of heat lightning momentarily brightened the sky. The trees and Queen Anne's lace along the road were cloaked in dust, and the mingling sachet of honeysuckle and wild summer grasses filled the dusk like lusty perfume, so heavy that you could almost reach out and hold it in your hand. I knew then that nothing I might do, absolutely nothing, could ever obliterate from my memory the mother and daughters at the grave. I knew the thoughts of the men were there, too. I wondered what Georgia was doing. So often when I was in this masculine company, I thought of her, my antenna of love and feeling and fear.

After a time one of them asked Luke, "When's the next one?"

"Don't know."

Silence again. Then Sarge Jennings spoke in soft monologue, as if to foil the hush, more to himself it seemed than to the rest of us: "Do you know I fired volleys for General Featherstone in '28? Just been made commander at West Point. Died of pneumonia. His mother died of a broken heart in the bathtub the next day."

"That's the truth," Son Graham said. "I was at that funeral."

"Pershing came," Sarge Jennings said. "Right here to Fisk's Landing. Telegram from Coolidge. Monoplanes droppin' roses. Had a sergeant play 'Taps' that played for Woodrow Wilson. Did you know Featherstone was fuckin' MacArthur's first wife in the damned Ritz Hotel? She sent a dozen orchids to the funeral. Potter showed me the card." He chuckled at the thought.

Everyone — men and boys — was thinking this over.

"That's the truth," Son Graham repeated, and chuckled proudly too. "It was common knowledge."

We had reached the final hill coming down, and the familiar green and white sign: "Fisk's Landing Corp. Limits: Pop. 10,184." Below us, the lights of the town were coming on.

"We can't let them little shits whip us like this," Roach Weems said.

4

I REMEMBERED Durley Godbold from childhood days. On Friday evenings we would wander about the town in a pack, Arch and I and the others in our blue and yellow Cub Scout caps, playing war games or kick the can on our random walks down the cracked mossy sidewalks of the boulevard to see a war movie, perhaps *The First Yank in Tokyo* or *The Purple Heart*. If it were really hot, we might steal onto one of the lawns, turn on a faucet, and kneel down for a drink of water.

"What're you *doin'*, boys?" a voice from a darkened porch might ask.

"Borrowin' some water, Miss Nelson."

"That's fine. Just don't step on my gladiolus."

One late afternoon we watched a long troop convoy come through town on the highway from the flatland. Soldiers in the ugly olive drab trucks had white and red Second Army patches on their sleeves. They were smoking cigarettes and looking bored until they saw us. Then they threw us chewing gum and shouted down in their sharp northern tongues: "Holy shit, look at *this* burg!" Or: "Where's the nearest subway, boys?" Or: "Boys, any *pussy* in this joint?" (The women on the street corners complained about such language and went to the Baptist preacher, who wrote President Roosevelt about it, but Roosevelt never replied.)

As we strolled in our group toward downtown, Durley and a

few of his contemporaries, who were in their last year in high school, would sight us from Durley's red prewar Ford. (How he got the gasoline during the rationing was a mystery, but he did.) They would leap maniacally from the car and start chasing us. We scattered in all directions, like rabbits flushed from the brush, each to his own devices, into alleys or side streets or the whole backyard world of victory gardens and clotheslines and barns and garages and hen houses. But they always caught us, and when they did they would gather about us in a circle and frighten us out of our senses, these brawny football players, tossing us in the air and letting us thud to the earth on our posteriors, or smacking us with the red and white paddles that they used in their F. L. Lettermen's Club initiations, or sending us sprawling onto the grass and tickling us on the ribs into such awful paroxysms that we almost suffocated, for tickling is surely one of the most underrated of the human tortures. "Leave those little boys alone!" some aged and tremulous feminine voice would sound from one of the houses, but this was no deterrent at all.

Durley was the worst of them. I recall one night in particular. It was a cool evening of late October with gusting leaves and a big burnt orange moon at the horizon; we spotted Durley and his cadre in the Ford half a block down the boulevard and began dispersing instantly. I sprinted alone around the darkened Darnell house and circled the barn into the alleyway separating the boulevard from Independence Quarters. I thought I was safe; I stood there trying hard to catch my breath. But all of a sudden Durley Godbold emerged from the backyard into the alley. I was hopelessly trapped. He had a paddle in his hand, and he approached me slowly, ominously, with a crooked, malevolent grin. He caught me by the neck with a powerful forearm and twisted me to the ground. *"Please!"* I implored. *"Please?"* he mocked me in his hoarse and curious tenor. "Why *please?*" and began pounding me on the rear with the weapon. The paddle had evil little air holes in it, the better to make blisters, and it hurt so much I started to cry. *"Sissy! Sissy!"* he repeated. Never in my life had I been so much at the physical mercy of another being; as I lay there helplessly on my belly in the gravel, choking with the autumn dust, feeling the accumulating pain with each stroke of the paddle, a nightmarish fear raced through my brain: *he wants to kill me.*

When he finally stopped, I staggered to my feet. We faced each other, a man and a child. There was one more whack. He whirled me about and caught me with such a staggering blow that I crashed headlong into a garbage can. I could feel it to my teeth. As he spun around and walked away into the Darnell yard, I knew in that instant that if I had had a gun and known how to use it, I would have shot him dead on the spot. Insanely I picked up a large piece of gravel in the alley and let it fly toward the back of his neck, and in the very act of throwing, dashed into a narrow pathway between a fence and a garage. *"Goddam!"* I heard his startled painful cry. I hid myself facedown in a cluster of dense nandina bushes as he came searching for me. I lay stolid and low and held my breath and heard footfalls in the leaves. With another cursory oath he finally gave up and disappeared into the night.

One day the following week Arch and I chanced across Durley's familiar Ford in back of Crenshaw's. What followed was Arch's suggestion and an ingenious one. We found a big empty garbage sack in a bin by the parking lot, also a rusty shovel, and darting furtively among the buildings and sheds, we went to the open pasture near the municipal water plant and shoveled a large pile of fresh cow dung into the bag. Retracing our steps, we hid momentarily in some bushes abutting the back of Crenshaw's, making sure the path was still clear, and then, like the infantrymen we had seen under enemy fire in the war shows, ran in crouched posture to Durley's car and emptied the entire mess onto the front seat. We escaped down the alley unnoticed. I felt good for days.

We had always heard a great deal about Durley — about when he was a Cub Scout and went to summer camp and his father sent a Negro to tend to him, about his freshman year in high school when the older Godbold punished him for some idle transgression by taking away his Ford and Durley drove one of the plantation tractors forty miles to Monroe City to a dance, about the time he beat up the class president for saying something disparaging about the skunk tail he had on the fender of the Ford. I would see him in all his musclebound bravado on the main street or the fringes of the town, hauling day laborers in trucks from the Quarters out to Godbold or shouting *"Caddy!"* in front of the Dew Drop Inn, where little black boys waited to be hired to carry the golf bags at the country club.

One afternoon just before high school graduation, Arch and I were sitting in a rear booth in Carr's Drug Store downtown. Durley came in with Amanda Pettibone, his younger brother, Porter, and a girl named Honey East. The Godbold boys were expensively dressed in the casual regional mode of the day. Durley's dark glistening hair was closely cropped, his eyes were stony blue, and he had his father's high, narrow, lackadaisical face. He leaned against the soda fountain, his taut athlete's body now in authoritative repose. He glanced at Arch and me with casual indifference, then he snapped their orders to the milky-pale country girl behind the counter — hot dogs, onion rings, cherry Cokes. They and the girls poured one nickel after another into the jukebox playing melancholy love songs of the war. "I'll be seeing you in all the old familiar places, that this heart of mine embraces all day through."

At one point Durley squeezed Amanda tightly around the waist, then picked up an onion ring and put it teasingly to her lips. His teeth gleamed as he laughed. "Let me spoil you," he said. The beautiful Amanda seemed for the moment a supplicant: she nibbled the onion ring, and when she had finished,

Durley gingerly dabbed her lips with a napkin. He held her closely and kissed her lightly on her cheek. She kissed him back. When I saw her there with him, the person I hated and feared most, her kind, wistful beauty touched my boy-child's heart with a mysterious sympathy and affection for her. To this day she is etched and defined by that swift passing moment so long ago.

Durley had gone off to the state university for two and a half years, where he enrolled in the ROTC. He was a reserve full-back on the football squad and apparently its most aggressive member, and he acquired the reputation as the second most unpleasant Sigma Alpha Epsilon on that campus, the first having been dismissed from school for trying to burn down the fraternity house for the insurance money. Then, against his father's wishes, it was said, he enlisted in officers' training at Fort Benning along with Luke's cousin Billy Permenter and acquired his second lieutenant's bars one week to the day after the climax of the war in the Pacific. "I wanted to kill Japs," he said, "but I was one week late." He was posted to Germany, where he reportedly cruised the autobahns in a prewar Renault convertible and had a liaison with a voluptuous German actress widowed by the war. When he returned home in '47, he decided to forgo his remaining time at the state university. He would work with his father.

To his credit the son had a faculty for self-interested rebellion, which meshed well with his hard and petulant constitution. People began seeing him with Amanda, though his father had blustered to the country club crowd that Amanda Pettibone was a redneck and she would never have Godbold, or its money. Durley had bought a sparkling sedan, one of the first new ones in town since the war, and the two of them could be observed driving around the town and countryside or in the restaurants of the capital city or the lobby of the Peabody Hotel in Memphis or at the country club.

In the rustic hall of the country club one evening — it was

Georgia's thirteenth birthday, and her parents had brought us there for a supper dance — she and I were trying to negotiate a fox trot. By coincidence, gliding next to us on the floor were Durley and Amanda. When Georgia saw Amanda she smiled and waved, and Amanda smiled in return. Durley glanced at us with his cool, black disdain. "She's sweet," Georgia said, and added precociously, "I don't think she's after Durley's money, do you?"

Amanda was stunningly pretty, willowy and full-breasted, with ash blond hair and gray eyes and an affecting diffidence. She was descended from small farmers in the hills, not too far from Luke's people. Like Luke's, her mother had died when she was young. Her father had gone bankrupt in the Depression, and they lived at the slender line of destitution: then he managed somehow to set himself up in a thriving service station and garage in a country hamlet that walked the hills. If a country girl lived out in the flatland, she might be one of the belles of the county, but the daughter of a failed yeoman-turned-small-time entrepreneur was disqualified from the social circles of the town girls and would never attain entrance to the exclusive sororities at the state university. But Amanda was quiet and nice and trustworthy and smart. She went to the state teachers college during the war to study music and returned to teach piano on a vintage Steinway in the town high school.

Sometimes she provided the accompaniment for my mother's tap dancers in their endless and noisome recitals. Once when I was just approaching my teenage years, I was sitting with her in our uncomfortable wrought-iron lawn chairs in front of my house, while she waited for my mother to finish a lesson.

"Do you want to be a tap dancer, Swayze?" she asked, in the soft, unadorned voice that much later became so familiar to me.

I frowned.

"Then why don't you let me teach you the piano?"

"I'm learning to play the trumpet."

"You can do both. And what can you do with the trumpet?
You can do anything with the piano — entertain others, entertain yourself."

I wanted to change the subject, so I turned my attention to
the passing cars. Ever since the war ended, I had enjoyed sitting
out here and watching the new cars come by. At first they had
mostly been Fords, reworked '42 models, and then the fancy
ones began to appear, like Durley Godbold's. Then I glanced secretly at Amanda. Even in her loveliness she had a vague sadness about her, evanescent and indefinable, an air of being a little outside of things. For a moment I even considered learning
the piano.

"I'd like to visit places," she said in a near whisper, as if
I, out of the whole world, were her accomplice. "Wouldn't
you, Swayze? Wouldn't you like to visit Paris and London and
French Morocco? I've only been to New Orleans."

I'd like to go to New York, I said. I had only been as far as
Memphis.

"Wouldn't we have fun in New York, Swayze? Let's save our
pennies and go."

One afternoon the following week something memorable occurred, all the more stunning because it was so accidental,
and unexpected, and embarrassing. My mother had asked me
to deliver some sheet music to Amanda. I went there unan-
nounced on my bicycle. Her apartment was in a wing of an old
house not far from the school. Her green prewar coupe was
parked outside, but when I climbed the porch steps and rang
the bell, there was no answer. I rang again. Still silence. I tried
the door. It was unlocked, so I opened it and went inside; I had
been there before on similar errands. The parlor was modest
and the light dim, and it opened into a brightly lit corridor. I
paused there in the parlor with the music in my hand. Suddenly
the bathroom door adjoining the corridor opened widely. She
stood there for a moment in clear view. Her hair was wet and
she was holding a bath towel. She was naked.

I was paralyzed. Then she saw me. She seemed briefly caught there. "Oh, no!" I tried to avert my gaze, but something strange inside would not let me. I had never seen a grown woman naked before. Her sudden nude beauty transfixed me, and to this day I have not forgotten her generous breasts with nipples as round as quarters, the dense swirl of brownish curls. Her whole body was golden and glowing, and I felt a surging feeling I had never in my life known. Caught there for the instant, she stood exposed before me. Her features were stricken and flushed. She desperately put her towel over her whole lower form.

"Swayze!" she cried, then turned and rushed out of sight.

It had happened in seconds. I left the music on a table and fled the house. The next morning I was sitting in the same wrought-iron chair in my front yard, listening to the tapping sounds of dancers inside. Before I was aware of it, Amanda had parked her car and was walking in my direction, carrying the sheet music. She was wearing a pink cotton blouse and a pleated skirt and sandals. She sat down beside me. Her own hot blush must have matched mine. "Swayze, I'm so sorry." She looked at me with concern. "Forgive me." I was about to attempt a response, but just then my mother appeared at the front door. "We're ready for you, Amanda." She rose and, glancing at me once more, disappeared into the house.

Why was Mr. Leroy Godbold so adamantly against her for his son? She was sweet and handsome and bright. He was an egregious snob, rich with a titan's land, and possessed by the indifferent green thread of greed. I suppose the chasm in lineage was too monstrously embarrassing — the feudal grandee with his medieval unit and the failed serf with grease on his overalls. The fecund baronial acres and the weak, scrubby homestead. The thoroughbred old university and the little teachers school. The powerful son and the powerless daughter. Perhaps only someone like Governor Fielding L. Wright's girl would have done for the scion. Or did Godbold in his clever, impermeable sagacity feel he had divined something — had she promised, like Scarlett, never to be hungry again? I know now that cunning and ambition were never in her nature. Yet Mr. Godbold must have thought they were, for the simple, inextricable reason that they were in his.

As it happened, Durley called his bluff. It was easy. He threatened to give twenty years to the United States Army.

"I'm going to get married," she breathlessly reported on another visit to my mother. "Swayze, I really do love him."

"Congratulations," I lied.

"We're going to Nassau for our honeymoon."

Where was that?

"The Bahamas Islands. In the *Caribbean*. And then we're going to build a house."

They were married in the little frame Methodist church in Marshall. My mother and I sat on a back pew and watched the clan of Godbolds stoically endure the service, a frosty retinue of detachment. Amanda's attendants were her friends from the teachers college, Durley's groomsmen his former fraternity brothers at the university; one of them was so drunk he stepped on the flower girl's toes. After the vows, when the bride and groom kissed, I felt a deep, vain stab of malice.

They built a modern brick palace in a burgeoning subdivision of town called Tara Estates, with all the latest domestic accoutrements, a kind of stage set: wall-to-wall carpets, dark walnut paneling, a deep freeze and dishwasher, an electric can opener, an automatic record player, a brick patio with a built-in brick barbecue grill, a fuel-run lawn mower, a kidney-shaped swimming pool (the second one in a private dwelling in the town), Bermuda grass on a fine, sloping lawn, and the only self-operating garage doors in Fisk's Landing.

The earth took a couple of turns; the years passed, the long seasons came and went. People said I was growing so fast I buzzed like a bee. Arch Kidd was bitten by a copperhead in his back-yard. Dusty turned four. The Ricks Funeral Home was the first establishment in the town to get air-conditioning, beating the Rex Theater by ten days; most of the churches would hold out for years, presumably because air-conditioning was not mentioned in the Scriptures. (When asked whether his church was air-conditioned, the Methodist preacher answered, "No, it's not, and Hell ain't, either.") One summer the rumors circulated that the Negroes would rise and cause mayhem one midnight, and the men bought shotgun shells and locked their windows and doors, but nothing came of it. Coca-Cola went up from a nickel to six cents. A tornado ripped through the far side of Blackberry Hill, killing eight people. The *Merci, America,* Boxcar Number 10, arrived in town for two hours on its national tour as a thank-you from the people of France for U.S. support in World War II. Floodwaters reached to the main street one spring, prompting talk about the Corps of Engineers diverting the course of the river. The *Sentinel* reported that 20 percent of the farmland was not in production and 30 percent of the houses had been abandoned. Fisk's Landing got a five hundred–watt radio station with the call letters WFLL. Some high school students drag-racing in the hills at seventy miles an hour collided, and Potter Ricks and Woodrow had to wash out the flesh with a hose; there were five funerals in one day. Durley Godbold bought a thirty-five-foot cabin cruiser and kept it docked on the gulf. Mr. Leroy Godbold enhanced his honorary colonelship on the governor's staff by being named an honorary admiral in the Confederate navy. They opened the new section of the cemetery. Georgia descended into nihilism. One morning I awakened to find my mother bent over the bed examining my nose, ears, hair, and neck with a magnifying glass.

Although Amanda still helped my mother on special occasions, I did not see as much of her in those times. One afternoon I ran into her in front of one of the stores.

"Oh, how've you been? You're getting *big*. Are you ready yet to take piano?"

No, thanks.

"I don't play much anymore, not since I stopped teaching. I'm trying to take up golf, but I'm not very good. The ball's so little, like a mothball almost." She seemed to have a brittle, distracted air, an uncertain and fugitive unease. She gave me a light, careless embrace and was gone.

There were rumors. That Godbold and his wife were curt and condescending to her. That they never visited Amanda and Durley in Tara Estates. That they scheduled a family reunion for a day Amanda had to be out of town with my mother. That Godbold would not allow Durley to take her to lawn parties for the privileged luminaries at the governor's mansion. That Durley was drinking heavily. That he called her "common" and had belittled her in front of four or five other couples. Georgia's mother claimed to have seen her with a bruise under her eye, which she had tried to mask with makeup. Then there was talk that he was spending time with a divorcée in Memphis and had been involved in an incident with her ex-husband in full view of several onlookers at the Peabody.

I too witnessed a fateful occurrence one evening at the country club. I had gone outside away from the bingo game for some fresh air. It was a still, cold evening in January, and on the gallery down the way I noticed two figures profiled against the dim interior light. Durley was sitting on a bench with his back propped against the wall. Amanda was standing before him in a red dress. By the slur of his speech he was plainly quite drunk.

"I love you, Amanda," I heard him say. "I never could help it."

"I love you, too. But it's time for us to go home."

"I'll never leave you." Far from sounding tender, as one might have expected from the words, his tone was urgent and cruel, like a reverse demand.

"Please. Let's go home."

"You're no good, you know," he said.

He reached toward her, pulled her down to him, fumbled his hand into her dress. "Durley, not here! Wait till we get home. Please don't." He silenced her with a strong, swift kiss on her lips, then a longer one. After a time she got up and moved away from him. There was a glazed look to her eyes. She began buttoning her dress. He also rose, and they stood there for a moment whispering. I watched from the shadows. She kissed him. Then my voyeuristic eye shamed even me, and I slipped stealthily away, around the building and back into the hall.

The gossip persisted. This mosaic of hearsay was a staple of the place, and my vainglorious heart has long inclined to sense that humans crave it because the afflictions of their fellows therapeutically diminish their own. The women were the worst. Bored, pampered, unlettered, unread, and Christian, they were on the telephone among themselves all the livelong afternoons sharing their embittered tattle, and inviting the latest intelligence from their confreres, and sometimes indeed from the very victims themselves, though this in an outward mode of solicitude. Amanda and Durley surely gave them hours of exuberant gratification.

It took me a long time to comprehend Amanda's relationship with Durley. I would learn some of it from Luke as that year unfolded, but only later did I piece much of it together; one must live and experience and suffer to fathom such mysteries. She had been in love with Durley, I know, but it was a constrained and honest kind of love — he was not her knight in armor. Yet did he not offer her the security and comfort that a dignified, self-respecting girl from a poor hill-country past must have found assuring? He was good-looking, rich, and socially and politically powerful, and he had to have been a man, to put it as it must have been, who made her hot. After their marriage, his true nature must have surfaced; he began to play God with her.

One afternoon of that summer, returning from Georgia's, I

saw Amanda's car in our driveway. All the windows to the house were up, and I saw her in the parlor talking with my mother. She was sitting with her hands tightly clenched before her. My mother was nearby on the sofa. As I stood there in the shadows, Amanda's familiar voice was as kindly as always, yet there seemed a stinging edge of anguish in it.

"He treats me like dirt. He makes me *feel* like dirt. He thinks I'm just another possession, like a . . . *tractor.*"

"Surely it can't be *that* bad," my mother was saying. "Can't you . . . ?"

"It's the worst feeling I've ever had. I know I'm not all that wonderful, but no one's ever treated me this way. He doesn't even speak to my father. He's always telling me I'm a peckerwood, a redneck, white trash . . . *a slut.*"

I could almost feel the sharp sudden inhalation from my mother. Why on earth was Amanda telling her such things? I struggled to see the logic of it. Amanda needed an older woman to talk to. Amanda knew her, was with her frequently. My mother must have seemed a worthy confidante to her. She was a widow who had her own career; she had had disappointments.

"I know a person never gets everything she wants," Amanda was saying, "but . . ."

"You think I don't know that?"

"But he makes me feel he's so much *better* than I am — that he gives me more than I deserve."

"Have you talked to him about this?"

"It makes him *laugh.* At first I thought he was really different, and that I could help him. I wanted to very much."

"Maybe you ought to just ignore all the bad things. Go your own way. He's rich, after all."

"I've tried to ignore it. I can't. I've got my self-respect." Her head was bowed now, and she began to cry. The sight of her tears was almost too much, and my own careless heart reached out for her. "I've got to live with myself. I won't be *degraded.* Isn't there more to life than being rich and having a fancy house? And there's the other thing."

"The other thing," my mother repeated.

For a moment the room fell silent.

"There's a girl," Amanda said. "In the capital. I guess I could ignore *that.* But I know her. I went to school with her." The last was said hopelessly.

I retreated into the backyard. I felt sorry for Amanda. But I did not want to see her, for her to know that I had heard. Later that day I overheard my mother on the telephone. "He calls her a *slut* . . . and there's another woman."

Then the fighting in Korea came, and the activation of the guard. Lieutenant Godbold went with them. He had departed from the armory on that bright, windy morning the many weeks before. Right now he was somewhere near the 38th parallel, on a hot mountainous spine, in the miserable Korean rain.

One warm, cloudy late afternoon in July, I was in the backyard practicing my two-handed set shot. Basketball was my game. For reasons unknown to me I could run fast, and I was getting stronger. Someday later in high school I would play a little football and baseball, but there was something about this game that especially attracted and excited me, some soaring sense of beauty and adventure and even mischief. When you wanted to, you could play it all by yourself, and use your imagination on your own private fantasies. And it was *fun,* putting the ball into the hoop and then hearing the melodic whish of the wet strings when it was true — it was the sound of the whish that mattered so much.

My father had put up this goal for me when I was hardly tall enough to get the ball to the rim, but over the years my solitary practices in all weathers and seasons had earned me a place on the junior varsity; I was not unproud of this singular attainment. It seemed a long time before that I had first started coming out here in my backyard alone, shooting the ball through the lonesome moments until it was too dark to see the hoop or the ball against the sky, succumbing to lazy thoughts and daydreams, a formless rite of solitude, trying to figure out things, I guess, and over time the bouncing ball and my own footfalls wore away the grass, so that the ground around the goal was spare and hard and useful.

I had just made an improbable shot at the final whistle to defeat the loathsome, arrogant Kentucky Wildcats, when I saw Luke park his truck in front and walk slowly through the yard in my direction. I was already preparing myself for the next burial and was relieved to learn he had seen me from the boulevard and merely wanted to pass the time.

"Let's see if I've still got it," Luke said, and extended his hands for the ball. I tossed it to him. He whirled around with a hook shot, which sailed errantly over the backboard. Dusty pushed it toward us again with his nose.

"I guess not," he said. Luke started shooting from everywhere, and after a while began making a few baskets. I knew he had been the star of the Fisk's Landing Choctaws years before, and later a substitute at college for two seasons, and I was impressed with his limber dexterity, until he began to hobble.

"My old bad foot. Let's see what *you* can do." He sat on a tree stump and watched. "Not bad," he said after a while, a trifle begrudgingly, I thought. "Let me show you something." He got up and demonstrated a one-handed jump shot. "This is the new thing. Gets you up in the air. The college players are starting to use it."

It was hard, I complained, as one after another went astray.

"Work at it." Then we took turns together shooting free throws.

"Your mother came down to talk to me yesterday."

I felt a sharp thrust of apprehension, then anger. What about?

"She says she don't want you playing the 'Taps,'" he said, bouncing the ball as he talked. "Says it takes too much of your time. Says you come home depressed. Says you can't stand it. She don't think it's good for you."

Even before my father died she had done these things. In elementary school she would talk to my teachers without telling me. In the seventh grade when I was one of the assistant "managers" for the high school football team, a sinecure that involved washing the uniforms, keeping the balls full of air, mopping the locker room, and distributing the Toughskin and analgesic balm and athlete's foot powder, she telephoned the coach and wanted to know if this appointment was an *honor.* "Darn right it's an honor, ma'am," the coach later told me he had replied. "An honor to serve his school and its ball team."

What, then, did Luke say to her?

"I said I disagreed with her. I told her I thought it was your *duty.* I told her I didn't think you felt about it the way she said you did. Was I right?"

Yes.

"I even suggested in a nice way that it wasn't really any of her business. She didn't like it. Sorry about that."

He held the ball under his arm and looked at me. "Why does she give you such a hard time, anyway?"

"I've never once seen her happy. She's lost something." My own perception, the unfamiliar words, surprised me.

"Well, that's a problem."

There were things I could have told him, about the magnifying glass, the hairbrush and the pompadour, the aggrieved and silent stares, the nights I would find her waiting for me on the front steps when I had been out with Georgia. That when I started shaving two years before, she wanted to shave me herself. That recently she had tried to clip my *toenails*! Even in this moment I saw her looking out at us through the purple curtains of the kitchen window. Only that morning she had said to me:

"I wouldn't have much to do with Luke Cartwright. He just works in a hardware store."

I missed seven or eight of the new jump shots in a row. My mother had disappeared from the kitchen window, and Dusty went after a squirrel in the hollow near the alley. Suddenly, a shiny black hearse halted behind Luke's truck at the front curb, and Potter Ricks and Woodrow approached us through the side lawn.

Both of them wore dark suits and ties. They had obviously just concluded a regular funeral.

"Want to shoot some baskets?" Luke jocularly asked them.

"Bad news again," Potter said. "Very bad." He glanced at us, then at Woodrow. "Terrible fighting."

"Who?" Luke asked.

"Chisholm and Jetter dead," he said. "Lank Hemphill and Pounds seriously wounded."

"*Damn!*" Luke whispered, and threw the ball so violently into the hedges that you could hear the crack of the branches. "Why in God's name does it always have to be us?"

The Fourth of July came, and people were angry over this spiritless constellation of death and defeat. In this province they had ceased celebrating the Fourth in the 1860s because that was the day the big river town had capitulated; many southern towns had not resumed their commemorations until well into the twentieth century. On this day almost a hundred years later the Stars and Stripes were at half-mast everywhere, on the houses and storefronts, at the post office and courthouse and Elks Lodge, and on the flagpole at the end of the main street. To the news of the deaths of Chisholm and Jetter, hill-country boys and guardsmen, was added that of Lieutenant Commander Harvey Tidwell, a U.S. Navy pilot who had flown thirty-eight missions in the Pacific in the previous war, was a state university graduate in the law and descendant of one of the most venerable and honored families of the town, old quiet money, munificent benefactors of the museum and the school and the Afro-American Hospital. His F-86D had gone down near Pusan the week before while he was leading a squadron, and as Arch and I drove up the boulevard on the afternoon of the Fourth, a row of cars more than four blocks long stood in front of the Tidwell house, and people spilled out onto its porch and lawn.

At the traditional barbecue in the park, the whites milled in clusters around the speakers' podium, the blacks out at the fringes of the crowd. Mr. Leroy Godbold briefly spoke first. He attacked "the subhuman Russians and Chinese and their ambition for global conquest." He called the men in Washington "cowards" and "parlor pinks" for not using "the great major weapons at our disposal. The time has come to search out disloyalty in this country and strike it dead." Mayor Fink delivered the main speech. He had the sunny, expansive, almost innocent countenance of the southern Jew, and he wore a double-breasted navy blue suit with the wide lapels pressed flat; as they had to Mr. Godbold, the holiday assembly listened attentively. The mayor eloquently declared that the nation had considered World War II a bloodstained victory for our ideals, and that America had been the strongest military power on earth, and that its young men were now dying again "in a little ol' country nobody around here ever heard of until last year." American casualties, he said, were already averaging fourteen hundred a week. He spoke of "despotism" and "Red rule," and declared himself against every "ism" but Americanism. "We are uncomfortable," he intoned, "with a policy not aimed at total victory. We must prevail." Surely human civilization requires such steadying and unpacific rituals, and to the applause, led by Sarge Jennings, Son Graham, Roach Weems, and the other old veterans, he asked for a "renewed national purpose" and read from the most recent list of the state's dead and wounded. The townspeople bowed their heads in silence and then sang "God Bless America." In our church the next day, the vicar read two prayers: "For the Army" and "In Time of War and Tumults," and the choir sang "The Sewanee Hymn":

> For the warfare train us, Father,
> God of battles, God of might,
> That no mists or Hell may gather,
> Darken or obscure the right.

Shortly after the Fourth, Arch and I were in Crenshaw's Drug Store having a hot dog during the noontime break at the Jitney. Roach Weems of the honor guard was on one side of us with a long-necked bottle of beer. "How're our *trumpet* players today?" he amiably inquired. Herman von Schulte, the Kraut, sat on the other side of us with a sausage and two ice-cold beers. No sooner had this gourmand finished one sausage than from behind the counter Sarge Jennings would emphatically place a new one on the pile.

A black woman came in and asked for "female medicine."

"The bottle with one baby on it, or two?" the Sarge needled, and negotiated the transaction. Then he flipped on the radio, and the broadcast described the brutal, static, inch-by-inch fighting. At both the white and Negro counters everyone stopped talking to listen.

"Sounds like '18," Sarge Jennings said.

"Damned if it don't," Roach Weems said.

"Not as bad as '18!" von Schulte said.

"You crazy Kraut!" Sarge Jennings said. "We whipped your ass *twice.*"

"Not as bad as '18," he repeated. The old adversaries stared at each other in righteous distaste across an ageless divide. That was the way of things in that bellicose summer.

Arch and Georgia and I finally got a letter from Lank Hemphill or, more accurately, a letter written for him by an army nurse in the Tokyo General Hospital. His left forearm had been blown away by a grenade in the ruins of Seoul, and they had patched him up at a MASH unit and sent him on to a rear field hospital and then Japan. "But don't feel sorry for me," the letter said. "I'm lucky to be alive and out of it." Many of the guys in his rifle company were already dead, he said. He was homesick and looked forward to coming back soon.

Durley wrote vivid, if infrequent, letters to Amanda, and she showed one of them to my mother and me.

> As of now it's been raining for 48 hours straight. The mud is like chewing gum. I'm tired of the stinking yellow rivers. I hate this damned place and the proposition we are here under. Americans are fools. The Koreans are contrary to everything you find that the Japanese are. For my money these Koreans are no good for anything, not the powder to kill them with. It takes a gun to make them work. That's the workers. Their soldiers are no good either. We ought to just leave and let the N. and S. Koreans butcher themselves. That's what they really want anyway. I'm sitting here while my boy is issuing to the Dutch. The Dutch attached to us ain't worth a damn either . . .
>
> The best officer in our outfit shot himself through the head last night. Not too neat a job. His name was Thompson. Already had 2 silver stars. Beats me. Our "K" Company was wiped out by the Chinese. Men don't come back much from night patrols. Don't worry about me, though . . .

"I hear Durley's a pretty good officer," Luke said one day. "Sons of bitches sometimes are."

In these days when I was seeing more and more of Luke, he was acting furious and impatient about things. I would see him in the ragged little poolroom on the main street bent down over the ancient table with its old leather pockets and bulbous mahogany legs. "Eight ball off the end rail and side rail in the cross corner pocket," he would say, and then strike the ball with such savage force that I thought it might splinter the wood. He spent many afternoons in the library reading the newsweeklies. "Why do we fight those wars against these Orientals?" he asked me. "Is it our fault, or theirs?" And a few days later, bitterly, and more to himself, it seemed, than to me, "There simply ain't enough boys here to whip the Chinese and look after Europe, too. It's not enough to ask them to get shot up for. That's just common sense."

I was sweeping the sidewalk in front of the store one morning when Potter Ricks walked by on his way to the funeral home from the coffee shop in the Earl Van Dorn Hotel. He had just completed, he said, an article on military funerals for a morticians' trade journal. Would I drop by his establishment after work and check it for spelling? I told him I would.

The funeral home was adjacent to the gray, fortress-like post office and across from the Presbyterian church. It had been there much longer than I could remember, a forbidding abstraction in red brick, a nest of tribulation and esoteric practices. There was the small lawn in front, always well tended, and a wooden gallery abutting its nondescript facade. I opened the door and went inside. The main parlor was slightly frayed, with a worn brown carpet and overstuffed Victorian sofas and chairs and a portrait of the first Potter Ricks over an unexpectedly ornate mahogany mantel. A muffled hush suffused the place. I had been there only once before, when my father died. He had lain in an open coffin in the large room next to the parlor. My mother had made me look at him. I complied, but only from a distance. The mute waxen figure, so quiet and still, the rouged and fallen features, the grave and sedate half smile, the prim and contrived clasp of his hands as he lay there on white satin, filled me with cold and unbearable awe and sorrow and anguish. *That's not him.* The words silently welled out of me.

"Please Ring for Service." I pushed the buzzer on the parlor wall. In seconds Potter Ricks emerged on noiseless feet from the shadowy hallway.

"Hello, Mr. Ricks."

"Good of you to come," he said. "Please call me Potter, if you will." In that time and place, certain adults — Luke Cartwright, for instance, and Georgia's parents, and Roach Weems — liked us to use their first names, although I was a little surprised that he would too.

His office was at the end of the corridor, with a big scarred wooden desk piled high with papers, an old Smith-Corona typewriter, an immense oak filing cabinet with six or eight ample drawers in a corner, and three or four plain straight-backed chairs like the ones used at the burials. Sitting in one of them before a smaller table was Woodrow, who was sorting documents and withdrawing one every now and then from an elegant eel-skin briefcase; I could never quite relate him to that case.

On the floor against a wall was a sizeable bookcase filled with books: Emily Post's *Etiquette* and some mysteries and Dale Carnegie's *How to Win Friends and Influence People, The Funeral and the Mourners* by Ernest F. Irion, *Modern Mortuary Science* by John H. Echols, *Techniques of Embalming* by R. Mortimer Jeffries, various novels including *The Grapes of Wrath* and *The Great Gatsby,* and a grand welter of periodicals and pamphlets — *Cemeterian, Southern Funeral Direction, Armed Services Specification for Care and Remains of Deceased Personnel.*

In public, Potter was recognized for his kindly, inviolate decorum, his delicate *ben trovato* and appreciation of therapeutic silence — he was a practiced suppliant to all despairs and sorrows, which he approached with a regard for proximate rather than ultimate goals. But in private he had an air of alert and controlled restlessness. He sat behind his cluttered desk like an anxious and skittish schoolmaster. The creases around his eyes were deep, but other than that, with his rosy complexion and large paunch and his sunburned bald pate, he looked robust, even wholesome.

He reached in his papers and handed me the article. It was written in pale black typewriter script. "I'm not a good speller. Idella King was always on me for that."

One paragraph read: "We should not forget that mourning is intensified with the military deceased. The mourners will look for reasons for what has happened. The bereaved will need and deserve more solace than usual. It should be the funeral director's responsibility to befriend the bereaved family at the first notice of tragedy. The interval between the actual tragedy and shipment home of the remains is often a lengthy and prolonged one. This is a trying period." And three or four paragraphs later: "In our small town, due to the large incidence of casualties accruing from the local National Guard's activation, we have had a community-wide effort, which has strengthened national pride in hard-to-understand events. Our honor guard of World War I veterans is a calming influence. So is the decorated World War II platoon sergeant who works with us on behalf of the American Legion. In the absence of military buglers, two young men in our high school have performed nobly and well." After considerable helpful counsel and detail, the article ended: "God bless Fisk's Landing. God bless America."

While I was reading, Potter leaned back in his swivel chair and contemplated the ceiling fan. "Have we heard from the army about Mrs. Scuttles's benefits?" Woodrow asked him as he rustled papers from his station in the corner. "No. No, we haven't. I'll write again tomorrow." I read his article carefully but found only one misspelling. That was when it occurred to me that Potter was not seeking my help at all. He wanted companionship in his despondent rituals and grotesque responsibilities.

"What do you think of it?" he asked.

It was good, I said.

"It's *really* good," Woodrow said.

"Do you like the part about the graveside service?" Potter persisted.

"I like it a lot."

He beamed, his broad features flushed in sunny contentment. "Well, I meant every word. Luke said he liked it. He gave me that suggestion about the preachers being briefer at the grave, and the best places for echo. Sarge liked it too. Showed it around at Crenshaw's." In the grim days that followed, we became unlikely but needful allies, dating I believe from that afternoon in his office, when at one week from age sixteen I endorsed his article for *Deep South Embalmer.*

"I sympathize with these boys," he said. He pursed his lips and dabbed at them with his handkerchief. "They don't want to be out there. I volunteered for Graves Registration in the last war. They wouldn't take me. They said I was in important work on the home front. They wanted to know who'd run my business. Also, I have flat feet. I knew a lot of them who didn't come back. I know their families. I've watched their children grow up."

Years before as a teenager he worked after school and on weekends for his father. He could remember country funerals back then where the coffins were loaded on horse-drawn wagons and plow lines were used to lower them into the graves. When he graduated from high school, he had spent two years at the Gupton-Jones School of Embalming in Nashville. One day that following winter, when the omnibus broke down at a burial far out in the flatland, and Luke and I caught a ride with Potter back into town in the hearse, he told us about his professors there. By then he had become unembarrassedly candid and graphic with Luke and me in his talk, so much so that I grew accustomed to it, which compounded the strangeness of that uncommon, long-ago season. He never forgot the sage words of an ambidextrous old embalming teacher: "Each individual leaves his own mark."

He told about the night Woodrow went out into the countryside to bring back someone who had been killed in a wreck. When he got there the man was headless. "Where's his head?" Woodrow asked the people who had telephoned. "Back up the road somewhere," one of them said. Then Potter Ricks reached into a drawer and brought out a photograph he and Woodrow had taken of the severed head. I could hardly believe it. There it was, sitting doll-like on a porcelain table, the gaping tissues dangling horribly from the shattered neck. "That was '44," he said. "I sent a copy of the photograph to my old professors in Nashville. They still use it in their technique classes."

He returned from school and joined his father as an associate, and, when the older man died in 1936, Potter assumed, at age thirty-three, the directorship. "I guess we're like the old family doctor," he said to us. "We're part of the family. We know each other. We're old-line. We respect dignity. We have the patronage of *old* Fisk's Landing." The best and most venerated families used him and also, of course, so did the United States military.

There was another white funeral home in town — called Warwick-Hudson and Sons, a recent competitor. It had located itself near the development of Tara Estates and was housed in a contemporary structure with white columns and spacious verandas, which Luke called "counterfeit antebellum." Mr. Leroy Godbold had made a sizeable early investment in this now flourishing institution. It had a haughty interior decor: lush wall-to-wall carpeting, concealed lighting, sedate pastoral paintings, placid Muzak hymns, and a stylish "slumber room." From every appearance it was doing more trade now than Ricks ever had. For years, there had also been a Negro funeral home, the Centennial Burial Association, and its proprietor was the richest black man by far in the town. We often saw him in his black Cadillac and expensive suits smoking long cigars, the only black person in town, it was said, who was allowed to vote.

"You have to be conscious of what people *see*," Potter explained one day. "Most flower arrangements are too thick. Flowers ought to cover a coffin easily." Also, he said, nothing looks deader than a human hand. "I like to put a little sponge under the hand to plump it up." The head ought to be turned a little to the right, like the dead person is recognizing you. Don't put flowers in a coffin. They've got mold spores, and bacteria. Make a person look relaxed, not tired. A little cotton on a Q-Tip under the muscles of the mouth makes a gentle smile. The right lighting has a consoling effect. "I like all that to look correct from *my* standpoint too. *I'm* responsible. No matter how good the minister does, or the organist, if anything goes wrong it comes back to me."

"I've known Potter since he worked for his daddy," Luke said to me. "He's not an undertaker so much as a *philosopher*. The problem is, he ain't got nobody to talk to, except Woodrow. You and I may be the first white men he's seriously talked to in years. Who in this town wants to sit around and listen to him talk about what he really *does*? Can you imagine him talking to Godbold? Or Georgia's mama? Or yours? Or your boss at the Jitney? You've seen him at funerals. Seen how good he is with the families. We need him." He paused for a moment and then asked, "Why do *you* sit around and listen to him?"

"I think it's interesting. I like him."

"Does your mama know you go down there? Don't tell her."

I was in his office one day when the mother of Oscar Goodloe, the first boy we had buried, came in. She was a slight little figure of indeterminate age, wearing a frayed green dress and thick Woolworth's eyeglasses. I knew that she lived in a small unpainted house in the hills with a sick, unemployed husband. Potter stood up and greeted her with a tidy flourish. "So nice to see you again, Mrs. Goodloe." He offered her a chair, and Luke helped her into it.

"You've got to help me with this," she said, and handed him a piece of paper with the formidable letterhead:

Department of the Army
Office of the Adjutant General
Demobilized Personnel Records Branch
St. Louis 20, Missouri

Potter removed his glasses as was his habit and rubbed them with his handkerchief. "Does this pertain to the insurance?" he asked.

"I don't think so. I can't tell."

"I wouldn't think so. We got all those forms in last month. I have a file on all the letters. You should get the insurance money in a month or so." He solemnly directed his attention to the document. "Ah, yes, *combat pay*." And he read aloud:

> Combat pay is at the rate of $45.00 per month for combat service rendered. The law provides that payments will be made only if the individual served as a member of a combat unit. Under the interpretation of the law, payments are authorized only for the part of the month in which the individual was in an institutionalized pay status. For example, combat pay not to exceed $15.00 is authorized for an individual who died on the 10th day of the month as a result of service with a combat unit. This amount for the month in which the soldier died would be in addition to the combat pay to which he may have been entitled for previous months.

"Does that mean I get fifteen dollars?"

"Oh, no, no. It means we have to fill out this form and send it back to this man in Missouri. It would help if we got some information on how long Oscar was in combat."

"I don't know that," she said, and looked at him in bewilderment. "All I know is they killed him."

He reached across the desk toward her, a little gesture of care. "Let me write a letter or two. I'll handle this. Do you have a way home? Why don't you let this young man drive you home in our van? Would you mind, Swayze?"

We rode in silence down the boulevard, up the ridges into the hills. She was clutching her purse in her fingers, burying her knuckles against it so hard that they soon turned white.

"Are you the boy who played the horn at Oscar's funeral?" she asked.

"Yes, ma'am."

"It was warm, wasn't it? Five weeks ago today."

Sometimes Woodrow would be in the rear driveway polishing the black Cadillac hearse and the creamy white ambulance that they used for emergency calls, or in front clipping the hedges or mowing the lawn. But more often he would be in the office doing paperwork with his employer. I noticed that he always said "Mr. Ricks" in public, but with no one around but Luke or me, he called him "Potter." Woodrow and Potter were almost the same age and had known each other since they were boys, when Woodrow first went to work for Potter's father. He was in the eighth grade then and quit school. His full name was Woodrow Wilson Lee, and his father had been the yardman for the Darnells on the boulevard. "When I was born," Woodrow told us, "Ol' Man Darnell tried to get my daddy to name me 'Robert E. Lee.' Offered him twenty dollars. My daddy agreed to name me Woodrow *Robert* Lee. They only gave him ten dollars, so he changed it back to Woodrow Wilson but didn't tell nobody."

Woodrow was a religious man, and he liked to talk most when the burials were over and the mourners had departed, resting in a chair under the canopy while the gravediggers shoveled dirt. "Any time you hear a plane's crashed," he might say, "it's sad. There's nothing man's made that didn't have a wreck. But if *God* made something, it never stops running. What He made don't have no accidents. Look at the moon and sun. They ain't stopped once since the Lord put 'em up there."

I had never seen such a relationship between a white man and a black man. It was almost a brotherly one. In the office they constantly engaged in their fretful riposte. "Potter, you *got* to write the army people about this," and he would hand over a piece of paper. And Potter would jot down notes while Woodrow criticized the United States Army on body shipments, insurance payments, or some other faulty piece of work.

Potter told me that Woodrow's son worked for them sometimes when they were really busy. "He's eighteen now, Woodrow Junior. He usually works in the Chinaman's store. I can't even remember the first time he touched a dead person. He just grew up around us. He was a funeral home boy, like Woodrow and me."

Enhancing this singular melange was an elderly black man named Silas Delaware, who had worked at Ricks off and on for many years. The funeral home had one of the two ambulance services in the town, and Woodrow and Silas Delaware had gone out on an emergency call in the hills one stormy midnight in '36. Woodrow was driving and hit an icy patch in the road just west of Marshall; the ambulance turned over twice. Woodrow emerged without injury, but Silas Delaware was almost blinded. "All I can see is little purple blurs," he told Potter. Still, Potter said, he retained his intuitive sense of touch in the embalming work and continued to contribute his skills when they were most required "in the back," as he called it. We saw more and more of him as the year progressed. As thin as a wisp and obsidian dark, using his hands to find his way, he had a voodoo priest's precognition of urgency and distress, and he usually arrived without summons when needed.

So, in the subsequent frightful days, there would be Potter, assisted by three Fisk's Landing blacks: a middle-aged one named after a president, a seventy-year-old who could not see, and a teenager. "We all know when we bring someone in," Potter would say, "that the body is sacred. We're respectful. A live body can tell you not to do something. A dead body can't." In the funeral home on evenings in that forthcoming autumn and winter, there would be soft music from Potter's record player, the abiding hymns — "Rock of Ages," "The Old Rugged Cross," "In the Garden," "Faith of Our Fathers." The velvety sounds would float into the darkest corners of the homely building, making it a tranquil and eerie island right there on the main street of Fisk's Landing.

The coffin room was in a separate building in the back, next to a larger windowless one with a heavy black door bearing the sign *"Private — Absolutely No Admittance!"* The cool, dark chamber was filled with coffins of every shade and description, copper and lead-coated and wood, some rectangular, some kite-shaped and pewter-hued, with satin sheets and tufted pillows and eggshell bedspreads and foam rubber mattresses and various kinds of grips and handles. For some reason they reminded me of boats, just sitting there waiting to be launched to sea.

Potter became a central figure in those days, the talisman and necromancer and conjurer of the tale, the sad, the gruesome, the funny. "If we didn't have some amusing things along the way," Potter once said, in that precise, rippling voice of his, which became a shrill lisp when he was amused or disturbed, "I doubt if we could do what we do without a little humor. Do you understand?" Sitting at the desk in his swivel chair, he would giggle at such things as a schoolgirl might and shake his head in sly amusement, and look over in the corner at Woodrow, who was giggling too, as if despite himself.

"Now I know you wouldn't tell anyone this," he began as usual one day: "In '39 we had Mrs. Ventress in her coffin two or three hours before her funeral. People were filing by to look at her. Older people, you see, especially widowed ladies, like to come to funerals for the company. Miss Mary Sims Stovall — you remember her? She was sort of an old busybody. We buried her in August of '45. She came rushing back to me in this very office, and said, 'Potter, Cora's alive! She's breathing!' Well, I knew she wasn't breathing after all that had been done to her out in the back, but I went up there with her and looked. It was a hot day and all the ceiling fans were on. Her blouse was fluttering in the breeze. Several other old ladies were standing in the corner with their eyes wide open. All I did was turn off the fans and showed them what it was. Quite frankly, they didn't seem all that disappointed."

One afternoon a little later in the summer, I was sitting on my front steps after the tap dancers had dispersed, when the hearse pulled up to the curb. Potter had just finished another civilian funeral and merely wished to pass the time. He reclined in a wrought-iron chair, a man relaxing after a diligent day's labor. At the sight of the hearse, people slowed their vehicles and looked out at it aghast — another death on the boulevard? I waved them on. I saw my mother, who had just appeared behind the screen door. When she sighted the visitor, she glared at him a moment in apparent distaste, then quickly turned away. "I used to sit here with your daddy," Potter said, "on late afternoons, you know, just to cool off. You were about *this* big, crawling around in the grass."

He was talking about desultory summer things when Amanda Godbold's Buick came to a halt behind the hearse. She emerged from the car with her sheet music. She looked radiant, brimming with vitality. She greeted us with a happy smile.

"Hello, Swayze. Hello, Potter."

"Hello, Amanda."

"Isn't it a fine day?" She tarried before us in a bantering mood. "I'd *hoped* no one was sick, not in this house. You're not sick, are you, Swayze? We don't want you sick." And she climbed the steps and went inside. Where was the desperate girl I had overheard crying in my parlor that afternoon months before?

"A pretty, sweet young lady," Potter said. "Durley's a strange boy, but promising. He's got a good career ahead of him when this is all over. Don't you think?"

I certainly did.

"When he was in high school," he said, shaking his head, "he came to us wanting to rent the hearse. For some Halloween party out at Godbold. I didn't want to, of course, but . . . well, I did."

The generations of jokes about his calling, the radio caricatures and all the rest, had elicited in him a vague and secret paranoia and, disguise it though he might, a feeling that he was unappreciated in Fisk's Landing, maligned and misunderstood, not taken with the seriousness he felt was his due. Was it not also true that others actually feared him — feared his power over them, feared the terrible authority he might someday exert over their very own flesh? That no elixir of longevity existed to countervail that authority?

"People in this town look at me, and all they think of is death," Potter blurted out to us after an especially trying army burial that fall. "We're human too. Sometimes I don't even think they like to shake *hands* with me."

"Then why do you do it?" I had thoughtlessly asked.

"That's none of your business, is it?" Luke said.

"It's what I was brought up to do," Potter said.

The fact was that with his own hands in his grim sorcery Potter Ricks had sliced and eviscerated and pumped and sutured and drained and trussed and distended and tubed and augured more than a generation of the Fisk's Landing dead, then ceremoniously led the mourners toward the murky pit of the grave. Yet I found it hard to associate his horrid craft and forbidding duties with the decorous gentle man I knew. Childless, friendless except for Woodrow, living alone in a house on a hill with tombstones for sale on the front lawn, Potter had developed, it was obvious, a real tenderness, indeed a *fondness,* for the dead, with whom he and Woodrow shared their countless hours.

Before that summer I would have considered this proclivity malproportioned. Then they began shipping the soldiers home. I grew gradually to sense the fragility of human life, to become aware that all of us — Potter and Luke and Georgia and Arch and I, Amanda and the Godbolds — were enveloped in something so elemental that it summed up the town, its miscellaneous ordinances and the flow of its generations and the powerful land that encompassed us. Potter by trade was custodian of our past. Is it not true that the past is the only thing we truly possess? He *remembered.*

5

LUKE HAD a large cabin three miles east of Fisk's Landing in the hills, surrounded by thirty or so wooded acres, isolated but with a distant prospect of the town below, a terrain of tall wizened pines and funny misty hazes in the nighttimes, and I started going there in the early summer evenings to let Dusty run around and swim in the creek. Sometimes Arch would go along, or Potter Ricks, but most of the time I would drive out there alone. Luke had built the cabin with his own hands, with the help of his cousin Billy Permenter and Woodrow from the funeral home, when he got back from the war. He had a good deal of back pay and some disability, he said, and he needed a place to get his head straight.

He had been sent first to one of the hospitals around Paris, where the men he had fought, the Wehrmacht, now prisoners of war, worked in the wards. He had two operations on his foot there before being sent to England for convalescence and rehabilitation; the king and queen even visited his ward one day. He was sent home in August 1945 on the *Queen Elizabeth*, then used as a troop carrier, and they were halfway across the Atlantic when the word came that the Japanese had capitulated. The captain gave an elegant celebration banquet for several dozen officers, and Luke's C.O. got him an invitation. He was the only noncom in the first-class dining room of the great lady,

with her lights ablaze again and her horns sounding grandly after the long dark of the war, while far below on the ocean's bed
lay the dead sailors and ships, the remnants of shredded pain
and decay. On arriving in this country he needed further surgery; he was not like a Roman conqueror returning home with
his treasures. After his release from the army he was consuming
a quart or so of gin a day and engaging himself in barroom
fistfights up and down the whole Atlantic seaboard, usually
with pushy civilians who had made a lot of money during the
war. Once in a saloon in Norfolk he hit a sailor over the head
with a pinball machine. He did not fight anymore, however, he
later told me. He used to hunt, birds and deer and squirrels, but
when he finally got home it surprised him what little use he had
for guns; he did not keep any in the cabin, and he did not even
hunt for pheasants, perhaps because he did not like the look of
open fields. When the work was finished on the cabin, he spent
half a year sleeping and reading books before he became a partner in the hardware store on the main street.

His cabin was built to be lived in. It felt *safe* to me, a small
oasis of tranquility, and over the weeks it became a haven from
my mother and her dancers and school and "Taps." It was of
pecky cypress indoors and out, the wood almost apricot in hue.
The ceilings were fourteen feet high with exposed beams, the
floors were heart pine polished with beeswax, and there was a
substantial fireplace, modeled from a photograph of the fireplace in Patrick Henry's kitchen in Virginia, with old rust-
colored bricks and a mantel of unhewn oak. On the mantel
were a large number of arrowheads he and Woodrow and Billy
Permenter had unearthed while digging the foundation. The
kitchen was of thick paneling in a deeply figured grain the color
of cherry.

Many of the furnishings had come from a house sale in the
hamlet of Marshall, where Amanda Godbold's father had his
garage, and consisted of an exceptional blend of Early Ameri-

can and Montgomery Ward. An old Hammond upright piano stood in a corner. On the wall was a photograph of his company, taken near Winchester, England, not long before the Normandy invasion. Inked on the chests of more than half of the men were the letters *K, W,* or *MIA.*

Wandering about one evening, I noticed a legal-sized piece of typing paper thumbtacked to a bulletin board in his bedroom with various other notes and reminders. His penciled handwriting was almost illegible, but the words leapt out at me:

F. L. Pub. Library, April, '46
Copied from a book by man who fought in WW2

There had to be something somewhere in all of them, in all of us, that loved it. Some dark, aggressive, masochistic side of us, racial perhaps, that makes us want to spray our blood in the air, throw our blood away, for some damned misbegotten ideal or another. Whether the ideal is morally right or wrong makes no difference so long as the desire to fight for it remains in us. Fanatics willing to do for ideals. It was territory, back when we were animals. Now that we have evolved into higher beings and learned to talk, territoriality has moved up a step higher with us, and become ideals. We like it. Cynical as it sounds, one is about led to believe that only the defeated and the dead really hate war. And of course, as we all know, they don't count. All war is civil war between brothers.

I could never have expected the array of articles in his dwelling, or his regard for finely crafted things: carved wooden objects, American Indian jewelry and rugs, leather items, belts and belt buckles, Randall knives, an old dartboard, an antique checkerboard, a dueling pistol with a mother-of-pearl handle, an old Victrola with a shiny brass trumpet, a telescope and a microscope and a pair of captured Wehrmacht officer's binoculars so powerful that you could see people's noses from a mile away. Empty boxes of Padrón cigars were scattered here and there, and in the kitchen was a long cotton-grading table made, in fact, of cottonwood, sanded down and oiled, on which bales had once been sliced when they came from the compress so that the fiber could be judged. It was on this table, as Arch and I watched in amazement one night, that the tough platoon sergeant whose fighting days were over was chopping onions and bell peppers. "A dull knife's more dangerous than a sharp one," he said. "Nobody's careful with a dull knife." Then he made a vat of beef stew, and began mixing up a salad dressing, wordlessly stirring oil and vinegar into an earthen bowl dabbed with mustard. "Now that's what you call a *vinaigrette*," he said at last. "Learned it in France. Can you guys pronounce it?" Some men like Luke, especially ones with country antecedents, could *cook,* and relished the process.

Outside the cabin, along its entire front, was a roofed gallery with the same rust-colored brick for a floor. All around were loblolly pines with their clean, dry needle smell and wild plums and catclaw vines and dogwoods and red and white and black-jack oaks and wild holly that stayed green all year and great shady hickories that turned flaming gold in the fall and black-berry vines, which had taken over the fencerows and which burst into delicate flat white blossoms in the spring. In a clear-ing beyond was a sizeable plot for vegetables — tomatoes, cu-cumbers, field peas, collard greens (which Luke washed in the washing machine before boiling), okra, snap beans, squash, corn — and in a slough near the creek bed a dozen or so drakes and guinea hens and a funny wild albino turkey, which Luke said was as reliable as a watchdog. A crude brick walkway led down a rolling incline to Potter's Creek, so named for Potter Ricks's grandfather, the first mortician, who had harvested tim-ber in the vicinity for his furniture store and livery stable and, of course, his coffins.

Luke had a smart cat, named Andy, who thought he was a dog. This maverick creature had appeared several years before out of nowhere. "When a black cat takes up with you," Luke said, "it's a sign of good luck." Andy's eyes were yellow and purple and looked straight at you, an Old Testament kind of look. He wagged his tail all the time like a dog, and he would come to you the moment you called him. His dining habits were democratic. Luke would give him hot tamales, barbecued beans, rat cheese, potato chips, spaghetti, chicken livers, ice cream, fried catfish, and boiled collard greens. At first Dusty did not care for Luke's cat. But after a while they got along fine.

Late one afternoon that month, the foliage all around us dry and brittle with dust, Luke and I were sitting on the porch snapping beans from the garden. A ponderous ceiling fan provided a breeze, and whippoorwills cried from across the shadowy hills. The cat lay on the porch beside us as we slapped at the mosquitoes.

"Has Dusty had any puppies?" Luke asked, stooped over the bucket of beans.

"I don't think so."

"Better let him get some puppies. He'll need them to be *remembered* by when he's gone."

I had never thought of it in quite that way, although it made a certain sense. Yet, watching his mad energies on this evening, I knew Dusty would never die.

"I had some girlfriends then. I even knew Amanda Pettibone — Amanda *Godbold* — back then. Our people knew each other. She's even prettier now than she was in those days." He paused, and a strange expression crossed his face, one that I had never seen before. "I had a real serious girl in town, a Ferguson girl, but then I had to go off, and when I got back, she was married to a dentist in Memphis." He pulled the bucket closer to his chair and stooped down again. "I guess I let a lot of things slip by when I got back. Didn't think I was good enough for any of 'em."

It was not too late, I suggested. Like Dusty.

"Son, you're damned right it's not too late!" he said, and came out with his ridiculous high-pitched giggle.

He seldom talked about the war with me, and even less about his role in it. Sarge Jennings of the Legionnaires had told us Luke had won the Silver Star for stealing toward the German lines in a night action under fire and bringing back a wounded soldier. He had listened to him cry out all night in pain. Luke's commanding officer later wrote Sarge Jennings as head of the Legion post. The C.O. was a graduate of a fancy northern college in the "Ivory League," Sarge proudly reported, pronouncing its name Dart-*mouth*. The C.O. said Luke was the most fearless man in the outfit and once had single-handedly prevented some hysterical tankers whose best friends had been killed from shooting several German prisoners. But mainly, the captain wrote, Luke had gone through the third wave at Normandy into Germany, a hundred miles or so north-east of the spot where Sarge and the others had landed with the Thirty-first Division twenty-seven years before, seven months of nearly constant combat, sometimes from first light to last light, and this had involved everything — fighting tanks, paratroops, and infantry, attacking pillboxes, defending little towns. "How Luke and I and the others survived I don't know," the captain wrote. "Near the end our casualties were more than 50 percent. Many was the time our company had more men in cemeteries and field hospitals than present for duty. We knew we were the walking dead, but Luke always cared for the men. In my humble opinion he was the best damned platoon sergeant of our whole outfit."

Luke was usually reticent about such things, but on two or three occasions, when I first started going out there, he was not. On our insistence that summer, he was teaching Arch and me poker. "If you play poker," he said, "you'd better *learn* it all the way. The worst thing's to learn it halfway. You'll end up on the poor farm, or in jail. Treat it with *respect*. Faith and love ain't got much to do with it." And he began to instruct us in what he called "enlisted men's poker" — cool, studied, covert. Whenever he lost a hand, which was infrequently, he might complain, "Christ, that's not the way it's supposed to come out." But he was a disciplinarian on the complicated points: "You got to learn how to turn a busted hand into a winner," he would say — a lesson I learned so well that when I eventually got to college I paid a good portion of the tuition from my marathon nights of poker playing. I prayed my gratitude to the tutor.

We had stacked away the cards after one such session. Luke was rereading a letter from his cousin Lieutenant Billy Permenter on stationery of the Hotel New Sokawa, Tokyo. Meanwhile Arch, as was his habit, was exploring the cabin, getting into things; his inquisitiveness about the possessions of others bordered always on the larcenous. He returned from the back room to the kitchen with a small tin box.

"Are these yours?" he asked Luke.

"Yeah."

Arch laid his discoveries on the table — an assortment of medals and ribbons — and blew off the accumulated dust. I had rarely seen him so honestly enthusiastic.

"Why do you keep 'em in your closet?"

"Because they don't do no good."

"What's this one?"

"That's Good Conduct. They took that away once and then gave it back."

"And this?"

"Silver Star."

"This?"

"Theater ribbon."

"Shit!" Arch's eyes gleamed. "Look — the Purple Heart! I've only seen these in picture shows."

Our host was stirring sheepishly but seemed grandly amused.

"This one?" It was a replica of a rifle on a field of blue with a silver wreath around it.

"Combat Infantryman's Badge. That's the only one any of us wore when we shipped home."

"Why?"

"Spoke for itself, I guess. It was just an unwritten rule. If you wore any of the others, the men would've laughed you out of town, or maybe whipped your ass."

"Were you a hero?" Arch asked.

"What do you mean, *hero*?" Luke said.

"Well, you were brave, weren't you?"

"It didn't have nothin' to do with being brave. It didn't even have to do with who you were fightin' or America or any *ideals*. It all had to do with your buddies, not to let them down. But you don't know about that." I do not believe Luke liked Arch very much.

Another evening later that month Arch and I went out to Luke's for supper and met a friend of his, Dr. Patterson, who had driven over from a nearby town. They had gone into France at about the same time. The doctor was a major in the medical corps, the assistant regimental surgeon, and they met by chance near Bastogne during the Christmas fighting of '44 when Luke brought in two of his wounded riflemen. They discovered that they lived seventy miles away from each other back home, and they had stayed in close touch ever since.

Luke called him "Doc." He was a garrulous and agreeable widower in his fifties with a sharp pointed nose, a tuneful basso voice, and a small, square mustache, like Hitler's. We were sitting around the big cottonwood table in the kitchen. The crickets were coming out, and the dying light fell on their faces and made a dancing mosaic on the doctor's wild shock of graying hair.

They were recalling the liberation of Paris.

"August 25, '44," the doctor said. "There was blood on the walls and people were singing 'The Marseillaise' and the French girls were giving us flowers and wine. They were hysterical."

"And two blocks away, rifle shots in the streets," Luke said. "One big party and people still getting killed."

"And the French girls!" the doctor added. "You could get two bottles of Chanel Number Five for a pack of cigarettes."

"I went into the cathedral of Notre-Dame," Luke said. "They let us take our M-1s in. That's the prettiest church in the world. Then we had to ship right out. Didn't even drink the wine." (Many years later, when I found myself in Paris, I tried to envision Luke of Fisk's Landing in '44 swinging down the Champs-Élysées, or on the Île St.-Louis, carbine over his shoulder, going into Notre-Dame. Much as I tried I could not see him there, although I felt his spirit.)

Then Luke began talking about the World War I cemeteries they marched by, set out in huge, strange squares, the bleak gray headstones everywhere. "I'll tell you why Europe's so damned green," he said. "Every blade of grass has twenty drops of blood on it."

"Things got complicated after that," the doctor said. "In those villages the closer you got to Germany, those people were waving swastikas one minute, Tricolors the next. You couldn't tell who they were *for* half the time."

Sitting with them around the kitchen table, a solitary brotherless and fatherless boy growing up in a house full of tap dancers and a crazed mother, I had never heard this kind of talk — two adult men drinking beer and smoking cigars and talking between themselves about something that mattered to them. I was mesmerized, and even Arch was subdued. The sounds of the summer evening drifted in from the bluffs, in melodious counterpoint to the doctor's talk about the field hospitals of the Bulge.

"The frozen corpses were stacked up everywhere like cordwood," he said, "more than the length of a football field, as far as you could see. Germans and Americans, you couldn't tell them apart. It broke my heart, I'll tell you, Luke. It was so cold you could see the bullet holes all the way through their heads. Ours were young enough, but a lot of the Germans were thirteen and fourteen. You'd give 'em a shot and they'd spit on you in the eye. Hitler Youth, I guess."

The two of them fell silent. But when one of them chuckled, the other did too. "Thank God for the paratroops," the doctor finally said, "and that screwy old horse cavalryman Patton."

"I'm sorry I've never been in a war," Arch said.

Luke looked at him and did not say a word.

Surely the memory of one's youth is stronger than thought — that tacit feeling of the shape of things as they were. I think now that Luke was becoming the older brother I lacked in blood, and as the days passed we became closer, and I needed him, just as I sensed that for some reason he needed me: we were confidants and conspirators. That summer he talked — as we were hoeing weeds in the rows of vegetables or walking along the creek with Dusty and the black cat who thought he was a dog or taking turns looking at birds through the commandeered Nazi binoculars or cooking in the kitchen or playing a hand of poker. But more often we were just sitting on the porch watching the hot sun go down. Sometimes the phone would ring, and he would go inside and enigmatically close the door and talk at length in hushed tones and return with a slightly distracted air, then sprawl in the wicker rocking chair again.

As we sat there on those torpid, sonorous evenings, the sounds of the nocturnal things all about us made a wild and impossible symphony: tree frogs, crickets, owls, and from the longest distance an incessant screeching moan, like a tortured lament, which made the skin crawl.

"What's that?" I asked.

"That's a *loon*. I think it's the same loon I've had for years. He must like it up here."

He would really talk when he brought out his cigars, almost as if a strange interior dam had burst and he had a purgative need. Between long silences he told me things. About one of his leaves in London in early '44: one night the blacked-out city was as solemn as a ghost, the next rife with flares and fires and explosions from the German bombs, all white and gold and red and pink, and he imprudently stood with some friends on a balcony near a curve in the Thames and watched — "and you won't believe this, Swayze," he said, "but it was just about the most beautiful sight I ever saw." About being on the line for thirty-five days without rest, the endlessness and hopelessness. About the artillery barrages and the booby traps and the bombs and the dead men and animals and machines and houses after a firefight, and the tenseness of muscle and nerve, the deaths of buddies, the bestial things men learned to do.

Did his friends, then, die in vain?

"They always die in vain."

"Were you scared?" I foolishly asked.

"You're damned right I was scared. Everything was life and death. It was luck, most of it — pure damned luck."

Then, over the days, he began recalling for me his own boyhood in Fisk County. I was a town boy, and his memories of the difficult times from the far backcountry past were as alien to me as the remotest Congo might have been. "You got to think," he would say to me that summer. "America is a sad country. You got to think and remember."

When Luke was growing up, his father managed a large farm owned by one of the planters, eight hundred acres or so, half hills and half flat, no more than three or four miles from the immense Godbold holding, in a community called County Spur because there used to be a dummy line, a railroad that carried logs out when they cleared the flatland; the tracks had long ago been taken up. His mother died of congestive heart failure when he was twelve years old. He grew up "behind a mule's ass" in the fields. His family had some bad years, when they had to trade chickens for shoes in town, and an occasional very good one. After one of the exceptional ones, his father took him to Memphis to an exclusive men's clothing store to buy him his first suit of clothes. "The clerk looked at my daddy in his khakis and work boots, and said, 'The cheaper suits are over here,' and pointed to a corner, but my daddy pulled out a big roll of fifties and said he wanted to see the expensive ones." Later, when he was at the university, he needed $60 to get through the semester. He telephoned his father. "Daddy didn't have it. He cried. I damned near cried too, I felt so guilty about having hurt him that way. So I borrowed five dollars and went to one of the fraternity houses and took the rich boys at cards. Should've done it in the first place."

The worst year he remembered was '29. "We were a colony of the Yankees then, even more than now — cotton and timber, that's blood and guilt money. This county was so poor, when the Depression came, people didn't even know it. We were in a depression before there *was* a Depression. It was a terrible crop. My father didn't have any money — the sharecroppers didn't have any money. No money for Christmas. Nothin'. The niggers were almost starving. One day when I was sitting in back of their church, I could hear the stomachs growling. A woman had a baby nursing at her breast. When the baby finished, an older kid, probably about five, took its place, and nobody thought anything of it. I never forgot that."

One evening he said, "If it wasn't for the black folks, people around here wouldn't have nothin' to talk about."

I pondered this; it was indeed the simple truth. Black people were everywhere; they were blamed for everything wrong under the sun, and, like Georgia, I felt sorry for them, especially the old gray-headed men with not a thing to their names. "A servant of servants shall ye be unto his brethren," the Bible says. In town almost every house had its black maid, who for 15 cents an hour left her own home early in the morning and did not return until late afternoon. The maids spent the days cooking, laundering, ironing, mopping, sweeping. Sometimes they would take the dirty clothes home with them and boil them in iron washtubs, scrub them on their washboards in their backyards, press them with irons heated over wood fires. Every second house or so had its yardman, Shorty or Potluck or Shenandoah, who wore soiled sweaty bandannas and had his own private jelly glasses to drink tap water from and who would aimlessly pass the time with you as you walked along the boulevard. From the womb to the tomb the blacks tended to the whites of Fisk's Landing, the women raising the white infants, the men digging their graves.

In the proper seasons the town blacks went out in trucks to the plantations to work from dawn to dusk. If through some precipitous act of nature the black people of Fisk's Landing had suddenly vanished from the Lord's earth, the town would have been strangely noiseless and empty. They lived in Independence Quarters behind my house, in Love Quarters, in the Bottoms out on the state highway west, and on New Africa Road, Blackberry Hill behind the cemetery, and Shaky Ground beyond the sawmill ("if you go there at night you're on shaky ground"), sprawling precincts with gravel or dirt roads and situated without design, sometimes separate from the white sections, sometimes bordering on and even mingling with them.

They were *different,* and their ways seemed to me exotic and intriguing. Potter Ricks knew this as much as any white man: the tempestuous flamboyance of their grief, the tolling and tolling of their church bells, the ceaseless days of mourning before they put their dead in the earth, their revelry in the very midst of bereavement — the crap games and the whiskey, the kettles on the big fires with boiling chitterlings, the ritual collecting of cash, the hand clapping and the singing and the high, melodious laughter. "Now, the Negroes, they really know about dying," Potter would say.

*　　　*　　　*

"When I was a boy," Luke told me, "I remember telling my father: put me in charge of all the black people in the state, I think I'd be good for them. I knew the ones on our place as well as I knew anybody, and their children too. We played together, swam together, worked together. We worked from sunup to sundown, then ate supper and worked again till midnight in the spring. They still farmed most of the land by mules back then. The black folks got three dollars a day, then after dark till midnight two extra dollars. You don't know what it was like.

"My daddy never cheated the blacks. Leave that to the Godbolds." Owners like Godbold who were going broke on 10-cent cotton, he said, started getting the big Roosevelt money. And the Godbolds also ran the local relief programs. They funneled the federal government's relief money to the workers in the off-season and then shut it down when they needed the labor. Luke called it "Godbold heaven." Also, for many years the Godbolds were landlords in Fisk's Landing itself, owners of broken-down hovels mainly in the Bottoms and on Blackberry Hill. "Worst things you ever saw," Luke said.

"Two or three times my father went into Godbold," Luke said, "and got Negroes out in the middle of the night after they'd told him they wanted to run away. That's how we got Shotgun. He and Sarah, they were with Godbold thirty-five years. He came to us in about '25 — couldn't read or write, fifteen cents in his pocket and the clothes on his back. Godbold and one of his men came to get him the next day. We had him and Sarah hide in the back section down by the county line. Daddy and Godbold got in a shouting match, but that was all. Daddy was a big man. Godbold had picked the wrong anthill to piss on."

Luke was nine when Shotgun came to them. "I remember the first time I saw him. Maybe fifty years old then. Picked cotton all his life from dawn to dusk, two hundred and fifty pounds a day. He always wore a cloth hat that had a front but no back. In no time he became our best worker, but he was more like a member of the family. He loved me, and I loved him. He never went to school and couldn't read or write. His mama and daddy had worked fourteen, fifteen hours a day, and I think for the first time in his life he found somebody who really loved him — me and my daddy. I don't want to sound fancy, but we were all in it together against the land.

"Then my mother died. Shotgun said to me, 'She was a woman among women.' My brother and sister had grown up and gone. I think he knew I was a lonely little white boy, and he wanted to help me."

Sitting there on Luke's porch in the dying light, I recalled how frightened I had been after my father died, how I could not sleep and developed the rash and the warts and threw up all the time and thought I had polio and started praying in the church. I had never told anyone before, but now I told Luke, maybe because he had the kind of gentleness I remembered in my father.

"Oh, I know," he said. "I remember your daddy. He had really serious *eyes*. And you got to feeling sorry for yourself. You got to worryin' what everything's about. That's normal, I guess, although you sure don't think so at the time."

Luke wanted to talk some more about Shotgun. "After his wife, Sarah, died, Shotgun moved into the shed in our yard. He ate with us at the kitchen table and washed the dishes. When Daddy started courting and was in town a great deal, Shotgun and I'd eat together and listen to the radio until we went sound asleep together in his big chair. We didn't have a lock on our front door, and when Daddy and I were both gone, he'd sit in the kitchen and guard the house. When I was fourteen and started drivin' the old truck, every Christmas Eve I'd take Shotgun to his cousins in Green County. An old toothless woman always hugged me and thanked me for bringing Shotgun. They were so damned glad to see him, especially the children. I owe Shotgun. He was my mainstay. He helped me grow up. He did a hell of a lot more for me than I ever did for him."

During Luke's twilight discourses, I could hear in the distance the rumble of the train, the hoot of the owl, the breeze in the pines. The cat would jump into his lap, and the lights of town would begin to appear far below. "Well, that's the way it was then," he would say. "All that will go someday, but nobody around here seems to know it yet. I'd look out from my porch at night when I was a boy and see all the coal-oil lamps in the blacks' shanties and wonder what they were thinking that night with their little lamps blinking and throwing shadows. Now I know they were thinking the same things *I* was. Lots of nights when I was little I prayed for the niggers more than I did for myself. I thought I could help 'em, but I couldn't. I didn't know no better. And then, of course, the war came along," and his words trailed off into the dark.

Sitting there on those evenings with Luke, I saw the mule hand Shotgun grow to proportions of pastoral myth, along with the others who had labored so against the earth and lived now in the Bottoms, or had moved to Memphis or Chicago for the stockyards or Detroit for the car factories or Gary for the steel mills, but mostly Chicago, to which they had drifted in hordes with their belongings in cardboard boxes and cheap suitcases tied with cotton clothesline, or who lay now as Shotgun's Sarah did in pine boxes in the very soil they had once tended.

I grew to perceive how all of them — the Negroes, the whites, even the mules themselves — were consumed by the unrelenting land, and how the earth itself would sooner or later absorb them forever. It was mysterious and cruel and profoundly interior, that merging here of the great European and African sources, yet vital and even life-giving, although I could not have begun to put any of this into words then. It was as if we belonged together, and yet did not, the barrier between us acute and invisible. It was very strange and hard.

"The Negroes didn't sail past the Statue of Liberty when they came to this country," Luke said. "They *made* this place down here. They worked to death and got nothin', except just the ground itself, and that wasn't theirs either."

Where was Shotgun now?

"Lives in the Quarters by himself, down by Number Two. He's *old*."

I would like to see him, I said.

"Oh, you will."

The talk always came around to Leroy Godbold. Before his father started having trouble with him, Godbold had offered Luke a menial job on his estate. "A Cartwright's never worked for a Godbold," his father said, "and ain't going to now."

"Five thousand acres are *big*," Luke would say. "In antebellum days *two* thousand were big. The rule of thumb then was what you could walk around in one day. A plantation was like an old medieval unit, just like Godbold's today. Mr. Godbold charges the Negro sharecroppers for their shacks. Charges them for everything. My father would always halve the cotton — the sharecropper took half of the income from sales and Daddy took the other half — even when money was low. Not Mr. Godbold. Godbold built a wood church on his place. Encouraged the Negroes to be religious, to expect their reward in the next life.

"When I was a boy I was on my bicycle on the front side of Mr. Godbold's place. It was a cold afternoon about the first of December. I saw Godbold and a crowd of blacks in a clearing. There was a lot of activity. I snuck up into a patch of thickets close to the crowd to see what it was all about. There was a big number-three tin washtub on the ground filled to the top with $1 bills, $5, $10, maybe a few $20 bills. Mr. Godbold and his foreman had put up a couple of card tables with three or four dozen pint bottles of Four Roses on top. Little Durley was even there, about two feet tall, standing next to his father and laughing at the niggers. Godbold and the foreman were handing out the bottles to the niggers, who started in on the whiskey. The foreman was standing next to Mr. Godbold with a big ledger in his hand.

"After a while, they got the niggers to stand in line by the washtub. Godbold said: 'Boys, we had a long year. Not a good year. We got your books figured out here. Looks like you owe me about $128 apiece. We could count against you. But I know you need Christmas money for you and your family. Have yourself another swig. That whiskey's yours; just hold the bottle in your hand. Get in that washtub with the other hand. Each of you gets exactly three seconds. *Go!*' The niggers were a little drunk by now and laughed and shouted and grabbed in that damned tub, then left with the whiskey in one hand and a clutch of bills in the other. Two of them walked right by me and stopped to count their money — all they had made for a whole year's work. One counted $98. The other had $105."

Why *were* the Godbolds so rich and powerful? I asked.

"Well, hell — the *land*. And they know how to exploit it. They get everything out of it that can be got. Land's the currency. Money's slavery. Always has been, always will be. Especially *land* money. The South is the history of greed."

Then why should one family have so much land? Wasn't it God's? Why couldn't it be split up?

"Oh, oh! There are a whole lot of theories about that. Better wait till college to get into that."

Would all that land be Durley's one day?

"*Durley.*" He paused, and gazed oddly into the distance as he spoke. "Knowing a little about Durley, I'm sure he'll get that and more. It wouldn't surprise me if he won the Congressional Medal of Honor and came back and grabbed Georgia's daddy's place. Or somebody's."

Did they think it was their *right*? What exactly was it? I was confused.

"Listen to me," he said, in a tone suddenly tender and proprietary, a mood I grew to know. "The day of the Godbolds is almost over down here. By that I mean *all* of what they got and do. They still want us to believe the blacks and rednecks are the trouble, but the trouble is them. Right now the Godbolds and the bankers control everything. We're in for some bad times and, knowing you, you'll probably be right in the middle of it when it happens."

But why *would* it change?

"I'll tell you why. The crazy damned *country* won't put up with it forever. I learned that being in Europe. If the war didn't kill you, it sure got a man to thinking. I just hope they don't take us all down in the process. It's not beyond them to allow the whole *state* to burn. But, when the time comes, they'll turn it over to . . . the thugs, and the men in the business suits and the country club men, and they'll be with the Godbolds. The Godbolds will *orchestrate* it, bring in outsiders, comfort the killers, the price to be negotiated. Wait and see."

One afternoon late that month, as Georgia, Arch, Zamma Bailey, Dusty, and I made a country exploration on an off-day at the Jitney, I found myself considering the things Luke had told me about Mr. Godbold. I had seen him only that morning in front of the post office talking with Potter Ricks. Potter said hello to me, but Mr. Godbold merely jangled some car keys in his hand and glanced at me vacantly, as he might some harmless anthropoid. When I walked past them, I heard them talking about the war.

"How is Durley, Mr. Godbold?" Potter Ricks was asking.

"He says the whole damn country of Korea stinks. Says it's not worth the trouble."

"Well . . ."

"And that's probably pretty much the truth."

As we drove out into the flatland, somehow that unmitigating terrain with its glutinous and devouring earth seemed of a piece with Godbold, existing with him in urgent symbiosis.

"I wonder if Amanda misses Durley?" Georgia said.

"I'm sure she does," Zamma Bailey speculated. Zamma was given to forms. In her vacuous beauty she sat on the front seat next to Arch, putting braids in her hair, then drew a little mirror from her purse and examined her lips and cheeks. "He sure is handsome, I know that," she said with her customary rising vowels and accentuated diphthongs.

"I'll bet she doesn't," Georgia said.

"Doesn't what?"

"Miss him."

"How do *you* know?"

"I just guess."

Arch was roguishly smoking cigarettes, finishing one and lighting another. It is unlikely that he was listening to Georgia and Zamma Lou Bailey. Zamma rolled her window down, turned sideways, and propped her bare feet with their brightly painted toenails on the upholstery.

"I saw her in the Sears today," Zamma said. "She was sending something Durley wanted — a radio or something, I think. She had on the prettiest white dress I ever saw."

In the distance were the spooky old Indian mounds where we had come as children in search of arrowheads. In the flatness they were the only rises, miniature grassy hills. We had been told all about them during "Indian Week" at the town library, and they never ceased to taunt our childhood imagination. They belonged to *our* Indians, a small tribe dwelling along the river, always going to one war or another, so much so that the river, it was said, often ran heavy with blood. The librarian had chilled us with the words of their chief, named Mingo Chitto: "I will make the white man red with his own blood, and then blacken them in the sun and rain, and the buzzard shall live upon his flesh," and after that Arch had boycotted the rest of Indian Week. Many were finally annihilated by the French many years ago, and the others merged with the Choctaws. All they had left behind were these strange haunted mounds of earth, and their place names — "place where the duck fell off," "place of the rising swamp," "place of the water eyes of the hills." Funny, from what I had heard of them, they were not terribly unlike the *white* people of the place now: violent, flamboyant, garrulous, a little eccentric, and unpredictable.

All about us was the warm, deep aroma of summer. The asphalt road on which we were traveling was built a little higher than the land; flourishing in ragged profusion along the sloping shoulders were wild grasses and burdock and elderberry, and the uncommonly beautiful thistles. We passed the occasional Burma Shave sign and a small concrete cross or two off to the side where someone had once died in a car accident. Amid the swamplands and thickets, the river appeared and reappeared in unremitting twists and turns; we could track its course by the graceful willows that lined its banks. The duckweed was thick and emerald green in the melancholy brakes of cypress, and pink cotton blossoms flittered in the whispery breeze. In the furrows field hands were bent low, chopping with their hoes, ebony silhouettes in the sunshine, and in an adjacent pasture a dozen or so Angus cattle grazed. The vista was of black earth, black people, black beasts, and we could hear the muffled song: "I ain't got too long now; that man be coming for me soon."

Then, more or less by chance, we found ourselves on Godbold itself!

Mr. Leroy Godbold's land, almost five thousand unbroken acres, began at a tortuous little creek seething with crawfish. All about us the cotton showed green in the rows, and occasionally there were deeper green patches in the farther fields with pipes leading to them, which meant they were experimenting with irrigation or rice. "Posted" signs were nailed to fences at regular intervals, and not a soul was in sight. A strange sense of doom hovered over the land.

As we drove farther, a few black people ambled along the

road or leaned on hoes in the cotton. They all waved when we went by, as if the car itself were a magnet that made ripples among the flesh. Now and then, we would pass a tiny unpainted shack, with chinaberry trees at its corners and sometimes a sturdier oak out front with the inevitable tire roped to it for a swing, a vegetable garden with corn and tomatoes, and a slumping outhouse in back. After a while the shacks appeared more frequently, in clusters along the road, with barefoot black children in ragged clothes staring vacantly at our approach, and scrawny dogs lazing under the trees. We went by a schoolhouse, a gaunt wooden structure set back from the road with a sloping rusty tin roof and, as if in afterthought, a whitewashed porch filled with broken furniture. And then to the commissary — the plantation store — also unpainted and unadorned, where three or four black men were lifting sacks of flour from a truck and an enormous new mechanical cotton picker was parked in back, the first one in the county.

Beyond this, the road suddenly ended. I had never been out this far. I thought the road cut right through the county. I did not like it. We were at the edge of an immense pecan orchard surrounded by barbed-wire fences. Towering fan-shaped trees formed a dreary shade, and a substantial "No Trespassing" sign was nailed to one of them. Parked in a circular drive were a new black Cadillac and a pickup truck. There, to the right of the orchard, was the bend in the river, swollen now by the passing midsummer rains, and not far from it, under a grove of venerable oaks, the Godbold house itself, an imposing antebellum manse embellished with recent wings, open green shutters, all in need of a coat of enamel.

Let's go back, I said nervously to Arch.

He swung the Plymouth around in a circle and began retracing our route.

Suddenly, in front of the commissary, we saw Mr. Leroy Godbold. Standing among the sweating blacks with another younger white man, he wore a broad, stylish white Panama hat and khaki work clothes. He was smoking a thin brown cigar.

He motioned for us to stop, then approached us. From the back seat, Dusty growled.

"What are you doing?" he asked, his voice seething with paternal contempt.

"I thought this was a through road," Arch replied.

"The through road ends two miles back to the highway."

"We apologize," Arch said.

"You know where you are."

I looked through the window at his thin, imperious face. There was hair stubble in his ears and a pale scar on his temple.

"Okay," he finally said, as if having weighed us and found us harmless, and with a casual gesture of his forearm waved us on.

"How did he know I'm not lost when *I* didn't know where I was?" Arch asked us.

Late that afternoon, after I returned, Luke came by. We were in my backyard, shooting baskets.

"Is Georgia your girl?" he abruptly asked.

I said yes.

"Do you love her?" He did not wait for a reply. "It's a mess, ain't it?" he said, and then sank a long, impossible, off-balance jumper.

Of course I loved Georgia. How much do you need to know about love to love? The myth of young innocence is a sulky, sly culprit. One loves at that age often more deeply, faithfully, passionately than at any other. Even though it was secret then from Luke, and perhaps even from me, I loved Georgia more than anyone I had ever known. Perhaps you cannot help whom you love, simply cannot help it whenever you do. It is so intense, you try to hold on to that first feeling — a wonderment, like a twilight. But there will always be the memory of that feeling as long as you live, coming back to you like the wistful measures of an echo. Georgia would go anywhere and do anything — sit with me on her front porch and watch the cars go by or play for me one of her hundreds of records, or drive the back roads with Dusty and me on smoky afternoons, or dance to the love tunes of that time while I stepped on her feet, or explain to me why she was a connoisseur of strawberry milk shakes and Dr Peppers, or tell me insidious secrets about her mother and sister, or study with me on school evenings and peevishly ask for help.

"Who cares who was president in 1839?" she would say, and crossly toss the book on the sofa.

Martin Van Buren was president in 1839.

"*I* never heard of him. Who down here ever talks about Martin Van Buren? When was the last time you heard his name come up?"

Or "Why do we need to know about the Wilmot Proviso? What's a proviso, anyway?"

Well, it was an important document about slavery.

Or "Why are we reading all this Chaucer?"

It was about people.

"Then why couldn't he write in English?"

Or "I don't know about this *onomatopoeia*. Why's she so big on that?"

Well, it has to do with sounds.

"Then just say *sounds*. You think Truman goes around using onomatopoeia? Or General Eisenhower? I'll bet they never heard of onomatopoeia."

Soon the leaves of a dozen colors would begin drifting down out of the trees in those sad and tender days. We remember what we wish to remember. It is all there to be summoned, but we pick and choose, as we must and will.

We are sixteen. She and I are standing on the side lawn of her house, under an ancient water chestnut. She is still tanned from the summer's sun, her long blond hair is tied at the back, and her green eyes glow in indulgent mischief. We stand in an amiable embrace. Arch and Zamma Bailey suddenly speed by in Arch's Plymouth and shout their greetings. I gaze down from the summit of the years, all the losses and guilts and rages and shames, the loves come and gone, and ravenous death, and I conjure now that instant when I was standing in the shade of the chestnut with Georgia, and I am caught ever so briefly in a frieze of old time, the high school years stretching before me as in a Lewis Carroll dream: "Come, lad." Artifice, all of it. In four days we would be burying Thomas Jetter. And after that Arnold Crosswait.

One lazy afternoon in the summer we were lounging in the grass in the park. The heat was so heavy you could see it in shimmering waves. Georgia was lying next to me with Dusty's head on her lap. Arch was perusing his sheet music, and Zamma Bailey was painting her toenails again, this time in bright lavender. Amanda Godbold drove by in her Buick and waved.

"I hear she's gone back to teaching piano," Georgia said.

"She taught me once," Zamma said. "I gave it up."

"For *cheerleading*!" Arch said testily. He had been like this since yesterday, when I had won the toss in the store for Harvey Tidwell's burial. Or perhaps he had a more profound concern, although I always doubted if Arch were much different on the inside from what he was on the surface.

"That one looks like God," Georgia said.

"What looks like God?" Arch asked with the same choler.

"That big cloud up there."

"For Chrissake, Georgia, you're dumb."

I looked up at the cloud, all pillowy and proud, and it *did* look like God, if you looked at it from a certain angle.

Georgia had a way of looking at things from angles. On one such summer's day later that month the two of us took a ride to a weird and seductive spot we had all known since childhood — a petrified forest twenty miles or so from town, deep in some rough little canyons hollowed out from the precarious hills, where more than thirty million years ago a prehistoric river had brought live forest giants down as driftwood. The logs had turned to stone, like mummies. A reclusive scientist from a small college nearby had put in nature trails and wooden bridges and hand-carved signs among the crevices and ravines and a high bluff formed of intricately textured soil — the loess bluff, they called it — and all of this was eerie and out of piece with the enveloping land; and it was in the middle of nowhere at the end of a tortuous country road. Hardly anyone came to it except those in the vicinity who had more or less grown up with it.

It was a warm Saturday in August, breezeless and deep-country blue, when Georgia and I drove out there. I have never forgotten the mood and texture and caprice of that day, mind-less, happy moments of burgeoning youth. Georgia wore a blue silk scarf around her hair, and we had the place all to ourselves, and as we strolled hand in hand on the thick carpet of needles and cones, it was easy not to take the large ghostly stones too seriously. When you are sixteen, and in a living forest of ver-dant pine and locust and cedar, the tracks of living deer and fox and rabbit underfoot, how do you absorb thirty million years?

"That one looks like a giant turtle," Georgia said of one of the stones. "And look, that one's a giant lizard." What must the Indians and the early pioneers and the Civil War soldiers in their spectral bivouacs have made of all this? It cast a haunted spell, this silent and vestigial terrain, the channeled and sculp-tured earth, the deep and gloomy declivities, the weathered soil, the dark crevices and outcroppings and dens, and we stood there wordlessly for a moment, her arm lightly on my shoulder, as if together and alone listening for something lost.

Later that day we drove over to Poindexter, my familial vil-lage, a serene old settlement ten miles outside of the capital city with an antebellum courthouse and lovely tranquil mansions perfectly restored from its earliest founding. We saw the one my great-grandparents had built, situated under a mammoth live oak on a stately rise. Then we visited the old crumbling section of the graveyard. The gray stones and obelisks of the Poindexter plot were enclosed by a rusty iron fence entwined now with summer vines. We went inside, pausing before my father, then my grandparents, and my great-grandfather: Major Winter Mead Poindexter. B. Alexandria, 1822. D. Poindexter, 1893. Georgia knelt down and picked a few wildflowers and put them on the graves.

We looped around and drove the few miles to the capital city. It was a brisk and expanding metropolis, not the somnolent political town it had until recently been. Its faintly ruined mansions on the main thoroughfares had been torn down for parking lots or transformed into offices for the substantial insurance and mercantile and commercial chains — private swimming pools here and there now and country clubs risen over old swamps, hotels twenty stories high with nightclubs on top, where people brought their own whiskey, and placid woods and meadows ripped out in lusty abandon for the new subdivisions and shopping centers.

When we got to the state capitol building, we parked the car and went inside to look at the mummy of the Indian princess, as we had when we were younger, and the grand rotunda with its fiery Civil War murals and then the portrait hall, an imposing chamber of archways and vaulted ceilings and paneled walls lined with dozens of portraits of the leaders of the state over the many years. Our footsteps echoed in the deserted quiet, until we found the portrait of Georgia's great-grandfather and the one of mine. "Wouldn't they be glad to know we're here?" she said. "It's funny — that they were friends. Do you think they know *we're* . . . friends?"

If so, would these worthy old warriors and Whigs of their more platonic day venture a high-minded judgment of their sixteen-year-old progenies parked in those evenings of a driftless mid-twentieth-century summer in a tail-finned American sedan in an isolated glade of the Fisk's Landing cemetery or out at a secret eminence overlooking the flatness or in the little wooded cul-de-sac behind the Episcopal church or behind the cotton gin, dark and desolate with only the moon reflecting on the rearview mirror of the car or the tin roof of the gin, her warm lingering kisses, the tilt of her body, her careless touch?

I had never known this tenderness before, and I can recall the exact smells of the land, the trembling radiance of the August sky, the sultry stillness, the summer fragrance of our guileless embraces, the soft feelings, the gentle sounds. The moonlight through the opened window would catch her face as she sat next to me on the front seat. Resting languidly there, she would look out into the heavens. "They say that for every billion stars in the whole sky," she whispered to me one night, "is a person who died on earth. Do you believe that, Swayze?" And later her impish laughter, her head reclining a little as she turned whimsically toward me. Somehow we always came back to the glade at the edge of the cemetery, and I wonder why — perhaps from similar motives much later in life when I would see *Casablanca* fifteen nights in a row, read the same book four times in a month, go to the same restaurant six evenings a week, or visit the same people every other day for a year, to retain as long as possible the magic of first discovery.

And when I got home later, of course, my mother, the other living Poindexter, would be waiting on the front steps. *"Where have you been?"*

I suppose now I must have had a little courage to be with Georgia. Yet I felt for her so, had grown up with her in the good and bad times, knew her heart better than anyone. The older boys deemed her too good for them and intimidating. "I'm going to take Georgia out," I heard one of the town seniors say to his comrades.

"All she'll say is no. She's a damned snob."

"She's a freak."

But I knew they would all love to go out with Georgia, to take her to a dance, to sit close to her in the Rex, to touch her just one time.

Luke said to me, "I'm glad you're parking with her at the edge of the cemetery and behind the cotton gin."

How did *he* know?

"Cops told me. I told 'em to watch after you. *Don't* park out in the flatland. Some drunk might sneak up and knock you in the head."

Luke's cousin Lieutenant Billy Permenter was still writing him three or four times a month — "to let off steam," he said, and besides there was not too much else to do over there in the off-hours.

It was ironic, Luke said: in the last war he had written young Billy V-letters from Europe, and now here Billy was writing *him* from this war. Luke let me read the letters; he had a whole boxful, and I enjoyed sitting on the porch of the cypress cabin absorbing the words from halfway across the world. Billy's letters when he started writing from the fighting zone, unlike those from Lank Hemphill and the others, were cheerful and amusing, seldom gloomy or bloody or gruesome — "good therapy," Luke would say. "Funny, despite all the shit," Billy had written early on, "I kind of like some things in this country — the old people, the little kids. I really don't understand why we're here, but I feel sorry for them. It can be very pretty here — spring flowers, mountains with snow still on them, white clouds like back home in spring. And they grow soybeans here, just like home."

Only as the weeks went by did his letters become more stoic and embittered, then in the end desperate and sad.

May 30
Here I am in the hills above the Imagine, right where the Chinese chopped up a whole British regiment not too long

ago. You remember R. D. Bird, how high-strung and excitable he is? How the coach could get him fired up and he was hell on the other team? Well, our platoon helps support an orphans home in Seoul and once a month we take them supplies. After Payday we take up donations of money and candy, blankets and ciggeretts. (They can trade for food, etc.) I took the supplies to Seoul last week, then went to visit my friends at 24th Evac. Decided to spend the night and go back next day. We had a good visit and a few beers. R. D. was on guard duty that night. And Buddy Tate said "You know how nervous R. D. is, let's scare the hell out of him." Royce Lampkin said "The Norwegians have a damned old horse, for a mascot, let's steal that horse, slip up close to R. D., slap the horse on the ass and make him run straight at R. D." So we did and everything went fine except R. D. whipped out his carbine and shot 15 slugs in the horse, killed him dead. Now we are in trouble. I went back to my platoon. Yesterday I went back to R. D.'s outfit again. Because I wanted to know what happened. I figured they could all be in the Brig. Royce told me this: "The Norwegians had a big funeral for their horse and they cried and carried on. The C.O. decided that R. D. did an excellent job of being alert and guarding his post. They had a dress formation, called R. D. out front, and gave him some kind of service medal." Royce said: "Shit, I should have gotten a medal too, I stole the damn horse."

June 12

24 pts. earns the right to go on R & R for 5 days. Rest and Relaxation, the Army calls it. We call it I & I for Intoxication and Intercourse. Because that's what it is. (Don't tell Dorothy!) We flew to Japan, got new uniforms, baths, got de-liced, slept in a real bed and had the best breakfast meal I have ever eaten.

July 19

We got a Korean houseboy that lives with us. His name is Chee-Si ("Shorty") 14 yrs. old. His real name is Lee Bong Ku. Lee is his last name and Bong Ku is the given name. They also make a sentence that way. We say "I will go to town." They said "Town I will go to." I told him that was Dumb, he said

"English is Dumb." He washes clothes in the creek by pounding them on a rock, then folds them up while they are damp and when they dry, they look pressed. Some of these boys are lazy, dirty and will steal but Chee-Si is neat and honest. I don't know where he gets his morals from, maybe he had worked for a chaplain before us. He's amazed at our big wide-open eyes. Yesterday Chee-Si was telling me how to get somewhere and he said "You go down this road and there is *Big* sign and you have *Big* eyes — you will see." Last week there was a wounded Chink in the aid tent down the road. Morgan and I took Chee-Si over there and I jokeing-ly said "They got your brother in there." He said "Where? Where?" We showed him the Chink. He got mad and said "Aw you speak-a bullshit, I no like-ie fucking chink" and he kicked me in the shin. Chee-Si really idilized Capt. Fry and when he rotated home Chee-Si was hart-broken. The day that Capt. Fry left Chee-Si went up in the hills and did not come back till dark. He just could not say good-bye. He would meet mail call every day looking for a letter from Capt. Fry. But they never came.

July 29

They've told us that early on in this war the North Koreans were killing American prisoners, and the word is that we were shooting prisoners in revenge. It's not as bad now as it was. The worst is among the Koreans themselves. There's a South Korean captain I know named Thinh, an educated man, speaks good English. He runs an infantry outfit. He once told us Korea would be an outstanding country now if the Japanese had left them alone. Our C.O. told us Thinh never takes any North Korean prisoners, that he takes them way out somewhere and shoots them in the head. I can't believe that, but everybody I know says its true. This is really a civil war, and ain't civil wars the worse? You know what I miss the most? Bread. Plain old American bread. And *spaghetti*. What I'd give for a big bowl of spaghetti! And I'd give $50 for some of the Chinaman's hot tamales.

And so they went, Billy Permenter's letters, through the fall and into the bleakness of winter.

As the summer died, Georgia sprained her ankle throwing a

football with me on her lawn. The high school band association in the capital city named Arch Kidd the second most outstanding trumpeter in the state, an honor he failed to appreciate: "I'd like to hear the *other* guy," and he forthwith began smoking cigarettes in public. As usual, the Godbold plantation won the prize for the first cotton bale of the year, surpassing the earlier record by five days, and the *Sentinel* predicted the most lucrative crop since '43, reporting also that there were at least fifteen of the new mechanical cotton pickers in the county. On the same page a headline declared: "Fisk's Landing Has 89 Television Sets." A new plant named Finewear, Inc., located itself on the outskirts of the town, and Luke Cartwright called it "another runaway underwear factory from Connecticut." Commander Harvey Tidwell's parents donated twenty transplanted elms for the new section of the cemetery, serving to enhance that barren, sparsely tenanted ground. My mother's tap dancers took third in the statewide competition, and Dusty was missing for two days before we found him with a half dozen other dogs at the farthest edge of Independence Quarters.

While von Schulte was up in the hills collecting loan money, his omnibus split in two, to the merriment of the old veterans. Our older Ruston Hill classmate Lank Hemphill with his mutilated forearm wrote that he was on his way home from Trippler Hospital in Honolulu, where he had been transferred from Tokyo. Potter Ricks got word that the remains of Marine Corporal Arnold Crosswait were en route from Japan to San Francisco — the marines moved quickly, he said. Leroy Godbold donated $1,000 to the state university to help purchase the marching band a giant Confederate flag that would cover the entire football field. The black man who had been convicted of axing Mr. Godbold's convict yardboy was sent back to town from prison and electrocuted in the state's portable electric chair in a truck behind the jail; a number of local denizens, it was said, stayed up late and had all the electric lights in their houses on so they could watch them dim at the precise stroke of midnight.

Lank Hemphill came home. The last time we had seen him was those many months before, in front of the armory the day the guard shipped out, as spindly as a scarecrow and uncertain about where he might be going.

Arch and I were in the auditorium of the deserted high school with Amanda one late August afternoon. She was at the piano as accompanist, and we were practicing a baroque duet to be played at church. It was arduous, and Arch complained sourly about my performance. Even Amanda was critical.

"The timing's important," she said. "Let's take it slow."

"This might be better as a solo," Arch said.

"Oh, no!" Amanda said. "Don't we always get it right?"

The three of us were working on a particularly difficult section when Lank suddenly stood before us. He had come down the aisle unnoticed. I was not aware that he was there until Amanda suddenly stopped playing. She obviously did not know who he was, and she was looking up at him with a startled, almost frightened cast.

He was thin to emaciation, with dull circles under his eyes, and his once ageless young-old face was pallid white and creased with spidery lines. The left arm of his army shirt was empty to the elbow and pinned high to his shoulder. He stood there ambiguously, with a dubious grin. Amanda was staring unsteadily at him one moment, gazing distractedly at the keyboard the next. He grabbed me with his undamaged arm in an awkward embrace. Then he and Arch shook hands.

"Well, I'm back," he said, "made it back," in the flat nasal hill-country drawl we knew from grade school. "You boys have *growed,* especially *you.*" We introduced him to Amanda.

"Lieutenant Godbold's . . . ?" he began and paused.

"Yes," she said. "Lieutenant Godbold's."

"I was with his outfit a little while till I got hurt."

"*Oh!* Well, welcome home, Lank."

Suddenly flushed, even anxious, she rose and gathered her music. "I have to go now," she said. "I'll leave you all together." She shook his hand. "We'll practice again tomorrow." And she departed up the aisle.

We packed the trumpets and drove in Arch's Plymouth to Georgia's. She must have seen us from inside the house, because she was soon out the front door. "Lank!" she ran to him. He stepped back in embarrassment, and as he did a shadow fell on her face.

"We'll have to fatten you up some," she said.

"I'm very skinny."

No sooner had he spoken than with no warning, he began to cry. His shoulders were contorted with sobbing. He leaned against a tree with his hand on his forehead.

"You're home," she said.

"You don't know where I been."

"Well, hell," Arch said, "let's go up to the Hill and get some *hamburgers.*"

"Let's do, Lank," Georgia said, and took him by his good arm.

It was simply called "The Hill," a long, low structure with a pink facade and white tiles at the base, which perched at the crest of the final swooping descent. There was a counter with red leather stools and individual booths with their own miniature jukeboxes set against the walls. We settled in one of these. From the windows we could look down on the fleeting, hot, sensual aura of the fifties — only an old summer's dream now. Georgia had Lank order two cheeseburgers, french fries, and a strawberry milk shake. "It's on me," Lank said. "I ain't never had this much money." He reached in his pocket with his serviceable hand, withdrew his wallet, and showed us several $20 bills. "I got a lot more at home. Ain't been able to spend all they owed me. Goin' to open a bank account. My mama wants a *eggbeater*. That Lieutenant Godbold, he's a good officer, far as officers go. Is she his sister, or wife?"

He had gotten to know an army nurse from New Haven, Connecticut, in the first hospital in Tokyo, he said, where he had stayed two months — she wrote his letters for him and helped him with spelling and grammar. "She told me to go back to school. I said I'm *nineteen years old*. She said so what? I'll probably start on up in September. Ain't got nothin' to lose. I'm not sure what grade I'm in. Am I with you or a grade behind again?" He seemed the simple child he had always been. "Graduate when I'm twenty-one or twenty-two. Time for my pills." He reached in another pocket and brought out a tiny plastic container. He handed it to me and asked me to open it; he took two capsules and drank them down with the milk shake.

"Hurts every day at dark. That's when I got hurt. Doctors said it's all in my *mind*. It ain't my mind — it's my arm."

The chimes from far below sounded four. For the first time he gleamed contentedly, as if the pills had something to do with it. "Can't believe I'm back," he said. "Can we buy that eggbeater?"

We went to Sears, where he not only bought the electric eggbeater, but also an electric carving knife for his brother and a Philco radio for himself. We drove him out to his house on Ruston Hill, that familiar lost neighborhood of eroded gullies and sunken ravines dotted here and there with its tiny houses and lean-tos, to give the present to his mother. Although we had known him since the fourth grade, I had only once been in his house set in the small grove of pecans and chinaberries; that was the day Arch and I had come out on our bicycles to see him after he broke his arm, the one he no longer had, falling from one of the sheds behind Arch's.

Lank's mother was also thin and sallow, with a pinched face, and she had on a heavy worn dress and woolen shawl even in that weather. Inside, the light from a kerosene lamp flickered on the drab walls and sagging, splintered furniture; the odors of coal oil and disordered poverty pervaded. She seemed embarrassed by her three sudden visitors from the boulevard but tried to cover it with her halting chatter. "Ain't it good to have him back?"

She secretly glanced at him from time to time. "Ain't it good?" She led us to the wall and pointed to a photograph held in place by thumbtacks in the wood. "Remember this?" It was our fifth-grade class in the schoolyard, Lank barefoot in the front row next to a surly Arch Kidd, Georgia and I two rows back among the outwardly casteless town and country boys and girls of that time. "You all growed up so," she said.

Lank went in the next room and brought back another photograph. It was his company, he said, just before it left Japan for the peninsula across the sea. There was a frozen quality to it, the young men caught there in a pause, such that it reminded me of Luke's photograph of his own infantry company in Winchester, England, in the earlier war. "Lot of 'em gone now. My buddy from Pennsylvania." He pointed to a small figure with a clipped mustache and an expansive, confident grin. "Eddie Dubow . . . Dubrowski. Never could say it. He was a *steel-worker*." He gazed down at the picture. "*Eddie*," he said to himself, so low you could hardly hear it. Then: "Eddie and I sure felt sorry for them poor little Korean kids. He wanted to bring one of 'em back with him."

We were leaving again for a hot dog party at Georgia's. "Takin' him away already?" his mother said. "Come back, son." As we walked to the car, I saw her aching face at the window. "I can't believe I'm home," Lank drawled. He nudged me with his good elbow. In his hand was the jar of pills. "Get out two more," he said.

Something disturbing happened later that week. It was a sluggish afternoon with nothing going on. I had taken a recess from the Jitney and walked down the nearly abandoned main street to Luke's store. It was empty. I walked about inside. From the storeroom in back I heard faint movements. Then, suddenly, through the half-opened door, I saw them.

Luke and Amanda were standing next to each other near a tall stack of boxes. She had her head on his shoulder, his hand rested lightly on her arm. She was whispering something to him. Then she stood on her tiptoes and kissed him.

I was stricken by this swift, unexpected sight of them. Nothing had prepared me for it. I slipped away without being seen. The next day Georgia and I were driving along a remote, sparsely used side road that bordered her father's land toward the river. Amanda's car sped by us from the opposite direction. The two of them were on the front seat, with Amanda at the wheel. The gravel flew all around us, ricocheting noisily off our car into the embankment.

Nothing was said for a moment.

"Did you see what I saw?" Georgia finally asked.

Yes.

"Do you . . ."

"Just don't mention it to anybody."

The following afternoon was Commander Tidwell's funeral. It was also my sixteenth birthday. The evening before, Georgia had given me a new all-weather basketball, and a red leather collar for Dusty, and a brown-handled jackknife with a corkscrew, a bottle opener, and five or six different-sized blades. My mother presented me with a new hairbrush. At the Jitney that morning Arch handed me a gift-wrapped box. I opened it to find a pile of old dried sheep droppings. In contrast to his recent noxious moroseness, he howled. Then he presented me with two packages of Levi Garrett chewing tobacco, a pair of orange socks from his father's store, and a small bottle of trumpet valve oil.

Luke came into the store later in the morning. He had been with Lank Hemphill most of the day discussing his future and getting him enrolled in the Legion post. Luke was already wearing his suit and tie for the burial, which as always made him look as dignified as a banker. As he stood before me, I was wordlessly consumed with my secret glimpse of him and Amanda in the back of his store.

He handed me a handsome embossed edition of *The Adventures of Tom Sawyer.* "Like it?"

"I sure do," I lied. I thought it a gift for a child.

"You're a little like Tom Sawyer," he said, "except he couldn't play the trumpet. When you get home, go look in your backyard." While my mother was away, he had gone back there with a ladder and repainted the backboard of the basketball goal in glossy white enamel.

The Tidwell service was in midafternoon at the Episcopal church. As usual, Arch and I arrived at the cemetery a half-hour or so beforehand to be greeted by the customary scenes. This burial was in the oldest part of the old section, a spooky childhood spot, with its proud stones for those progenitors who had settled and founded and chartered the town and cleared it for its schools and churches and courthouse and jail and installed the landing at the river's bend, where the keelboats and then the steamboats could stop on their route to the great river west.

The high obelisk in the Fisk plot was gold with lichen; its inscription said: "Their greatest struggle was against the forest." Thomas Jefferson Culpepper's identified him as a benevolent philanthropist who donated the funds to found the town library and the ground for the high school. "He gave back to the land," the words read, "what the land had given to him." And on *his* son Jefferson Davis Culpepper's: "He too was generous, like his father before him." The Tidwell plot was next to these. Whenever I came as a boy to these graves I felt the generations — *felt* more than thought about them, I suppose — and preposterously dwelled on who my own great-great-great-great-grandfather might have been and where he had lived and what he had looked like and whether he had owned a dog.

I noticed Luke motioning to me from a distant hill. I walked up there. "This is perfect, don't you think?" he said, then quickly departed for the grave.

He was right. Over the months of that year as it ensued, playing echo at that precise station, the finest spot in the entire old section for echo since it so ceremoniously commanded the flatter terrain and the town itself below, I grew accustomed to the wonderfully gnarled and ancient magnolia there. Standing at the highest crest, I could almost hear the long-ago voices, the vanished cries of joy and ecstasy and sorrow and pain; the tree would protect me from the heat, as now, and from the rain and ice and snow to come as I stood under it to sound my dirgeful echo. It rose at least 150 feet with its spreading branches and graceful twin trunks arching toward the sky — majestic and indomitable, a sentinel of authority. Its dark shade on this summer's day was cool and luxurious, the undersides of its leaves were a pale, slick green, the upper ones verdant and impervious, and I would remember my lonely notes in the frozen winter afternoons later that year when its icy leaves and branches crackled and trembled, making an eerie music, it seemed, a magic and caressing soprano, like the carousels in the European playgrounds I would someday know. Standing beside it one day after a funeral, Potter, who knew the cemetery better than any living man, said he thought the magnolia was at least five hundred years old, perhaps six or seven hundred. The Indians surely must have known it before they fell to the white man's sword and germs, when these hills were unbroken hardwood before the Anglo-Saxons came and dispossessed them and made this the place of their own bereaved. How many burials in the sloping grove of the Fisk's Landing dead had it seen? In its grace and strength it seemed to say: I was here before you and will be long after you, but I am with you.

Georgia was going with her parents to the service in our church, where the vicar as always would greet the hearse out front and then with an acolyte holding high the brass processional cross escort the coffin down the aisle. She had told me she would sit in the back pew and leave at the conclusion and join me at the cemetery if she could find me. Now, from far below, I saw her talking with Luke, who was pointing upward in my direction. She was wearing a dark linen dress and a wide-brimmed white summer hat and her great-grandmother's little string of pearls, and she came slowly up the hill, pausing once to lift each foot behind her and awkwardly take off her high-heeled shoes. She must have stepped on a briar or a thistle, because I heard her whisper "Ouch!" and then *"Damn!"* Despite the lugubrious occasion, the sight of her brimming so with young beauty and surging life as she stumbled toward me between the stones, then walking gingerly as if on an icy pond, her countenance so studied and serious, almost caused me to laugh.

The procession was coming now. It was the most impressive yet by far, an unending row of vehicles that must have reached from the cemetery gate all the way to the boulevard, an inexorable line, slow and grand. It took long minutes for the crowd to gather around the grave. Finally the coffin came out, and Potter Ricks and the official navy escort, an ensign in dress blues, led the family to their places.

Suddenly everything, the earth, the trees, the people, the whole enraptured landscape, became very still, as if time itself was for the most transitory moment suspended. It was so noiseless that from under the magnolia on the hill we could hear the Episcopal vicar in his vestments down the way, fragments in a buoyant tenor, his words drifting up to us like the murmur of a breathless sea: *"Man, that is born of woman, hath but a short time to live, and is full of misery. He cometh up, and is cut down, like a flower; he fleeth as it were a shadow, and never continueth in one stay. In the midst of life we are in death; of whom may we seek for succour, but of thee, O Lord, who for our sins art justly displeased."* Then his words were lost.

Lank Hemphill was standing near the old veterans in his uniform. Just before they fired their volleys, twelve silvery navy jets bearing a five-pointed star flew in twin V-formation high over the grave, dipping their wings in deference. There was a three-gun salute, and the breeze subsided again, and in the same stillness came the loud rumbling shots as always, and from our hill we could hear the bolts of the rifles working metallically in the quiet between each volley — and then Arch's "Taps," and I followed with mine. The notes wafted slowly away, dissolving into the hot misty hills, and Georgia and I watched the crowd disperse slowly back toward town.

The next afternoon Kinsey, who had flipped our coins, fell off a ladder in the back of the Jitney and broke his right wrist. Arch and I had to take him to the Afro-American Hospital. The wrist was bent at a horrible angle. "Oh, shit!" he said. "Just look at it."

"Don't worry, Kinsey," Arch said. "They won't cut it off."

"Cut it *off*?" Luckily the quarterback for Number Two high school was a southpaw — it was not his passing hand.

As we returned to the grocery store, a violent thunderstorm descended on the main street. The sheets of rain were so thick that we could barely see the "Jitney" sign in front.

Potter Ricks was waiting at the store for us when we came in.

"Durley Godbold is missing," he said.

6

THE NEWS about Durley was for days the only subject of talk. He had been out between the lines leading a night patrol. Of the thirteen on patrol, nine were killed, two severely wounded; Durley and another simply were not seen again. Lieutenant Billy Permenter, in a letter to Luke that arrived two weeks later, said he heard the unit had run into unusually heavy mortar and cannonade and machine-gun fire and later had been all but overrun by the Chinese; one of the wounded reported Lieutenant Godbold bodily hit by a shell. In Crenshaw's Drug Store one afternoon, Sarge Jennings and Roach Weems speculated that there probably was nothing left of him, nor of the private from South Dakota missing in action with him; that was the way it usually was. The deaths of Strong and Boone, two hill-country boys, in the same sector the following day seemed almost an afterthought.

They held a prayer service for Durley on Wednesday evening at the First Baptist Church. Mr. and Mrs. Godbold did not attend. We saw Amanda with Durley's two younger brothers walking across the lawn afterward. Her expression seemed one of pale, abstracted terror; Porter Godbold caught her by the arm as she half stumbled on the sidewalk. Later that week I saw Mr. Godbold himself emerging with a bag from the bootlegger's by the abandoned train depot. Unshaven and unkempt, he moved trancelike, a dim and spectral phantom, toward his muddy Cadillac.

The mood of the town was eerie. Some, like Sarge Jennings and Roach Weems, who knew of such things from the western front, had already consigned Durley to oblivion. Others were not so sure. Because Durley had always been such a forceful presence in the town, even in his high school years an avatar of power and strength, there was a nearly cabalistic sense that he was indestructible. In the little synagogue in the capital city that Saturday, Mayor Fink said a prayer for Durley, and later remarked that he was far from alone in being sanguine.

The days passed. Mr. Godbold gradually rose from affliction. We saw him about town again, clean-shaven and competent. Potter Ricks told us that he and the governor were in constant touch with the Pentagon, particularly a two-star general originally from the state. I wanted to talk with Luke about these circumstances, but I did not. "He's gone," Luke had told Potter.

"What's going to happen now, Swayze?" Georgia asked. "What's going to happen to our friends?"

Billy Permenter wrote a letter to Sarge Jennings. It had come from "somewhere in the mountains below the Yalu."

> I thought Durley would live forever. I ran into him in Seoul about a month ago and he looked like he was going to win the war single-handed. I believe the Red Chinese got him. There must be 50 million of these Red Chinese. The first ones we saw wore canvas shoes with rubber soles, and cotton caps with fur-lined ears. They're skinny, bowlegged little peasants. They ain't got anything like an "honorable discharge" — they sure ain't got a point system. They'll be here until they get killed or captured. I've seen some of the prisoners up close. You wouldn't think they had the strength to squeeze a trigger. But they're tough little heathens. It's kinda scary. They're the ones that got Durley. I never liked him much, but I like Amanda. I'm writing her now. Old Man Godbold must be in a fit to kill every gook there is.

The last country club party of the summer took place under a waning crescent of a moon in another heat wave of epic authority. Soon the light would change, taking on a benign and subtle sharpness after the stringent weight of August. People of all ages gathered a half-hour before twilight. We could look down from the hills into the saffron flatness, the sun enormous at the dusky horizon, and see the bright little red and yellow crop dusters still at work against the boll worms. The busy monoplanes looked like toys in the distance, dipping and ascending as swallows would, leaving behind their steamy trails of poisonous dust.

The clubhouse was a long, spacious pine bungalow perched on the summit of that hill; below it the golf course tossed steeply downward in neat symmetry, and the swimming pool off the parched fairways stood out like a little opal oasis. This was the second-oldest country club in the state, formed in 1912 on a slice of the original Fisk land by planters and bankers and lawyers and merchants and doctors. Its membership comprised a modest scattering of Catholics and Jews among the Waspish hegemony, but excluded the successful Lebanese entrepreneurs and their wives and progeny and the marginal hill-country people, but not the rich second-generation parvenus from the flatland, who garrulously conscripted the phrases and inflections of the aristocrats, only more so. It was a modest institution, but lavish enough for Fisk's Landing, and on this evening of departing summer there was the tinkling of ice in tall glasses, and the splashings of the swimmers down at the pool, and from inside the strains of popular tunes from a slightly off-key piano. People sat in their summer best at lengthy tables on the porches and around the dance floor, "festooned hypocrites" being Luke's description, "half of 'em hating the other half but lacking the will to show it." The grudge *du jour* involved a lawsuit between two double first cousins, women, over a tract of land, the combatants and their respective broods remaining on opposite sides of the room. Everything pertaining to prattle and the sound of one's own talk. Glossy middle-aged Saxon blondes in vibrant pinks and yellows greeted one another with a rippling "how you *doin'*?" and gossiped in corners, pointing like Minervas as they talked. The heavy, pungent scent of barbecue drifted down from the piney slopes above us, mingling with the sharp smell of the cotton poison from below in a rich, prolific odor that only summertime in highest synthesis could ever give.

Georgia wore a blue strapless dress and rhinestone clasps on the tips of her shoes that glittered as she walked. Although she was still hobbling slightly on her damaged ankle, we wandered about inside among the tables. The crowd was talking about the dazzling cotton crop on its way, and the blacks, and the war, and Durley Godbold, and the loathsome Washington bureaucracy, and all the threatened mores, and sick people in the hospital, and once more Durley Godbold, and there was a good deal of drinking.

"It's my best crop in years. Hell, even my *hay* crop's good. If it holds we're goin' to Mexico this winter."

"Not us. None of that Montezuma's revenge. We're goin' to New York for some ball games and shows. Never been to New York."

"I hate New York. It's okay to visit, but I wouldn't live there if they gave me the damned Empire State Building."

"Cancer's got him in the esophagus. They just sewed him back up."

"It happens so often."

"I feel bad for Mr. Godbold. He had a lot of faith in Durley."

"Well, Durley's a tough one."

"Bein' tough don't stop a cannon."

"They ain't *smart* enough for our schools. They don't take care of the ones they got. Scientists even say they got smaller skulls, not enough room in there for *brain capacity*."

"It'll never happen. Our maid says they don't want it either."

"If it was me, I'd drop the bomb on every airport in Red China."

"That ain't enough. How about downtown *Moscow?*"

In this rippling cacophony, which seemed to follow us everywhere, Georgia and I found the table where her parents were sitting with tall drinks. They were handsome in their middle age, and the only couple in town with sons or daughters our age who insisted, as I have said, that we use their first names; they thought themselves progressive, or at least said so.

"Hello, Swayze."

"Hello, Alice."

"How're you doin', Swayze?"

"Just fine, Jake."

"Ain't she pretty tonight, Swayze?"

"She sure is."

Her mother's eyes were oyster gray and set too closely together, so that they gave her pretty face an aspect of lowly and circumspect meanness. Given to using polite, glacial phrases, she had a serene and icy aplomb: thoroughbred hauteur and pinched conceit. Progressive or not, she was glancing at me appraisingly. Inferiority stirred in me like nausea. I doubted if she had ever forgiven me for separating her and her daughter in their frantic wrestling on the back lawn two years before or for my not having wholly appreciated the aristocracy of the 8½ quad-A foot.

Georgia's father, on the other hand, was consistently amiable in his bucolic simplicity. It was he, not his wife, who descended from my great-grandfather's ally. When Georgia defiantly took my hand, he looked on. "Lovebirds tonight, huh?" he said with an impudent yet not unfriendly grin, and took a mighty swig from his glass, while his consort sat before us with a blistering smirk, as if to suggest: You're just sixteen, and not good enough yet. "Georgia, Swayze," she said, "why don't you circulate and make some *small* talk, like me?" Then she rose and, fluttering like a moth before light, mingled briefly among the others.

I had been dreading the forthcoming performance of my mother's tap-dancing class. *Dread* is not the right word. I was anticipating it with the horror one might have reserved for a public dismemberment. Already she and about a dozen of her pupils were filing into the hall. The little scatterbrains were wearing short, frilly dresses and garish miniature hats of the kind worn in the carnivals by performing simians, and the taps on their shoes were clicking discordantly across the floor before they even started. As I gazed despondently at this gaudy platoon that had invaded my house for years, I saw Amanda.

She was standing by the piano ready to accompany the performance. Except from Arch's car as she stood with my mother on our front porch three days before, I had not seen her since the news about Durley. She was talking now with Mrs. Idella King, who was solicitously touching her arm. In a dark blue dress and without rouge or lipstick, she looked pale and unwell. Still, she was beautiful, like the bedridden Merle Oberon in *Wuthering Heights* or Vivien Leigh in the Tara turnip patch, with a blanched perfection that caused me against my will to stare at her as if hypnotized. Georgia's mother noticed this. She glanced at Amanda infelicitously, and then at me, then pursed her lips before taking a shrewd little sip from her glass.

I wish I could say the dance performance was as sweet and effortless as a Mozart minuet, but in truth it was some kind of Argentine flamenco, a sort of subhemispheric carioca, which ended with the impudent little troupers sprawled histrionically on the floor. The Fisk's Landing haute monde greeted the climactic finish with courteous applause. In moments my mother had come to the table.

"What a wonderful show, Ella," Georgia's mother said. "Please sit down."

"Ella, join us and have a drink," her father said. To my surprise she ordered a neat gin, ignoring Georgia and me.

A pianist from out of town was playing dance songs; couples slowly made their way onto the floor. My mother conversed nervously with Georgia's parents, then ordered another drink. I had never seen her with anything stronger than sherry. Her heavy cheeks had an uncharacteristic glow, and during a lull in the talk when no one was looking she reached into her purse and scribbled something on a piece of paper, which she firmly planted in my palm. Then she said goodbye, gathered her pupils, who had been kneeling in a corner watching the dancing, and departed. As Georgia's parents left for the dance floor, I looked at the note. *"Don't be late tonight!"*

Now Georgia looked at Amanda, who once more was standing by the piano alone, nodding every now and again to the dancing couples who said hello.

"She looks so sad," Georgia said. "Nobody's dancing with her."

"Why not?"

"Oh, you know why. Why don't you ask her?"

Couldn't *we* first?

"Okay."

She limped around the floor awkwardly, whispering a cursory oath. Yet she even stepped on my toes with a vestigial style. And she was perspiring as she often did in the summers around her eyes and ears, a good smell to me. Her father must have requested the song: "Georgia, Georgia, the whole day through. / Just an old sweet song keeps Georgia on my mind."

There it is, I said.

"It really *is* about me."

I held her closer, and we danced the song out. Then she saw Amanda again. "Now please go dance with her."

"I don't want to."

"I think you love her."

"I do not."

"That's why you're scared of her."

"I'm not. I love *you*."

"Then dance with her, the poor thing."

I walked over to Amanda and asked her. I did not know what to say, and I was as graceless as an invertebrate, especially since I was trying to avoid her breasts, a nearly impossible task. They kept brushing across my chest, soft and alluring, and I tried to keep my suddenly bursting loins out of contact. I remembered for the hundredth time the stunning image of her in her hallway when I was twelve, and that night months before with her husband here on the darkened porch when I saw him drunk, telling her he loved her, her opened blouse, her naked nipples, her sighs. Trying to move perfunctorily with her about the floor now to the strains of "Harbor Lights," I felt against my will a profound enveloping feeling, a dizzying little ecstasy, like a warm, swirling gulf. Even Georgia was safer than this.

"Haven't your mother and Georgia taught you to dance?" she asked.

"Georgia. She's *too* good."

A smile crossed her melancholy face. The song ended, and a few people began to leave for home with their plastic go cups filled with gin or bourbon. I thanked her for the dance and politely turned away. "No," she said. "One more." We were in the middle of the floor. She swayed strangely. That was when I realized she was quite intoxicated.

"When have you seen Luke?" she whispered as we danced.

What?

"The last time you saw Luke."

"Day before yesterday."

"Where is he?"

"I don't know."

"I can't find him," she said, so fiercely that her arm, which was lightly on my shoulder, caught me in a quick, painful vise. "Tell him I was wrong."

"You were *wrong*?"

"Yes." There was a desperation in her eyes. "Tell him I was wrong."

The next afternoon we buried Marshall Pine. Luke and I were standing under the towering old magnolia in the cemetery before the cortege arrived when I gave him the message. He listened, said nothing, then gazed distractedly down the hill.

I still recall the smoky autumn haze of that Indian summer, the leaves ever so imperceptively beginning to turn, the soft, indolent languor pervading the air. The days were getting shorter. The students from the town came back to school in new sweaters and shirts and starched slacks and plaid skirts and high white bobby socks, and those from the hills arrived on their uncertain yellow buses in the threadbare wardrobe of earlier seasons.

The high school was at the lower end of the boulevard, a substantial old two-storied brick edifice against a flourishing backdrop of oaks, with the words "Education — Knowledge" under a statue of Plato at the entrance, and on the front lawn a big burnished granite stone bearing the Ten Commandments, and three or four bicycle racks, and a graveled parking lot in back with cars like armored tanks with fins, driven there by the richer students. Behind the schoolhouse was a span of deep, unspoiled woods crisscrossed by Potter's Creek, which had come down from the hills, and by the remnants of Indian trails, often used as shortcuts by students who lived on the far side of this ground. Inside were the worn, spacious corridors carrying the faint smell of wax and ammonia, the half-rolled-down shades and secret enclaves and musty stairwells and Orwellian loudspeakers in every room for the principal's announcements and smudged blackboards not really black but sea green and pipes that growled and rattled incessantly in the winter; it was always too hot or too cold and seldom in between. The walls of the dark, humid basement where we awaited the bell on rainy days bore names and initials going back three or four generations, as if they were reminding us of life itself and its brief and immemorial rite of passage: *We were here.* The letter jackets with their crimson and white "F.L."s were everywhere, and the long, glassed-in trophy case outside the gymnasium was a sanctified spot with tarnished plaques and cups and emblems and ancient oval footballs and old autographed basketballs slick with wear and dim photographs of winning teams and proud Fisk's Landing boys and girls long since gone from the earth. These were the mellow days under the drowsy skies, but they soon gave way to the gray equinoctial rains, grim and thunderless, when the whole school seemed a cozy haven against the dark. And then came real October.

Georgia and Arch and I were in Mrs. Idella King's homeroom, where we convened every morning at 8:10 A.M. for roll call and the Lord's Prayer and the Pledge of Allegiance before leaving for our first-period class. Mrs. King taught four classes of English and one of French and had been there as long as anyone could remember. She had acquired her degree from the state women's college, and she had arrived in our town in '08 with her husband, who owned the American Steam Laundry. Now she was a garrulous yet infinitely competent and methodized and exhortatory widow who sang contralto in the Episcopal choir and played in the bridge tournaments at the country club and in her myopia ran into cars and trucks in her battered Chevrolet. It was commonly known that she did not have a driver's license. She had begun driving so long ago, at a time when licenses were the most indifferent of requirements, and the local authorities usually ignored this oversight more or less out of habit, and also perhaps deference. One morning she had been driving into town in her nightgown with a fur coat over it to fetch her maid when a young policeman pulled her over on the main street.

"Mrs. King, I'm sorry to stop you," he said, "but you ran a red light."

"How much is it?" she asked.

"Two dollars."

"Here's four. I've got another one coming to me." And when she and her maid returned five minutes later on the same route, she ran the same red light again.

Ageless and unconquerable, with coal black hair that Georgia and others suspected she dyed and her frumpish black dresses to match (although on some days without warning she would wear the most outrageously colorful frocks and blouses even in the throes of winter), she was a prolix and redoubtable disciplinarian, a vainglorious taskmaster, a zealous anatomist of the English sentence, the unstinting grammarian and savant and literary marm. "Talk well, write well, use the language well," she would constantly intone. "What's the good of having a mind if you don't use it? A person who doesn't read is no better off than a person who can't." Woe be to the pupils who used such expressions as "hisself," "that there," and "n'aarn"; she could give a lecture of Nietzschean dimensions on "n'aarn" itself.

On other things, too, she brooked no quarter. Among her most grievous resentments, the particular regional indulgence of certain possessives ranked high. It would not have been politic to say in front of her, for instance: "Bob Johnson from Lutherville's brother," or, as Arch Kidd once uttered during an oral report, "the black and white bird dog in the big backyard's collar." Yet beneath the peculiarities — for many learned and unusual women in the smaller stables of the republic of the day were known to fall back on quirk and eccentricity as a last bastion of impregnability, or perhaps survival — lay a shrewd resilience, an imperturbable strength and resourcefulness in the nether heart of her that allowed her to remain, I believe, precisely who she was. She was not ashamed.

Her nemesis was Arch Kidd, who once spelled "occasion" with three s's. Educating him beyond his manifold casuistries seemed her nirvana.

"Arch, are you going to be a sap all your life?"

"Yes, ma'am."

"You think you'll make a living playing the *trumpet*?"

"I'm sure gonna try."

"I hear you've been smoking cigarettes across the street in the firehouse," she parried, to which even Arch had no convenient reply. Then she would proceed to read to the class his report on *The Ancient Mariner,* in which he had described the albatross as "a king of buzzards first seen in Louisiana," or a paragraph from his disquisition on *Huckleberry Finn,* in which he judged Jim "one uppity nigger," or his identification on an examination paper of Sir Walter Scott, one of her favorites, as a native of Waterloo, Iowa.

She would read anything out loud, and on the most random whim. Her tastes were as eclectic as they were egalitarian — Shakespeare or Robert Service, Wordsworth or Ogden Nash, Housman or the recherché poet laureate of the state, Mrs. Orrissa Arlee Freemantle of the town of Homochitto. On a typical day she might read to us from *The Lady of the Lake,* Elizabeth Barrett Browning, the Brontë sisters, and *Beowulf,* and she was a zealot about anything in iambic pentameter, a heady melange that elicited dark, unhappy growls from Arch and the others in the back row. One day that fall, standing full height behind her desk, she said she was going to read a little passage from a Mr. Turgenev.

"Here comes another damned foreigner," Arch whispered.

In that season of the dead, she read us poems of war, reminding us as she did that she had taught Durley Godbold, Harvey Tidwell, Arnold Crosswait, and the others. I can hear her to this day in that somnolent classroom, the restless squirmings of smug and healthy teenage bodies, the brisk early-October sunshine on the oaks outside, the lyrics to "Danny Boy" drifting down the hallways from the glee club practice, her words so sharp and rhetorical that they echoed through the opened windows and likely could have been heard by the firemen across the way:

What are the thoughts that are stirring his breast?
What is the mystical vision he sees?
— "Let us pass over the river, and rest
Under the shade of the trees."

* * * *

Clad in beauty of dreams begotten,
Strange old city forever young,
Keep the dreams that we have forgotten,
Keep the songs that we never sung.

She was expert on matching a pupil with a subject for a theme. In the course of that year she assigned me "Secrets of Playing Echo," Arch "Secrets of the Trumpet" (he made the first A of his life on this paper, but only a C-minus on a later one that he entitled "Why Don't They Ever Have Women Pall-bearers?"), and Georgia "Secrets of Good Grooming," where she confessed one of her few deferences to cosmetology: in the summertime she would jump in the swimming pool to get wet all over, then come squeeze two or three fresh lemons on her wet head, then lie for a long time in the sun, a tortuous process that made light golden streaks in her tawny blond hair.

She liked to toss in Latin references, and sift and mesh them here and there into her monologues. It was the time for funerals, as she of course was aware, and did we know that the Latin derivative for *cemetery* was "dormitory of the dead"? "Who gives a shit?" Arch would mutter under his breath.

The other teachers did not like her very much, considering her high and magisterial and a touch condescending, and despite her cerebral pinnacles and the fact that she was unregenerately ignorant of every facet of organized sport, her best friend on the faculty, curiously, was the football and basketball coach, an ornate and complex personage named Asphalt Thomas.

Asphalt Thomas was a bachelor in his early thirties; he was a friend of Luke's and had a girlfriend who was a hairdresser in the capital city. He was as tall as Luke, dark-complexioned and wiry, as sly and feline in his movements as the ballplayer Kinsey at the Jitney, yet with the incongruous neck of a bull, and he had acquired his name from having developed his considerable basketball aptitudes in an asphalt parking lot with a regulation goal in a little town called Ludlow in the lower part of the state, where he once scored sixty-eight points in a single game. Asphalt's father was a carpenter, and poor. "Go to college and *grow*," he told him. "I got so many knots on my hands from hammers and nails they don't work right no more." He spent two years on a football and basketball scholarship at the state land-grant university, then joined the marines and was in heavy combat, including Okinawa. He survived unscathed. "Didn't even get a nosebleed," he said profoundly, "although some asshole from New Jersey carrying a bazooka once stepped on my big toe." He returned to the land-grant college, where he concentrated on basketball and was all-conference his senior year and got his bachelor of physical education with a C average.

Two or three times that summer Luke had brought him to my backyard to shoot baskets. "Give me that friggin' ball," he would say, and proceed to sink shots from all over the yard, one even from the far side of my mother's pansies. "Look, kid, you gotta have an idea of where you are at any given time. You gotta concentrate, but also hang loose as a goose. And be shifty-eyed as a Jap." Then he missed three shots in a row. "That goal ain't ten feet," he said. "It's one-eighth of an inch low." He went out to Luke's truck and returned with a tape measure and hoisted me onto his shoulders. It was an eighth of an inch too low.

The first thing he did when he arrived in Fisk's Landing and took over the football team was install the split-T formation. "You dumb boys been accustomed to the single-wing," he said. "That's for slow little rustlers. In the split-T you gotta move around at all times." He did not allow his football players to drink water during the broiling late-summer practices, appar-

ently considering them ruminant desert mammals, and he required of them a dozen or so wind sprints at the end of each
day that left them parched and limp and cursing. He had
brought two bluetick coonhounds with him to the town, which
he would run in the woods behind the school. Attached to
his belt was a ring of assorted keys that must have weighed
five pounds, as emblematic as a ceremonial mace; as he glided
along the corridors in his worn leather jacket or bright green
peacoat, their rattling and jangling could be heard from the farthest place in the building. "These rings will open every single
classroom and closet and office and cubbyhole in this whole big
schoolhouse," he would say, "even the rooms where the gals
wee-wee." Sometimes he got so angry at us in forestry class
that he would eat pieces of chalk and various other items. He
had about fifty different kinds of leaves on a long table. One
morning he said, "Some of you goatheads ain't been bathin'
yourselves too much lately. This classroom smells like an *outhouse*," and he picked up an oak leaf and proceeded to eat it,
explaining: "It's a damned sight cleaner than *you*." Mrs. Idella
King would invite him to her house once or twice a week to
eat the birds he and the bluetick hounds had gotten for her.
One evening that semester I went there to deliver an article I
had written for the school paper on the dead marine Arnold
Crosswait and found them sitting greasy-handed before a plat-
ter of quail, Mrs. King with a dab of flour still on her nose.

Mrs. King allowed the coach, and Amanda too, more or
less free access to her classroom, an exceptional dispensation.
Sometimes when he was not busy he would participate in our
weekly spelling bees; he and Arch were often the first two to
be eliminated. At other times he would drift nonchalantly into
the room and sit at a desk in the rear next to Arch and ask
the teacher to read some poems. Occasionally Amanda would
come in with him from the music room upstairs and listen.
Flattered, almost twittery, Mrs. King asked what poet he would
like to hear.

"Any of 'em will do," he would say. "You pick one out." And with deft alacrity she would reach for Oliver Wendell Holmes or Henry Wadsworth Longfellow or James Whitcomb Riley.

Despite his usually unconfined flamboyance, Asphalt Thomas's dark features and black eyes gave him a saturnine aspect, as if there were something remote and perhaps even dangerous that he was keeping to himself. In the team practices, as I would learn, he could be brackish and foul-tempered, a hard and restless perfectionist. In this regard his friendship with Idella King was not all that preposterous. He was tough. Luke told me that once at a party the coach and Durley Godbold had words over some arcane matter and went outside and fought half an hour to a grisly standoff. Like Luke and Sarge Jennings and Lank Hemphill and Billy Permenter and, yes, Durley Godbold, he was a warrior, and of a generation transformed by arms. Might coaching have been a natural extension of what he had learned in war?

Lank Hemphill enrolled in school as he said he would. At first he was a peculiar sight, in his army dungarees and laced boots with the empty sleeve pinned high, until he bought some modish clothes at Arch's father's store. His courses were English, forestry, history, carpentry, and typing. Typing? "It ain't that bad," he said. "I use one finger. The typin' ain't hard, it's *what* you have to type." He was being fitted for an artificial limb at the veterans hospital in the capital city. Three times in that new week of school he fell asleep in Mrs. Idella King's class, and the skittish taskmaster was benign about it until he began to snore in the middle of a stern recitation on grammar.

"Lank!" she said, stooping near his desk.

The lax scarecrow did not respond.

"Lank!"

At last he stirred, looking up at her with swollen eyes.

"You've been sound asleep. Do you want to go to the sick room and take a nap?"

"*Sleepin'?*" he said.

"Yes."

"Well, I'll be. I guess I got the habit of sleepin' wherever I can."

"But not while I'm talking about dangling participles."

"Danglin' *what?*"

At this Arch and the others in the back of the room laughed.

"Quiet, you saps!" Mrs. King said.

When Luke suddenly appeared in the corridor outside the classroom one Thursday morning, Arch and I knew, of course, why he was there; there would be other such visitations to the school by our special messenger. He waited there until Mrs. King saw him. "Come in, Luke!" and she rose from her desk and ceremoniously led him inside. "What have we done to deserve this visit?" Before he could reply she turned to us with her familiar flourish: "This is Mr. Luke Cartwright. You wouldn't know it, but when this boy was in school he made straight As in English. One of my best students. Isn't that true, Luke?"

"No, ma'am," he replied, and for the first time ever I saw him blush.

Arch and Georgia were at the blackboard diagramming a lengthy sentence. "We'll see about that," Mrs. King said. She pointed to the blackboard. "There's a serious error in that diagram. Can you find it for us?"

Luke stood there silently, hands on his hips as he deliberated before the blackboard. Then he picked up an eraser, rubbed out a parse, and chalked in another. "Absolutely correct!" Mrs. King said with a felicitous beam, and there was a scattering of juvenile applause.

The two of them conferred in whispers at the desk. Then he motioned to Arch and me to join him in the corridor. Arnold Crosswait and the escort had arrived in Monroe City late last night, he said. Potter and Woodrow had brought them back. The funeral would be Saturday at three in the new section. "No problems in that?" he asked. "Then go back inside and get *edu-*

cated," and he departed in his loping strides down the hallway.

Arnold Crosswait had been three or four years older than we. His father was a woodcutter who sometimes worked on the side for Georgia's father and for Mr. Leroy Godbold. He had enlisted in the marine corps halfway through his senior year in school. "I'm tired of not havin' enough money to go to the picture show," he said. "I'm gonna see the world. So long, Fisk's Landing!" He was a tall, attractive young man, well mannered and shy, courtly almost, and when he returned on leave after boot training at Parris Island, his transformation from woodcutter's son to spit-and-polish marine made a stunning impression, so much so that two other boys in the senior class enlisted because of him. When the word arrived that he had been killed by massive shell fragments in a reserve outpost slightly behind the lines, his old girlfriend, a girl named Ouida who worked one of the counters at Arch's father's store, went hysterical right there, flinging herself on the floor and into racks of clothes and toys. Arch's father summoned Potter Ricks, who took her in the ambulance to the King's Daughters Hospital, where she lay catatonic and sedated for three days. Potter told us Arnold Crosswait's mother too lay like a ghost in bed for one entire week, refusing even to eat until the doctor finally forced her to. And when the girlfriend Ouida said she was going to escape from the hospital and kill herself, the doctors knocked her out again with more pills.

The official escort was a marine private. I still remember his name — Bobby Ray Fairchild. He had straw-colored hair clipped short, his middle and index fingers were missing from his left hand, and even in his full-dress uniform he looked younger than eighteen or nineteen. Georgia and Arch and I had gone to the funeral home that Thursday evening where the closed coffin draped in the flag lay in the side room. Luke and Lank Hemphill and the escort and Sarge Jennings and the other Legionnaires were sitting in the parlor with Arnold Crosswait's family and his girlfriend, pallid and fragile there on the Victorian sofa; his father actually seemed to have shrunk in size. Potter moved dutifully about. The crowd was an approximate amalgam of town and hill people; some of them had spilled out onto the little front gallery.

On the porch where we were standing the night air was crisp and invigorating. From the interior of the Presbyterian church across the way the pipe organ resoundingly boomed with "Onward Christian Soldiers," and the august militant strains, in such contrast to the desolate scene at the funeral home, poured from the church and bounced majestically off the facades of the post office next door.

Luke appeared with the young escort and introduced him. When American strangers come together, I have long since learned, each wants to know where the other is from, and to compare places. "This town reminds me of mine, except it's bigger," Bobby Ray Fairchild said in a flat, nasal drawl not unlike Lank's as he gazed up the sleeping main street. "I can see it shuts down early, just like mine. The land's a lot richer around here, I can tell you that."

Georgia asked where he was from. "Guymond, Oklahoma — it's only about twenty miles from Kansas. Arnold wanted to come see me out there someday. Arnold liked a good time, but I ain't tellin' his family."

"How does it compare to Tokyo?" Luke asked.

He glanced at Luke with pale blue eyes, translucent almost in the chilled shadows. He had a slight tic under one of them, a fleshy little tremor that contradicted his otherwise calm, wholesome American face. "Nothin' like Tokyo," he earnestly replied. "Or San Diego. Or Seoul, either. Ain't much left of Seoul."

He was staying with the Crosswait family, he said — sleeping on a pallet in the front room. Luke suggested we invite him to the high school the next morning.

"I'd like to," he said. "I never finished school. Just like Arnold didn't."

"You'll have to come to the ball game tomorrow night, too," Georgia said. "We play Lutherville."

"A ball game?" he said. "I've forgot about *them*."

He accompanied us on the rounds of classes that Friday morning. In Mrs. King's room he talked briefly about Arnold Crosswait and answered a few questions. "Arnold was a good marine," he said. "We started out in boot camp together. I'm sure sorry I have to be here like this." He described the terrible rain and murderous cold over there, the frozen dirt and trails. "The hills is all straight up and down and one right after the other. When it rained it didn't know when to stop. One night it got down to ten below. Even a boy from the Oklahoma Panhandle ain't used to that. In winter the sun went down about eleven in the mornin'. My feet still feel cold." Then he said, "These are the prettiest girls I seen anywhere. Arnold told me."

From the back of the room someone asked, "Did you kill any *gooks*?" Bobby Ray paused and looked straight ahead. "I don't know." Then Mrs. King, who, as one may already have perceived, was equal to such moments, and approving of the heroic and kingly style, stood dramatically behind her desk again and once more read to us, dedicating the words this time to Arnold:

> Tho' much is taken, much abides;
> One equal temper of heroic hearts,
> Made weak by time and fate, but
> strong in will
> To strive, to seek, to find, and not
> to yield.

I was following the words from the textbook, and I noticed she left out the following lines after "abides":

> And tho'
> We are not that strength which
> in old days
> Moved earth and heaven, that
> which we are, we are —

Luke's cousin Lieutenant Billy Permenter had only that week sent him a poem that the troops were circulating over there. I brought it to school that day to Mrs. King, and naturally she read it, too:

> Located in the center of nowhere,
> Korea is the spot.
> We are doomed to spend our time
> In the land that God forgot.
>
> Down with the snakes and buzzards,
> Down where a man gets blue,
> Right in the center of nowhere,
> Five thousand miles from you.
>
> You sweat, you freeze, you shiver.
> It's more than I can stand.
> We're just a bunch of convicts,
> But defenders of our land.
>
> We're the soldiers of the Twenty-fifth Infantry,
> Earning a measly pay,
> Guarding the guys with millions
> For a couple of bucks a day.
>
> Staying here with our memories,
> Waiting to see our gals,
> Hoping while we are away
> They haven't married our pals.
>
> Few people know we're living
> And they don't give a damn.
> Although we are all forgotten,
> We belong to Uncle Sam.
>
> And when we get to heaven,
> St. Peter will proudly yell,
> These boys are from the Twenty-fifth,
> They have spent their time in hell.

Idella King was disappointed. "Well," she said, "it's certainly not Kipling, or Tennyson either." But the marine from Oklahoma said he liked it a lot, and so too did Lank Hemphill.

*　　*　　*

That Friday night before the Saturday burial was one of the important home football games, and the whole town was imbued with a fine undercurrent of excitement, for on Fridays in the fall you could almost feel the tension in the atmosphere. Everything, the earth and the trees, touched by the airy sunshine, was the soft golden brown of that sad and lovely time. There was a faint presence of wood smoke everywhere and the smell of leaves burning, and the sounds and their echoes — the train whistles, the courthouse chimes, dogs barking, dead leaves drifting — carried a long, long way, as across a vast and immeasurable distance. Surely it was one of the two most thrilling times of the year in the town, if one loves and remembers too the voluptuous and fragrant Aprils. The autumns there are not so fiery or magnificent as the eastern ones, but their sudden sharpened luster after the heavy summers, the bracing exhilaration of them across the invigorated earth, are a song yet in the heart. It seemed not the time to celebrate death, but rather a moment to indulge one's self in the throbs and melancholies of the living. Wherever you looked, there was a truckload of raw cotton coming in for ginning; along the roads and even the paved avenues of the town you could see the dirty fragments of cotton that had fallen to the ground. There was cotton in the very atmosphere, little floating particles of it. The cotton gin remained open all night, ablaze with light and rumbling with busy noise. The older trees in the flatland were covered in trumpet vine, the soybeans and bitterweed and goldenrod were a sea of yellow, and the gnarled cypresses had turned russet brown and looked for all the world like gaunt and undying sentinels. The leaves glided down out of the trees and whirled along the lonesome sidewalks, and the boulevard was a corridor of sudden and riotous color — the hickories awash in golden flame, the dogwoods almost purple now, the sweet gums bursting with reds and yellows. The weeds and Johnson grass in the gullies and ditches were already beginning to turn brown and seared, yet so teeming was the land that they still grew, half dead and half alive.

The World Series was on the radio, and the county fair was in town! Almost every night of that week we had taken in the 4-H exhibits — vegetables and bottled preserves in all the shades of the rainbow, and pumpkins and great slabs of meat. My mother, playing bingo with Mrs. Idella King and others, won — if it is to be believed — a hula skirt, and Coach Asphalt Thomas a pair of women's garters. In a large brown tent off at the far end of the fairground some of us had paid a dime each to see Flora, the belle of Memphis town. The breasts of the corpulent Flora in her bulging red tights bounced extravagantly to the beat of the bass drum: "Watch her shimmy, watch her shake, like raspberry jelly on a birthday cake." Some of the regulars at Crenshaw's shouted for her to proceed further, but the dim presence of a sheriff's deputy posted in the shadows cast a puritanical authority over any excess in this temporary Babylon. The announcer called it an airplane dance: "Wait till you see her tailspin, boys." A preacher from the hills brought his ladies' Bible class out to the fairground to demonstrate in front of the tent, singing "Bringing in the Sheaves" and other such anthems, which seemed to have the same kind of reverse effect as books banned in Boston.

In the freak tent Georgia, Arch, Zamma Bailey, and I stood mesmerized before a two-headed cow who stared back at us with four listless eyes while the Lord's Prayer played on the loudspeaker, suggesting, one supposes, the divine source of this miserable beast. Her main head was normal enough, but the second one, which went out at an angle from the other, was small and pitiful, and for some reason I felt sorrier for this cow than I did for the gnomish midgets, the fat lady, or the eight-foot, 490-pound giant who sat expressionlessly in his stall drooling chewing tobacco. I gazed blankly at the cow, for somehow she actually seemed to be admonishing us on that night that all is not what it seems, and that there was grief and sorrow as grotesque as she yet to be dealt with at Ricks Funeral Home and the cemeteries, and for all we knew in the whole world of living creatures.

"Poor thing," Georgia said.

"*Poor thing?*" Arch said.

"How would you like to have two heads?"

"People come and look at her," Arch said, "and she probably gets as much to eat as two cows." He laughed in appreciation of his own wretched profundity.

That Friday afternoon, after the marine escort Bobby Ray Fairchild had left us to return to the Crosswait family, the town resounded with band music from the football game at Number Two and the carnival tents at the fair and the baseball broadcast from New York. That night, under a colossal harvest moon, three thousand people turned out at the football field behind the school to see the Fisk's Landing Choctaws play the Lutherville Yellowjackets. When I was little my father had brought me here to some of these games. At one of them a Fisk's Landing player had his neck broken; he died a few days afterward, and lay now in the old section of the cemetery with the replica of an "F.L." football letter on his gravestone. Near the entrance to the field Potter Ricks and Woodrow were stationed by their ambulance, and along the home sidelines we saw Mr. Leroy Godbold, grim and distant among four or five other planters with their silver hip flasks. In the end-zone bleachers fifty or sixty black people were congregated, including the Number Two Black Choctaw ballplayers who had played the Lutherville Number Two Blackjackets that afternoon, when Kinsey had scored three touchdowns and passed for two more. From our perch with the band in the grandstand, I kept noticing the marine escort, sometimes sitting on the bench with the substitutes, or wandering among the crowds, or standing alone down beyond the end zone. The girls would walk up to him and say, "Now you come to the dance after the game, you *heah*?"

The game itself pretty much typified flatland football, indeed the flatland itself — a great number of crazy gambles, unpredictable passes, histrionic fumbles, laterals, blocked kicks, flea-flickers, double reverses on fourth and long, and of course an ostentatious multitude of unnecessary roughness penalties. Two players on each team were ejected for fighting, one of them for kicking an adversary in the testicles, as the boisterous and thigh-spread cheerleaders leapt about in their flamboyant red sweaters. A yellowed document in my attic testifies that we lost, 33 to 32.

The dance was at the country club. Everyone arrived on time, exchanging those Friday-night salutations that would later seem to me such a self-conscious blend of old South and modern black; then the dance music started from the band of black men in red hats, and the couples swayed and rocked on the dance floor and out onto the porches. During an early break, Arch brought out the singer, named Rufus, and accosted Georgia and me on the side gallery. As with Kinsey in the Jitney earlier that summer, he handed the man a 50-cent piece. Arch called heads, and that is what it was.

Back in the men's locker room, where the older boys hid their bootleg whiskey, the drinking was flourishing by eleven. The marine escort made frequent trips to the locker room and to someone's car, and by midnight I saw him weaving back and forth on the dance floor. At 1:00 the party gradually began to disperse. Georgia was dancing briefly with one of the seniors, and I did not enjoy looking at them, so I walked outside to the first golf green to breathe in the air. Under the luminous moon I saw the marine alone, leaning against a tree, then staggering helplessly around the sand trap. I asked if he was all right.

"Yeah, I'm okay. Just a little plastered."

Did he have a ride home?

"Yeah."

He paused for the briefest instant; his pale blue eyes seemed aflame with fever. "Arnold ain't in that casket," he stammered in a rush.

What did he mean?

"Just what I say. Just a little pile of burnt bones. About this big." He gestured drunkenly with his hands. "And his mother wants to open it up, and Mr. Ricks and I keep tellin' her she can't." He stopped for a second, and gazed down the sloping green fairway out into the cotton, glowing white in the moonlight. "And besides, it's against the rules."

I helped him back to the clubhouse. Then, turning to me, he said, "Don't tell nobody. I ain't told nobody else." I promised, and then a group of older boys met up with him on the road, and they got into a car. With a sharp screech of rubber and a rattle of gears they sped down the hill.

Next day a large crowd descended on the cemetery. The new section was not so barren now with the transplanted elms donated by the Tidwells. Only fifty feet or so from Arnold Crosswait's grave, I could see the recent mound of earth on Thomas Jetter, whom we had buried a few days before. As I stood at attention, under the canopy the preacher from the Second Baptist Church read from the florid eulogy I had written for the school paper, patterned, I thought, after Ernie Pyle: "His old desk is empty, but with his spirit it will forever be filled." The family sat there quiet and motionless next to the escort in his dress blues.

Shortly before I sounded the notes I noticed Luke standing just beyond the tent. Then I saw Amanda, alone down the slope perhaps twenty feet away. They were exchanging a long glance, a look of such quiet, secret intimacy that only I could have noticed it. Behind them, not far from the Jetter grave, was Mr. Leroy Godbold. His Panama was in one hand, and with his other he was holding the arm of his wife, who looked pallid and unsteady.

On Sunday morning early, the marine caught the Greyhound west. We never saw him again.

We did, however, see Corporal Wayland Bunch. He had been shot in the lung in the early summer. Four or five days after the ceremony for Arnold Crosswait, he returned to town from a rehabilitation hospital in the Midwest, where he had been released from the army. In his absence his wife had left him for a farm implement salesman and moved to Jonesboro, Arkansas. He had enlisted in the guard in '46, the year he graduated from high school, and had gone to work for his father, a bootlegger out in the county. Arch and I once telephoned an order of bourbon to be delivered to the front door of the Baptist parsonage, and another to Mrs. Idella King, who was rabid about temperance, and we hid in the bushes and observed the pastor's wife and later Mrs. King as they lacerated the unfortunate deliverer. Wayland had been responsible for making the runs into Louisiana to get the whiskey, and even then had the reputation of consuming a substantial proportion of the profits. It was apparent on the Saturday afternoon I saw him, a week after the Crosswait burial, that he was starting again where he had left off.

I was walking down the main street when I encountered Potter Ricks. Luke had just telephoned to say that Wayland Bunch was holding forth at the firehouse. Did I want to go with him? I did.

Firehouse Number One, in contrast to Firehouse Number Two across the street from the school, was quartered in a wing of the city hall next door to the jail, and largely because Roach Weems worked there it was the traditional axis for poker, dominoes, and sports broadcasts. We arrived to find Luke, Sarge Jennings, Roach Weems, Herman von Schulte, and three of the firemen sitting in various postures around the poker table in a room behind the fire trucks. The poker had recently ended, with cards and chips strewn in aimless disarray on the green felt tabletop, and in the middle three or four partially filled bottles of Four Roses; in the background there was a college football game on the radio, the state university against the Texas Aggies. The room was thick with cigarette smoke, it seemed. Roach Weems courteously motioned us to a pair of straight-backed chairs near a pool table.

Wayland Bunch was a thin, angular young man in his mid-twenties, with a weary, sallow complexion; a gray flannel shirt drooped on his frame. His eyes were red and swollen. It was still daylight, and he was already more inebriated than the marine escort from Oklahoma had been at the dance the week before. He was talking about Durley as we walked in. He had delivered a message to Durley in his dugout two days before that night patrol. Durley carried a carbine, he was saying, and had some notches on the wood.

"I was behind the line the night he got it. You could've heard the damned Chinks' artillery fifty miles away. I was afraid my ears was gonna explode. The next day I felt like somebody's beat me all over with a club. And I wasn't even *up* there. I went through boot camp with three of them guys on that patrol."

Sarge Jennings was smoking a giant cigar. "Tell us what it's really like over there," he said.

"The fuckin' Chinese is the worse," Wayland Bunch said. "All they do is kill and die. They come out of them mountains like bugs. Bragged they was gonna drive us into the *sea*. We'd get all of a hundred yards from the little fuckers, and they'd jabber like animals, 'Die, Yankees!' and we'd yell back, 'Fuck you, you little yellow shitheads! We ain't Yankees noway!' I had a good carbine with a telescopic sight, the best the damned U.S. Army can buy, and I'd blow two or three yellow heads off every day with nothin' at all better to do."

He poured himself an unsteady whiskey and looked threateningly around the room. Potter sat next to me; Luke glanced in our direction. Von Schulte was wedged between Sarge Jennings and Roach Weems at the poker table. "The Aussies was the best." Bunch's words were slurred and heavy. "I ain't seen an Englishman yet. Seen about ten Greeks, and about all *they* did was deliver the damned mail. And the damned Turks was crazy." They drove American vehicles, he said, like madmen, and when people saw a jeep with Turkey's star and quarter-moon on the sides, they ran off the road just as people do when they see a fire truck. "Meanest, toughest sons of bitches you ever saw. When they captured the Chinks they cut off their dicks. I don't know nobody who wouldn't shoot the South Korean soldiers quick as they would the North Koreans, or Chinese." He swept his arm across the table so that he almost scattered the poker chips. "They ain't no good — won't even help their *selves*. All they ever wanted to do was *eat*. Eat more of our goddamned food than you ever saw. You know what they ate before the war? Eels. Turtles. Dogs. Cats. Octopus. Can you believe it — mother-fuckin' *octopus*? I still get a knot in my stomach just thinkin' about it. I'm too fuckin' mad to talk."

But he did. It was not a visual poem, but there was a bitten-off eloquence to it. He spoke of the endless confusion, the growls of the T-34s, the roads in the canyons that did not go anywhere, the glazed landscapes and windswept ridges, the hills bare from napalm drops and mortars and strafings, the devastated villages, the treacherous minefields, the cold sunsets and hot tracers, the murky yellow rivers, the way they had to put halazone tablets in their water to chase away the bugs, the human-wave assaults of the Chinese in the nighttimes — the mortars, the rush, the great showers of sparks from the arming devices on their grenades. Once they were in a convoy going over the mountain roads. One side of the road was mountain straight up, the other a sheer drop straight down. Up ahead he saw an old papa-san standing by the side of the road with his back to the trucks, looking off down the cliff. He had a frame on his back loaded with long sticks of wood, so that he had to turn sideways to let the trucks by. When the truck ahead of them got abreast of him, a private on the right seat leaned out and put his foot on the old man's back and gave him a shove. He fell off the sheer drop at least two hundred feet and bounced on the rocks. "Crawford said to me, 'Did you see that?' I said I didn't see a damned thing, and Crawford said, 'Me neither.'"

The courthouse clock struck 5:00.

They were on the line, off the line, and back again, he went on. Seldom was the day they did not have plenty of casualties. His best buddy, from Mobile, lost his eyes. After some heavy artillery an officer named Armbrister would not come out of his bunker. Some captains and a doctor went to the bunker and tried to get Armbrister to come out, finally persuading him. The next day Armbrister took a bazooka behind a tree and waited for the tanks. He thought he could ambush the damned *tanks*. One of them rumbled down the hill and aimed its 85 mm at him. He shot off the bazooka. All the rocket did was bounce off the tank, as harmless as a firecracker. "Too bad," Wayland Bunch said, "because the shell from the tank sliced Captain Armbrister right damned in two." It was a good thing he had to leave his regiment when he did, Wayland said, because it was nearly wiped out by now. "The old shits don't fight. Don't die. They sit back somewhere and tell us what to do. That damned MacArthur was in *Tokyo*. Why wasn't *he* on the line. Them shits in Washington was probably goin' to *parties*. And who back *here* gave a fuck?"

Roach Weems retired to a closet and brought out another bottle. Luke was sprawled silently in a chair, Sarge Jennings was a dark figure in the hovering smoke, and next to me Potter picked at a spot on his coat sleeve with his handkerchief. The bootlegger's son was not finished. He was wavering in his chair, but he pointed toward us with a whirling, ambiguous thrust. "These little shits is jealous of us, can't you see? They ain't got nothin' but their stinkin' rice paddies, that's why they want what we got. Fisk's Landing's got more than all North Korea put together. They want our food, our cars, our fuckin' houses, our women. The assholes would take *Arkansas* if they could. But I'll tell you *one* thing" — and he glowered harshly through the smoke — "right now we're killin' five of them for every one of us!"

There was not much to say to this. The afternoon's monologue ended appropriately with a fire alarm — a brushfire at the end of the boulevard, called in by someone's yardman. Six or seven sober firemen slid noiselessly down the pole from upstairs, gathered their paraphernalia, and cranked up one of the trucks. "Looks like you better not go," one of them shouted to Roach Weems and his three colleagues, who had been sitting at the poker table drinking and were trying now to scramble onto the running boards. They went nonetheless. The siren began to sound as the slick red vehicle edged out, and it soon disappeared beyond the jailhouse in the enshrouding dusk. Wayland Bunch staggered forth to leave; Sarge Jennings had to take him home.

I thought of the drunk veteran often after that, and of the drunk straw-haired marine with the missing fingers on the golf green. I stood briefly outside the firehouse with Potter and Luke.

"Who the hell knows?" Luke said.

7

THEIR SECRET illicit match might have seemed an unlikely one. She was a pianist, a beauty, proud and alluring and true. She had married the Godbold heir and
lived alone now in her expensive new house with the walled-in
patio, the kidney-shaped swimming pool, and the self-operating garage doors. He was a country boy who had never married; he lived in a cypress cabin in the woods and owned part-
interest in a hardware store.

Together they surely made more sense in every way that mattered than did she and Durley Godbold. They had both come
up poor, she even more so than he. Given her attractiveness and
determination, she could easily have been the village coquette,
but she never was; and she married at twenty-three, as a virgin.
He might well have used his record in the war for other, more
ambitious enterprises, but he had not even used the GI Bill,
which transformed a whole generation of Americans, to finish
college. His father, who oversaw illiterate sharecroppers, died
penniless; hers ran an auto garage in an expiring crossroads
hamlet that was about to lose even its post office. She had been
damaged by childhood destitution on a collapsed farm in the
hills, he by months of infantry combat — each more than either might ever admit. They were intelligent and, in their different ways, remarkably resourceful. Most of all, I see now, they
were tender people who desperately wanted love.

Amanda and Luke had started seeing each other six weeks or so before the news about her husband. When that came she told him she could never see him again, certainly not until the war was over; as the days passed she changed her mind. Hence her bizarre message to me that night at the country club. They were very careful. They were together mostly in the countryside far out in the county or in adjoining ones, or at the home of his trustworthy World War II friend, the doctor, or sometimes even as far away as Memphis or New Orleans or the coast. It was that way then, compounded by war and circumstance.

I had never known such friendship as I did with Amanda and Luke, Georgia and me. We became conspirators in their little faraway affair. Hidden meanings to this day escape me, shadows without substance, yearnings and heartbreaks, yet they trusted us, and I understand now that they needed us. How can we forget about the things that quicken the heart? They were older, yet they treated us as equals, or as nearly as was possible under the circumstances. Georgia and I were children of the forties, but we were not so innocent or naive. The town itself was teaching us not to be. We were not really children anymore. As I comprehend it now from time's odd pinnacle, we could be thirteen one moment and thirty the next. We drifted into Luke and Amanda's love, and were ourselves enveloped by it, almost against our will. "Men and women aren't all that different," Amanda once said to Georgia later, when events threw us together more and more. "They're kind of the same. They need each other. The hardest thing for a man to give is humility. I love Luke. He has courage and passion."

More and more as the weeks went by, I began to confide in Luke, and he in me; half brother, half father, he began to tell me of these things between himself and Amanda, and I grew to trust his words as never before. When Durley left, Amanda fell in love with Luke, and Luke with her, and I perceive now as never before that it was a real love; the intensity of her faithlessness was surely in proportion to her feelings of desperation and need and hurt.

"Durley's dead," he said. "But still, you understand why it has to be secret, don't you? Hardly anyone ever comes out to this cabin but you two, and maybe Shotgun or Doc Patterson." There was a high fenced enclosure around his cabin, and he made a point of keeping the front gate locked.

Sometimes when Georgia and I were supposed to be working on Mrs. King's first-semester paper, we would go for supper at his cabin. It was getting colder, the nights clear and stimulating, and there would be a fire in the fireplace, with Dusty curled up in front of it like a furry, contented, Arctic creature, the cat lying next to him or sometimes right on top of him, and Amanda might play a love ballad of World War II on the upright Hammond, or a minuet, and often we could hear the hoot of the owl and dogs running deer in the distance. All this seemed perfectly natural and about as illicit as the stars.

And they were a striking couple. Beauty will sometimes breed the most arrogant ruthlessness and self-esteem, giving an authority others do not possess. Luke was a handsome man, but I doubt if he ever gave a thought to it, or more particularly if he considered that it amounted to anything. As for Amanda, she was literally the most beautiful woman I have ever known, yet I believe she was too ambivalent and exposed at the edges of life to consider that, or to flaunt it.

The light from the fire would catch her lovely features, and she would talk about growing up out there in the hills, and even about the Godbolds. On one particular night she was very sad and thoughtful. A fellow officer of Durley's from Wyoming had just sent her a box full of Durley's possessions through the personal effects quartermaster in Kansas City: a shortwave radio, a Chinese sword, photographs, a few of her letters. She was quiet for a long time, but then she began talking a little about the past.

"I can't believe we were so poor," she said, as Luke also had told me of the bad times. "It was about life then, everything. And the earth. We worked very hard, but we had nothing, Swayze, hardly a penny to come to Fisk's Landing. But we always had food to eat." They had a big garden of vegetables, which they ate fresh all summer and canned for winter, and biscuits and gravy and cornbread and molasses; they kept a few chickens and hogs. In the evenings occasionally there might be a small piece of ham out of the smokehouse and on Sundays fried chicken. They ground their own corn and only had one mule. Her father charged and charged at the planter's store. She had one candy bar and one Coke a month, always charged, paid for in part when the cotton and corn came in. "You had to put your heart into everything to get by. I learned you couldn't plant a cotton seed without everything being right — water, sunshine, fertilizer."

Her best friend in those childhood days was her father, she said. "He fought for me, wanted me to try and excel, to be something. And *then* my best friend was a piano — the old piano at the school. I'd spend hours with that piano. I played on a Steinway baby grand when I went away to college. I'll never forget the first time I played it."

She told us how rude Mr. Leroy Godbold had been to her father.

"Does he have *any* good points?" Luke said.

"Yes. He's frightened."

"Frightened?"

"Frightened of what he's got, and that he'll lose it."

I remember Georgia on these evenings, lying on the sofa with her head propped on pillows, looking into the fire. Later she would talk about them. "Do you think they'll get *married*? *Can* they? What's going to happen to them, Swayze?" On one such night a toothless white-haired Negro drove up to the cabin in a pickup truck so eccentric and dilapidated that it barely made it over the hill. Even before Luke shouted his name, I knew it was Shotgun. "Hello, Little Boss," he said, and they embraced.

"Where'd you get the truck?"

"Found it by the dump, fixed it myself. Can't afford the gas."

He already knew Amanda. He called her "Young Miss," and Georgia "Little Miss." He sat at the table with us; he was having a difficult time with the pork chops. "Your daddy's Mr. Jake," he said to Georgia. "Done a little work for him last year." And to Amanda: "I knowed her when she was *this* big," which by his measurement was roughly the size of the pork chop.

"How've you been?" Luke asked.

"Fine, but broke. Down in the back."

He told us about his children and grandchildren. Black Pepper's son Walter was the janitor in the Memphis bus depot. Baptiste's children had moved from Memphis to St. Louis but would be coming home for Thanksgiving. And the others were still in Chicago.

Once he turned to me and said of Dusty, sitting up now by the fireplace, "It says in the Bible, sugar, never sell a dog."

I never would, I replied.

"A dog's too good to sell. The Bible says it."

After he finished eating he talked some more. "I'm hopin' to find a little money to buy a car, have a nice little home. But if I don't, I won't be the first that missed it." Then he retired to a chair in the corner and was soon asleep. Luke got up and put a blanket around him.

Georgia had the countenance of certain young women that sometimes could be almost plain, as if she even judged this her prerogative, with her spare cosmetics and blue jeans and blouses — yet at other times, given the mood and the moment, she was distractingly vital and lovely; in her free spirit there was a hectic, compulsive allure. Half-innocent, half-lewd, half girl, half adult, she was imperfect and contradictory, and in hindsight's sweet clarity she was dear, and she exuded love. As for Amanda, her physical splendor was unchanging. Integral to her was an essence of honor and self-possession. She had courage, and knew the hardness of life. Both were warm and proud. Georgia was spoiled and unregenerate, and, except for the fragile moments that come to every one of us all, stubbornly self-reliant and free. Did all the complex eddies of Georgia's personality make her *stronger*? I am not sure.

"They're both better than us," Luke said to me once. "Love's like a butterfly — just as soon land on a cow pile as on a rose. I guess we're both lucky this time."

It is funny how things are so intertwined. The sense one makes of the past often derives from small, evanescent moments, seldom the grand designs; existence is sustained in the continuing. "People really need each other," Luke often said, echoing Amanda, "even if they don't have the sense to know it." I see now that Georgia and I were helping to make each other survivors, almost as though we were using each other, trying at that age to draw strength from our own mutual questioning, just to feel good about ourselves.

Perhaps that is why I wanted her to bear witness with me to the scenes at the Ricks canopy before a burial. In a peculiar way I needed her to be there. I watched as she looked at the mechanical lowering device and the great pile of dirt under the counterfeit grass and the gravediggers in the distance leaning on their shovels and the funeral home chairs in their fastidious rows, and then as she gazed down into the dark, yawning hole. *"Oh, God!"* she whispered, and looked at me in stricken melancholy.

Surely sexual love lies hidden in each individual, waiting to be summoned. It takes time and blood. She was what that generation called "passionate," yet we were the creatures of that time, too, young yet not young, if that makes any sense, and to tell the truth, more than a little afraid, and all this had to do with biological urges. It was the era when we furtively passed around *God's Little Acre* and *The Fountainhead* and a manual called *The Torch of Life* sold in drugstores in the capital city and the "ten-page books" from under the counter at Crenshaw's with their lewd drawings of Popeye and Olive Oyl, Dagwood and Blondie, Superman and Lois Lane. If the older students from town did not tell you everything when you were eleven or twelve, as if they were passing the torch itself to the next generation, then you could rely on your hill-country contemporaries to do so, and in more graphic and abundant detail. One knew there had to be something to it, if the Baptist and Methodist preachers railed against it so much.

Of course we knew about it. One might just as easily have exorcised the Book of Deuteronomy. The small-town adult world of that day was never for a moment so clever or discreet as it assumed itself to be, even when that year the pastor of the Second Baptist Church left town overnight after his suddenly discovered relationship with a manicurist in the congregation. The father of a boy in our class named Leslie Renfroe had been observed entering a hotel room in the capital city with a pretty, young second-grade teacher. A friend of Leslie's mother had seen them walking down the street together and followed them; swifter than Reuters, she returned home with the news.

"It's the quiet ones you can't trust," my mother said a dozen times, if once, to her confreres on the telephone about Leslie Renfroe's father, and then she would pause for the response before speaking again: "Always so quiet and nice . . . Oh, yes! Right there in the Davis Hotel . . . Has anybody spoken to Maggie?"

It had only been in recent weeks that I could hear her wandering about the house at all hours of the night talking to herself. Sometimes she tiptoed into my room when she thought I was asleep and quietly browsed through my dresser, and twice in the darkness I saw her holding up the trousers I had worn that night and sniffing them. Then, as she often did, she would lapse into a kind of vague and formless indifference. One day in the backyard Dusty chased a cat under the steps to the porch. I heard a mighty clatter of breaking glass, and poor Dusty rushed out with the whine of a javelina, woebegone and angry, nursing a cut on his paw. I looked under the steps and found a dozen empty gin bottles.

Returning unexpectedly early from a dance recital one afternoon, my mother found Arch, Zamma Bailey, Georgia, and me sitting innocently in the kitchen.

"What were you doing in there before I got home?" she asked later.

"Nothing."

"Oh, yes. I'm not stupid." Was Georgia driving her crazy? Or was I? Or was everything?

Although the house on the boulevard was dark and still, sleep did not come easily. I was lying awake in my bedroom one midnight. My mother was long since oblivious in her room in front. The carpet at the foot of my bed was piled with schoolbooks, and next to them Dusty dozed in fitful dreams. A solitary car whipped by in the night, and from the Quarters I could hear the sound of a radio and someone singing a lonesome song, but I could not make out the words. I drowsily began thinking about my father, trying to remember exactly how he looked when I was eight or nine, how he walked and talked, the red flannel shirts he wore. Somehow my thoughts turned to one of the poems Mrs. Idella King read that day, and then to a terrible burial weeks before at Locust Grove, and the long drive home with Luke and the Legionnaires. Suddenly with a stab of hot apprehension I recalled how two or three of the football players had glanced tellingly at Georgia that very morning in the corridor of the school, looking her up and down. Then the telephone in the kitchen rang. I knew precisely who it was, another night owl like me, using her own phone in her bedroom. I wrapped a woolen blanket around myself and felt my way to the phone. Strange, but there were things you could talk about on the telephone late at night in those days that were more easily said than when you were together.

"Hey."

My bare feet were cold and stiff on the linoleum, and the autumn moonlight streamed softly through the venetian blinds. I could hear the mellow chords of the train whistle become fainter and higher-pitched as the late train to Memphis sped northward.

What was wrong?

It was her fears, her secrets. She was failing French. Her father never talked to her, only worked, drank, and watched the new television, while her mother talked *too* much. Her mother had tried to read her diary. She had overheard two older girls calling her a bitch. An old, blind black man she knew was sick and alone, except for a scraggly yellow dog. She still feared for Luke and Amanda.

Once she called in the middle of the night and actually asked if there was a God.

"Of course there's a God." And I believed it.

"Are you sure?"

Yes.

"I'll take your word for it. I believe there is, too. I've just been lying here thinking about it."

Sometimes in darker moods she would call and say: "I don't get along with people very well."

Why not?

"I don't like anybody. I'm not sure I like *you*."

Me?

"Oh, I *love* you. But I don't like many people. I really don't. People are mean. *I'm* mean too. Don't you agree?"

The most unexpected call I ever got was about her father. That night after I had dropped her at home, her father himself had confronted her inside the front door. He was drinking.

"Where've you *been?*"

"Daddy, I'll talk to you about it tomorrow. I'm okay. Daddy, I'm a good girl."

"You're a damned liar," he said.

"This hurt me, Swayze. Daddy never talked to me that way." Why were all of them conspiring against us?

Draped in the blanket in the cold darkness, I would call her, too.

"Number please," the cheerful operator inquired.

"Nine-six-three."

"You won't guess what my mother just did."

"What?"

"Went through the pockets of my clothes in the closet."

"No! In the *closet?* I'll come over."

"At one A.M.?"

"Oh, is it that late?"

One night when she called, she was crying. I could hear her sobs, the deepest I had ever heard from Georgia. She had just gotten a letter from her sister in Kentucky.

"The things she said to me. The witch!"

What things?

"That I don't love our parents. That she's disappointed in me. That I won't ever amount to anything. That I'm going to ruin."

We were hardly going to ruin. Our only sin was growing up. But neither were we innocent. We deserved to be rebels.

There were my fantasies, my imagination scarlet with feverish secret images of her. I longed to tell her, but I could not. I was falling into pleasurable private trances. On leaving her in the nighttimes I would have to seek my own release.

It was Luke, of course, who saw and understood. We were in

the kitchen of his cabin. I was asking him about girls — what they really felt about things.

"They feel the same you do, most of them," he said. "Only more so."

He disappeared into his bedroom and returned with a small sack in his hand. He was almost shy as he handed it to me.

"Now don't be reckless. But if you have to be reckless, don't be dumb." I withdrew a package of condoms from the sack. "I'm sure you know Sarge Jennings sells them," he said. "A man's got hormones before he's got brains. Can't do much about that, I guess, except to be careful."

In our car on those faraway evenings, or at Luke's cabin, which he sometimes let us use — but mainly in the *car,* the hallmark of our hard-earned and mutual autonomy — our bond at first was in the kissing, and then, slowly, ineluctably, in the touch. After many falterings, it was she who finally led me with her hand to her small, taut breasts, and the kisses there — and then at last my fingers to the warm, deep mystery of her. I was afraid, and she helped me. I could not associate this warm, slippery openness with her, the deep wellspring of her, but then it *became* her to me, who she was. And then she turned to me with her touch. Alone and together in the secret dark, we tried to find our way.

It first came the night of Arnold Crosswait's funeral. The windows were down, and all about us were the clean scents and sultry rustlings of Indian summer. There was a mysterious unforbidden look in her eyes, a veiled, glazed expression I did not know, her lips gently parted and glistening, the light sound of her breath, the naked beating of her heart against my own. Surely it had been this way in Eden's bowers.

It was almost by accident. It hurt her a little, a piercing little cry. It hurt me too. Yet after a while . . . I had never before had a feeling like this. It is this way for the boy, the man: the glowing, pillowy rapture of joy. As she lay still beneath me, my whole lower being was engulfed in a new paradise of blissful pleasure, as if the highest crown of my feelings were lavished and caressed and embraced by the soft, ardent cauldron of her, the heat and pull of her lovely body. Suddenly I erupted in a sensation of maddening ecstasy, at the edge of pain, almost, so stunning and powerful, yet so tender, that as from some distant place I heard my own enraptured cry.

We were quiet afterward in our limp embrace. "Oh, Swayze." She gently stirred. She trembled when I moved away from her. She looked down and saw blood. "Oh, no." I slipped the used condom out the door onto the grass.

It was lucky her parents were away and would return late that night. We drove through the empty streets to her house in an odd and embarrassed quiet, a little like strangers; she looked straight ahead, and glanced at me only once or twice. I parked the car in the alley behind her house and walked with her to the back door. She fumbled in her purse for the key.

"Do you want me to come in with you?" I asked.

"No. I'll be all right. I'll . . . take a shower." Without looking at me, she touched my hand and disappeared inside. The next morning in school, as Mrs. Idella King diagrammed sentences on the blackboard, our glances swiftly met. Something secret had passed between us, ours alone. She creased her lips in a tiny, reticent smile.

And so, in those days of death, it began. We were young and lost. Yet against the dictates of our place and age, our very youth and uncertainty brought us together in a funny, profound alliance of discovery. I believe now that it lay in our loneliness and need, and that we knew each other, and that it was our fear, too, that sustained us, the fear itself a heady excitement. There was something in Georgia. Amanda and Luke's example? Curiosity? Defiance? Courage? *Life?* It was as if she wanted to *know* something, to memorize some new kind of lesson.

She really wanted to keep trying. I will not forget how much. We would kiss and embrace, then she would detach herself. "Don't kiss me anymore," she would whisper. "Let's just . . . *try*. I want to feel it." She would look down and help me with the condom. Then she would be very quiet and intense, opening and closing her eyes, moving her hips slowly up and down or in tense little circles — her high, arched thighs, her nipples long and stiff, her small, rippling sighs, her faraway look. "It doesn't hurt anymore. It's . . . nice." I would complete in her so quickly at first, loving her in spasms. And we would try again.

After a time it became a strange, obsessive rhythm. We could not help it. Our bodies were so young. It was horrendously new and consummate and wonderful, a supplication of feeling encompassing me and changing me — and it was incredible that someone I cared for could give such intense pleasure. It was *Georgia*. And when the dazzling ecstasies struck me, she would be a little stunned by them, and put my head on her shoulder and whisper to me. In the mornings in my own bed my wakenings were rich and slumberous, so distant and distinct from the bleak, dark insomnias of childhood.

It could not have been more blessedly fortunate that Mrs. King, in assigning the principal term paper of the semester, put Georgia and me together. The rest of the class would likewise work in pairs, but because there was an odd number of students, and more specifically because no one else wanted him, she soon added Arch to our team. The project called for thirty-five hundred words on a subject of our choosing, just as long as it pertained to the town, past or present. "Three thousand, five hundred words!" Arch complained. "That's longer than the Bible. That's twenty-five *pages*!" This little long-ago exercise now seems enmeshed with Georgia, with the way she looked and felt and remembered, with the things she did and said and heard, with the moments and moods of her, with the two of us together in that time of Luke and Amanda and Durley,

and youth and passion and mortality. It was Brigadier General
Miles Featherstone who brought us even more closely together,
and even more frequently, in our new and mysterious union.

It was my idea to do our paper on Featherstone, the intrepid
Fisk's Landing boy who had attended West Point and served
General Pershing so well and diligently in France in World War
I, then died of pneumonia before he could assume his appointment as commandant of his heroic alma mater on the Hudson.
I remembered the Legionnaires' stories of his funeral, the largest and most stirring in the entire annals of the town, and I was
likewise aware that Mrs. King herself had taught him English
and French long ago and could serve as an indispensable source
in our research. Georgia liked the idea, and Arch went along
with it, although I knew he would have acquiesced in the notion of studying Genghis Khan, Walloon verse, the Algonquin
tribal tongue, Ramakrishna, Planck's constant, the Maori
Wars, or Emperor Heliogabalus, for all the work he would do.
I was enthusiastic about the project, and it was not lost on me
that Georgia and I would of necessity be thrown together late
on school nights in the cause of history. Even my tenacious and
suspecting mother would have no answer to that and might go
so far as to acknowledge that sitting on the front steps waiting
for me could interfere in the interests of scholarship; thus, what
was an awesome task and a curse to the others in that class was
to me an act of the most intense independence and liberation
and pleasure.

Right after school one afternoon — I remember the day well,
for we had played "Taps" that noon only a stone's throw from
the Featherstone plot — Georgia, Arch, and I had a valuable
discussion with Mrs. King about the general. When she departed to set up the bridge tables at the country club, the three
of us remained in the classroom to confer. More accurately,
Georgia and I conferred while Arch moved nervously about,
misanthropic and edgy, then sat down at Mrs. King's desk,

carefully unlocked the three drawers with his penknife, and began searching them one by one. When he found her grade book hidden under a stack of papers, he thumbed through it and suddenly exclaimed, "D-plus! As of right now I've got a damned D-plus." "And you're lucky to have *that*," Georgia said.

Despite Arch, Georgia and I made a crude outline. I came across it not long ago in a box of high school memorabilia I brought from my mother's house after she died. Written in Georgia's erratic southpaw's scrawl, like veiled calligraphy or a half-secret hieroglyph, it brought back to me in a tender rush the fusty twilight orange against the windows of our school that day, the desktops carved with initials and impudent graffiti, Arch reading aloud from Mrs. King's private letters, Georgia supple and mocking and playful as she filched cigarettes from Arch, smoking them possibly because they were so forbidden in that academic chamber. Classrooms in old, settled American high schools have always had a certain smell, a faint layered scent of chalk and dust and talcum and old wood, the residue of youth and mutability and time and the rites of passage, and I remember that, too, as vividly as yesterday, and I will forever associate that scent with Georgia, with her lingering summer's tan, the cool touch of her hand, her teasing glances.

When we had finished the outline, Georgia yawned and stretched and smugly touched my arm. She put her head on my shoulder. "Aren't *we* smart?"

It was a school night, and Georgia told her parents we had to work on General Featherstone some more. Before we slipped away to our familiar spot at the edge of the cemetery, we drove by the Featherstone place on the boulevard and got out to look around. The looming red Victorian had long since been sold to a family from Memphis, the man an executive in the new liquid fertilizer plant, but there were no lights on or cars around, so we walked through the yard toward the back. In the moonless dark we nearly bumped into an immense red oak with something carved in its bark. Georgia lit a match and we looked. "*M.F. — 6/3/01.*" "Isn't that *something*!" she said, and we went up front again and stood near the steps of the broad, columned gallery, and in the darkness I tried to envision General Featherstone as a young cadet home from West Point sitting there with his hunting dogs and watching the people go by in their wagons and carriages and wondered what he would think of the latter-day Godbolds and the new liquid fertilizer plant and tail-finned sedans and the dead soldiers coming home now. It was as if the pieces of a sad and wondrous puzzle were coming together.

"I think you like this," she said. "Why do you like it, Swayze?"

The adventure maybe?

"That's it. I like it too. I like adventure."

The next morning at school Mrs. King summoned us, Arch and Georgia and me, to her desk between classes. Did we know Mrs. Alabama Darnell? Mrs. King had had tea with her the previous evening, and Mrs. Darnell mentioned she had some letters that Miles Featherstone had written to her daughter from France during World War I. She would be glad to loan them to us if we promised to take good care of them. She would expect us late that afternoon. "She's rather lonesome, I think," Mrs. King said, "and, well, wants to talk a little about Miles. Now, you be nice to her. Alabama Darnell's very old and frail and . . . not very much in touch with things, if you know what I mean. Although she was as lucid as could be yesterday."

"You two can go," Arch said to us in the corridor. "I ain't gonna be caught with that scary old crone. She's two damned *old* to live."

It was just before dark, and Halloween. Georgia's parents had departed for a party of state university graduates in the capital city, and as we left her house for Alabama Darnell's, the children were already engaging in their noisome trick-or-treats. On the boulevard great swarms of them were descending on the big houses, and along the side streets toward the Quarters diminutive black hobgoblins in sheets were making their forays toward the shanties. Georgia got me to stop the car to give them some nickels; the children surrounded her en masse.

It was as familiar to Georgia and me as anything in childhood, this irregular and formidable Darnell manse: the pewter fountains and ornate birdhouses built especially for bluebirds on its flat green lawn, the sweeping front porch with the cornices and fluted columns and the iron balconies at the second-floor windows, half-hidden now by the blossomless crape myrtles, all of it dominated by a high, steepled cupola that forever had looked to me like a witch's cap. We paused at the massive front door and rang the bell.

"Can you believe it," Georgia said. "I've never been inside."

"Me either."

"Let's don't stay too long, okay?"

The bell was answered by the aged mulatto named Isabella, who had lived with the dwindling family since anyone could remember, and she squinted out at us now into the fading, ambiguous light. She had high cheekbones like an Indian, and rich wrinkled skin, and she wore a bright checkered dress that fell shapelessly over her slender form.

"Oh, the children," she said. She ushered us into a large vestibule with a big brass chandelier and plaster medallions on a high ceiling, and we entered it as strangers in our own land. To my astonishment, propped side by side against the wall of the vestibule were two .20-gauge shotguns. "Don't trip over the guns," she said. I could hear Georgia's low whistle between her teeth. "I'll get Mrs. Darnell."

"I can't believe it," Georgia whispered. She took my hand; it was as cold as ice. "It's another whole world."

As we stood there waiting, we looked through to a huge, re-

mote parlor like nothing I had seen before, with a marble man-
telpiece and Victorian sofas and side chairs done in needlepoint
and an elaborate mahogany whatnot with mirrored doors and
French love seats and marble busts of Apollo and Venus and
another intricate chandelier and on the walls old Darnell family portraits and a prodigious mirror with cavetto molding and
ceramic figurines on its stand of a boy and a girl each holding
what I took to be an odd breed of dog. The dying twilight
caught the beveled glass so that it shimmered magically in all
the colors of the rainbow. In a corner a grandfather clock
ticked ponderously away. I tried to evoke Ulysses S. Grant of
Galena in this very parlor, as indeed he had been, a funny-look-
ing little man from the pictures I had seen in the library, with an
unkempt beard and a muddy blue uniform and the stub of a cigar in his mouth, and had the crazy, beady-eyed Sherman himself been in this room too, consulting with his superior on *strat-
egy*? Unlike the luxuriant manicured lawn outside, overseen by
two Negroes from the Quarters, the whole interior seemed
uncared-for, ever so disarranged, a little musty and smelling of
dust and the obscure accumulated past so heavy that we could
almost feel it as it hovered before us. Everything was dim and
amorphous and eerie and indistinct, with a sort of watery ambiance floating upon it despite the dust, as if we had entered the
ballroom of a failed luxury liner that had lain for years on the
crust of the darkest sea. Although only a little of the sun lingered outside, there was not a single light in the house. And
through it all the ticking of the clock.

Georgia stood beside me breathing lightly, inhaling with me
the patina of time, mute and solemn in the spooky gloom. Suddenly Isabella returned, and behind her came an incredible apparition of collapse and decay. As Georgia took her hand from
mine, I could hear her low, involuntary gasp.

Alabama Darnell's skin was the hue of parchment, lined with
crevices not unlike the formations of soil at the petrified forest,

her mouth a livid gash dabbed with garish pink lipstick. She too was a figurine, as delicate as an antique artifact in her woolen shawl, her eyes as indistinct as her very household, yet with steel gray hair clipped neatly about the temples, and a crawling step that defied all expectation, for there seemed not enough skin and bones for the faintest dexterity. I do not think I had so much as glimpsed her since that night years ago, when she had come onto her back porch on one of those wartime evenings and told Durley Godbold and his comrades to leave us little boys alone.

We knew that she had outlived two daughters, one of whom had married a rich young planter and after their wedding in '21 had ridden with the groom from the church to the reception in a gilded carriage driven by four white horses and tossed flowers to the children along the way. And that when her husband died years after the daughters, she had taken her meals outdoors by a beautiful rosebush he had planted, then gradually, like the slow receding of a tide, disappeared forever in tardy requiem into the shadowy obscurity of the house.

"Boys," she pronounced the word in a soprano, as high-pitched and brittle as a child's. "You're Ella Barksdale's boys?"

"No, ma'am. He is. I'm Georgia."

"Oh, yes. You're Alice and Jake's girl."

She played distractedly with a brooch as she stepped forward and squinted at Georgia; for a horrifying moment I thought she might reach out and touch her all over her face, the way Helen Keller was always doing in the newsreels. "You're a very pretty child."

"Thank you, ma'am."

"How old are you, Georgia?"

"Going on seventeen."

"Idella says you're interested in Miles Featherstone."

"Yes, ma'am," we replied in unison.

"I knew him," she said. "He was from a fine family. My

daughter went to dances with Miles. He became a . . . famous man. And died so young."

"Did he ever visit this house, Mrs. Darnell?" Georgia asked.

"Oh, yes. He liked to sit in *that* chair." She pointed to a high-backed Victorian piece. "Even as a young man he was a fine talker. He wrote several interesting letters to Melly from the war. You'll take care of them, won't you? Where did you put the letters, Isa?"

We followed Isabella into an antechamber. Our guide withdrew a small box from a desk under the windows and handed it to us. "She's tired now, I can tell. She talked too much to your schoolteacher last evenin'. I think you'd better be going now."

As we returned, Mrs. Darnell was sitting in a chair in the parlor, like a rag doll tossed carelessly there. She looked at us with a dim, uncertain gaze. "Who are you?" she asked in her tremulous voice. "What are you doing here?"

"Remember, they're Mrs. King's students," her attendant said. We departed quietly.

A quarter-moon had ascended over the trees and housetops and there were the sounds again of the Halloween children, happy shouts and squeals from the darkest recesses of the boulevard and side streets. Georgia turned to me in a long, shivering embrace. "Oh, Swayze, we'll be old like that someday. Dried up and old. Won't we?"

We'll never be old like that, I said.

"Poor thing. She scared me. I'll be that way someday. Don't let me. Look at me." I looked down at her in the equivocal half-moon light, at her smooth, fresh features, her soft green eyes, the warm, moist tears flowing on her cheeks.

Very gradually over the days something had begun to change in her, poignant and indefinable. I could sense it in her whole body, this strange responsive stirring. She had grown more playful, and she would laugh and pout and tease, then lapse into her quiet, all-feeling intensity.

At our secluded place, after our visit with Mrs. Darnell, she turned to me, trembling. I had never felt her so open and expectant and vulnerable. Her face was flushed, hot to the touch. She was shuddering, then she began to cry out, shrill, desperate cries I had never heard from her, and I could feel her as she pulsated, throbbing about me in her tight, thrilling embrace, as if we were melting into each other. As on that first night, she was like a stranger. It was terrifying and wonderful, this tempestuous rising in the well of her, this mighty crestful dervish, this passing of something ancient and terrible. Only when she was falling from this great new pinnacle did I follow her.

We needed a little time to cry; it was that magic, the dizzying joy shared with another being, freeing one, if briefly, from the loneliness and isolation. She lay still near me, her head slumped to her shoulders. Then she opened her eyes. "Oh, God!" she whispered, as she had that day at the yawning grave. "It was . . ." But, as before, she was strangely shy.

As the days passed, the old sweet song of her sexuality slowly began to course through her, and became part of her, and of my love for her. Going on seventeen, she was already warm and needful and orgasmic. Before our own eyes our lives were mutually deepening, moving powerfully away from ourselves toward . . . what? Our feelings were so close to the surface and would almost imperceptibly grow more sensitive and easily hurt than one could have ever reckoned. The adventure had begun, and with it the suffering.

Mr. Leroy Godbold put his wife in a convalescent home in the capital city for two weeks. It was rumored that she had had an emotional breakdown. Mr. Godbold himself looked healthy enough, and even participated in a three-day junket with the governor and his staff to New Jersey and Connecticut in quest of additional garment factories. The military had dispatched a lieutenant colonel in army intelligence from Washington to visit him — deferential courtesy, it was said; what could they do from Fisk's Landing? The Swiss Red Cross had sent Mr. Godbold several communications, Sarge Jennings reported, all more or less perfunctory. The information, the Sarge said, on Chinese and North Korean prisoners gotten through neutral sources was almost never accurate. Durley was awarded a Bronze Star in absentia. The mother of the South Dakota army private reported missing with Durley also wrote Mr. Godbold, the Sarge said, saying she had had a vision that their sons were dead and in heaven and dwelling sumptuously in a mansion on a gold-paved street with the Holy Trinity; she had enclosed a number of Jehovah's Witness religious tracts.

We had played a "Taps" earlier that week, on November 11, the old Armistice Day, for Raymond Strong. It had been a sharp, chilly day of lofty breezes, and rusty autumn leaves fluttered across the graves. Sarge Jennings had obviously been partaking of the vinegar jar at Son Graham's grocery all morning, and as he waited with us by the Ricks canopy for the procession he described the no-man's-land between the two foes on that distant day in 1918. It was the first time I had seen him stagger; he put his hands on a pole of the burial tent for balance, and Roach Weems and Lank Hemphill and Woodrow reached out to steady him. The end was to come at 11:00 A.M., and they had announced it at dawn, he said, amid a gray drizzling rain in France. No one cheered. All everybody wanted to know was, will we live till then? Then there was the sudden awesome silence. The last few minutes passed like an eternity. There were the fumes rising from the torn, petrified, bombed-out earth, the acres of barbed wire still miraculously intact, the dying stumps of men, the twisted blackened corpses blown up like balloons, the poor horses he said he always felt sorry for, the dead ones mutilated like the men, the live ones with their heads bent low in shock and exhaustion. "It was quiet. We'd forgotten what quiet was. Then the time came. We crawled out of our holes like rats, and so did they. We walked up to one another and looked our enemies up and down. Twenty minutes before, we were shootin' at their asses, but here we were now in broad daylight shakin' hands. It didn't make good sense. Some of them was cryin', brother — and to tell the truth, Roach and I was a little too."

"What did they look like?" Arch asked.

"Just like us, and just as filthy."

Papier-mâché poppies had been sold all over town by the Legionnaires that day. *In Flanders Field the poppies blow / Between the crosses, row on row*. People attended the burial with the poppies pinned to their lapels. Since it was also my dog, Dusty's, birthday, I attached one of them to his collar, and he seemed to like it.

And then we had the most unusual burial of all.

It was the first black funeral we played for all year; it took place far out in the hills. Since the church and the graveyard were so isolated — it was the Blackjack community almost at the remotest county line — the preacher had requested assistance from the town Legion post. The Centennial Burial Association was in charge, but they needed Arch and me and the veterans, and Luke, Potter, and Woodrow to help with the military rites. The soldier's name was Elzie Brown. He was twenty years old, in the regular army, and he had been killed when his rifle platoon was ambushed nearly two months before. Luke did not know much about him, except that he was a sharecropper's son who had gone through ten grades in the Blackjack school before enlisting in '49. The family had kept his body in their house for the better part of that week, until the official escort, a black infantry private from Pittsburgh, had finally persuaded them to put him in the ground.

Arch and I drove out with Luke. Arch, having lost this toss, looked as cramped and uncomfortable as ever in his dark suit and tie. We were into November now, and it was a raw, gray Sunday afternoon with a harsh, cutting wind. All around us were dreary fields of corn stubble and harvested cotton and dense, hovering flocks of squawking crows and blackbirds — one of those somber, ambiguous days poised between autumn and winter that only compound a melancholy mood. We counted sixteen red-tailed hawks in trees and on telephone poles between the town and the church. In '37 only eight or nine miles from here, across an abrupt and miasmic savanna, there had been a brief oil strike, the homegrown geologists employing a theory they called "creekology" — start drilling at the sharpest bends — which made about fifty poor whites and blacks (and a handful of Texas and Oklahoma speculators) rich before it swiftly expired. The chamber of commerce thought this unexpected bounty might make Fisk's Landing a honeyed metropolis like Atlanta, but that never remotely happened, Atlanta going its way and also Fisk's Landing, and naturally many of the lucky families moved to Memphis, and after that the rich of course got richer and the poor got poorer, just as always.

This was impoverished country, poorer even than the small-farm terrain around Locust Grove, and one of the few practically all-black enclaves among the hills. The unpainted lean-to shacks were as pitiable as the ones on the Godbold plantation, and the Blackjack school, with its rusty tin roof and grassless playground, where the returning Elzie Brown had finished the tenth grade, was less substantial than the one on Godbold. The branches of the trees here were so dark and sere that they stood like frozen strands of ink against the heavens. Beyond the school was the Letitia Screws Grocery, owned, Luke said, by the white woman of that name who had once been from a suitable family in town until her husband ran away to New Orleans with a seamstress and she came out here and bought a little store. (Her husband had also been the subject, Luke told Arch and me, of the most infamous headline in the history of the *Sentinel,* in '32: "Ben Screws Daughter in Recital.")

And beyond that, at the crest of a hill, was the Blackjack

Baptist Church, a modest frame structure, newly painted yet indistinguishable, with its humble porch and wooden steeple, from the dozens of others across the outback landscape. The graveyard was off to the side. Potter, Woodrow, and the Legionnaires were already there; the Centennial Burial Association hearse was parked to the rear. As we got out of the truck, the perfervid activity in the building was revealed in a mighty torrent of sound — moans and clappings and melodious hosannas, thundering hallelujahs that rolled across the fields and ravines and merged suddenly into a crescendo of such sweet mournful singing, of such terrible loss and yearning, as to grip one in the soul.

"They been doin' that for three hours," Lank Hemphill said, as he stood by the grave in his shiny new blue and gold Legion cap. "They walked behind the hearse up here from the house. That's two miles."

"They know how to do it," Roach Weems said. "We may be here all afternoon."

"Aw, shit!" Arch grumbled, and lit a cigarette. "Think what it'll be like out *here*."

"If they ever *get* out here," Roach Weems said.

The sounds from the church grew louder; the little structure seemed almost to tremble with emotional hysteria, and this cast a compelling spell on all of us as we stood there in the slicing wind. We sat down in the funeral home chairs and listened; only Potter and Woodrow, who were conferring with a large black man in suit and tie from Centennial Burial, seemed at ease. Spread out before us were crude handmade tombstones going back half a century or more. I went out to explore a high plot of ground in a thick copse of hickories, then shouted down to Luke; from the distance he nodded his head in approval.

Four little black children had appeared and were examining my trumpet when the singing from the church abruptly ended, and the earth around us was shrouded in a silence so immense and dreadful that one could hear from afar the flapping of wings, the cawing of crows, the rustling of leaves. Soon the pallbearers brought out the coffin, followed by the escort, the parents, and seven or eight children. The quiet did not last very long. The ensuing demonstration was even more feverish and emphatic, and on the wind orotund fragments of words from the baldheaded preacher, softened by the distance: "Lift up your heads, he died for the Lord . . . Our King of Glory shall come to us, Sweet Jesus . . . Comfort ye, my people. People of Israel done gone off to war. Comfort ye, my soul! Comfort ye, Elzie Brown! Amen! Amen!" The pulsating throng bobbed and bowed, faces fiery and grotesque, arms to the skies — the grave enveloped by a sea of moving flesh, like a dance of the living elements. The raucous and incessant crows sat so thickly on the arched branches of a distant pecan that they appeared as a dark, feathery fan, and dim slivers of lightning quivered on the horizon. Then a thread of sunlight broke across the heavy skies above the pines, a ghostly ephemeral orange, and the pines were caught in an odd, misty gloaming. It was terrifying and splendid to watch, and once again I was touched by a great surpassing sadness and melancholy — for Private Elzie Brown, for every son of Israel gone off to war — and a strange, profound emotion of desire and love and exhilaration and loneliness and fear, and I thought as always of Georgia, of her new impassioned cries.

And when the moment came for the echo, the black children with me in the woods stood there quietly and attentively, looking at me with such awe and respect that I felt not like an insignificant gargoyle of sorrow, but a little like a god.

"No more nigger 'Taps' for me," Arch said on the ride back to town.

8

GEORGIA AND I finished our paper on General Featherstone, Arch as usual dispatching himself to the wings.
We got an A-plus. For the next project Mrs. Idella King,
as deft as always in matching students with subjects, assigned
us a history of the Ricks Funeral Home and its influence on the
community, Arch due to contribute little because he refused to
visit that establishment again except on the most titular of missions. Georgia, too, fitfully complained that the funeral home
made her uncomfortable, but she promised to go to the library
and read up on the history of funeral practices.

It was early December now, and there was to be a funeral for
another black soldier, an army private named Dorsey Kimbrell,
who was from the town. The services were being supervised by
New Jerusalem M. B. Church and Centennial Burial, which
would provide the honor guard and trumpets, so Arch and I
were relieved of the duty.

Dorsey Kimbrell had grown up in the town and, before enlisting in '48, had played football and graduated from Number
Two; I remembered him as a handyman in the summertimes at
Son Graham's grocery at the far end of the boulevard. Shortly
after the coffin arrived, we drove by his little family dwelling in
Independence Quarters. People spilled out onto the bare, dusty
front yard and into the yards of the adjacent houses. The peo-

ple were in their Sunday best, and a small number of whites were there — Sarge Jennings and a few of the Legionnaires, Son Graham and his family, Luke, Potter Ricks. Mingling with them were several black veterans of both world wars who wore the blue and gold caps of their own Legion unit with the braided words: "Croker Simmons Post No. 106, Fisk's Landing." From inside came the same frenzied sounds we had heard at the Blackjack Baptist Church, in one moment loud and ravaging, then soft and indistinct like the unhurried coming of a tide. Late that night as I lay in bed, the soulful music rose from the juke joint across the alley almost until dawn, punctuated by weeping and moaning and shrill maddening laughter; I doubt if anyone on our block slept much that evening. The mourning continued unrelieved for four or five days, and toward the end of the week the throngs at Dorsey Kimbrell's house down Calhoun Avenue had grown so considerable that the constabulary had to cordon off the street and detour traffic.

In the afternoons after band practice I went to Potter's office at the funeral home. He was allowing me to peruse his files in my research for our assignment — certainly not the "Embalming" file, which he kept under lock and key, but a cabinet full of old newspaper clippings and photographs of the original livery stable and correspondence to his father and grandfather and an interesting packet of documents pertaining to the history of the cemetery.

One day I had the office all to myself. The whole building was suffused with its queer, discomfiting hush. I was immersed in esoterica when from behind me I heard someone come into the room. I hoped it was not the sightless freelancer Silas Delaware, and it was not. The intruder was a tall, burly soldier with swarthy Levantine features and olive skin and a prominent Roman nose, in his late twenties perhaps, so hirsute that there were coarse stiff hairs on the backs of his hands and protruding from the collar of his shirt. He was dressed in crisp starched khakis with corporal's stripes and a neat single row of ribbons, including the Purple Heart and crowned by the proud blue and silver Combat Infantryman's Badge.

"Is Mr. Ricks here?" he asked, in a knifelike northern pitch too loud for the tiny room. No, I told him, he was at the Legion Hut on business but would be back soon.

"Mind if I wait on him then?" He sat down in one of the straight-backed chairs and began thumbing the pages of the monthly *Morticians of the Southeast*. His cap was still on his head at a rakish angle, and he glanced about the room with a restless, distracted unease. After a time he got up and began walking nervously around. From the corner of my eye I noticed him examining several of the volumes in the bookshelf. He picked up *Techniques of Embalming* by R. Mortimer Jeffries, and exclaimed, "Holy Mother of God!" Then he sat down again. "You work here?" he asked.

Only doing an assignment for a high school class, I said.

"What assignment?" His gray eyes surveyed me curiously and with a muffled belligerence.

"The history of this funeral home," I replied.

"What kind of town *is* this, for Chrissake?" Fortunately in that instant Potter came into the office, followed in seconds by Luke.

"Corporal. Nice to see you again," Potter said. "This is John Righetti from Cleveland, Ohio. He's the military escort. Got here day before yesterday. Woodrow and I met him at the train in Monroe City." I was surprised. I had assumed the army's official escort would also be a black man. "John was in Dorsey's outfit," Potter said. "Anything I can do for you, John?"

"I went back to the hotel and remembered your invitation," he said. "I had to get away from the noise for a while. It's getting to me bad."

"I know, I know," Potter replied in his scrupulous little whisper.

"Wanted to be around some white people." Asprawl in his

chair, a little wild-eyed, he seemed baffled, yet curious as to what our response would be.

"I know," Potter repeated, and looked tactfully at the ceiling, then withdrew to the desk and plugged in the coffeepot.

"I'll put it this way — it ain't a Roman Catholic wake. Four more days of it, they say," and he held out his hands and mightily shrugged.

"Yes, that's their custom. And given these circumstances."

"Dorsey was popular," Luke said. "Last time we got the family to cut it a little short. With this, I doubt it."

"I do too," Potter said, and handed the visitor a cup of coffee.

"Got anything to go in it?" he asked.

"Cream? Sugar?"

"Something a lot stronger." His heavy olive features stood out in the room, as did his sharp, cutting accent, and his expression beseeched his host with a kind of mock exasperation.

"I'll take you back to the Legion Hut," Luke said. "We've got a bar. Same brands of booze as you get in Ohio."

"That's the best thing I heard since I been here. Never been this far south. What do people do here? You got a lot of Negroes here. Looks like they kinda outnumber you. I got to get home soon. My mother's sick. Ain't seen her in two years."

"We hope you'll enjoy the town while you're here," Potter said. "How's the Earl Van Dorn? Best restaurant in town, in my opinion."

"Not bad considering the places I been sleeping the last twelve months. Ain't even been in the restaurant. Dorsey's people been feeding me some strange shiny white stuff. Tastes like shit, if you ask me."

"Chitlings!" Luke said, and Potter smirked demurely while Luke giggled, such a high and goofy and infectious sound that I had to laugh too. "Soldier," Luke said, "you look to me like a man who could stand a drink. I used to know a few Ohio boys." He patted me on the shoulder and winked as he and the corporal departed.

The wake continued, and during the next two days we saw the Ohioan everywhere — on the main street, in the coffee shop of the Earl Van Dorn with Potter, in Luke's store, at the counter in Crenshaw's, in the firehouse with the firemen and the returned veteran Wayland Bunch, under the chinaberry tree in Dorsey Kimbrell's front yard surrounded by the grieving mass. With his clipped profanities and dusky countenance he might as well have been an alien from a faraway galaxy, sprung full-blown from the big polyglot city of the North and utterly unlike the marine private from the Oklahoma Panhandle who had come home with Arnold Crosswait, or what remained of him. He would never have set foot in the town were it not for Dorsey Kimbrell.

It was early evening of the day before the burial — December 7, Pearl Harbor Day — a dark evening of gusting winds and wan clouds against a cold half-moon. I took Georgia to the town library, where she had already begun the work on funerals, surreptitiously smoking Kools, snuffing them out on the floor, putting them in her purse, taking almost indecipherable notes from the *Encyclopaedia Britannica,* and complaining that she was learning a lot more than she cared to about how the pharaohs had dealt with their dead.

The library was a harmonious turn-of-the-century stone structure at the residential end of the main street with a minuscule rotunda inside the entrance and tapering wings on either side, a reposeful establishment of high ceilings and brass chandeliers and musty Victorian paintings of cathedrals and meadowed arcadias and incongruous stained glass here and there, and over it all the fine pungent scent of books and age. I had been here often in childhood perusing the long, shadowy stacks, or sitting at the scarred oak table in the side room on rainy afternoons reading the children's magazines or examining maps of the town and county going all the way back to its Anglo-Saxon genesis. The librarian, Miss Lydia Fortenberry, a hushed and reverential spinster, had been there forever, her black dresses with white lace covering shoulders so thin and stooped as almost to seem deformed and her delicate, childlike feet encased in flat-bottomed rubber slippers so that she could move about as silently as a spider weaving a secret web. She was the local antiquarian, a proud and qualmish curio. Her rule was that patrons could talk only in whispers. Once when we were in the fourth grade, Georgia put a thumbtack in Arch's chair while he was getting a drink of water, and the resulting scream of pain led to his being exiled from the premises for six weeks, a ban which, even at that age, he welcomed.

She saw us from behind her polished oak counter, looking at us with the pallid subaqueous eyes of a solitary creature who has spent most of life's hours indoors. She approached Georgia. "I found some more material for you," she whispered. "I didn't disturb your books from this afternoon."

"Thank you, Miss Fortenberry."

"It's nice for young people to be interested in history."

The big side chamber was cryptlike and deserted. Georgia sat down in a chair at the familiar table. "Rescue me from these damned Egyptians," she said. "Look at *this*." She pointed to the pages of another opened volume about the Hindus. "I found *this* today. What does *self-immolation* mean? I hope not what I think it does."

I left her there and went down to the funeral home for another visit to the files. Both Potter and Woodrow were doing paperwork in the office. Potter was dabbing his eyes with a handkerchief. "It looks now like we're going to have a ceremony around Christmas. The Pennebaker boy. Will you and Arch be in town?"

I said I would, and my collaborator probably would also.

"Some of the finest services are at Christmas," Woodrow said as he rustled his sheaf of papers.

"Did you know December's always our busiest month?" Potter said. "I don't know exactly why."

"No reason for these things," Woodrow said, and stifled a yawn.

In the interests of historiography I jotted this casual intelligence in my notebook, then the three of us worked on in silence. The wind rattled the shutters on the windows outside, and the courthouse chimes up the way sounded seven. I had promised to rescue Georgia from the Egyptians and Hindus at eight.

Suddenly the back door opened and closed with a ruthless clatter; we heard heavy, hurried footsteps in the corridor. The corporal from Ohio appeared before us, his duffel bag over his shoulder, tie askew, eyes vehement and flashing. He moved swiftly into the room and threw the bag on the floor with a thud.

"Corporal!" Potter said, as taken aback as I was by this unexpected apparition.

"I'm fucking outta here!" he exclaimed.

"You're *what*?" Potter said.

"Fucking outta here!" He stood glowering before us, as if at the smallest provocation he might go amuck.

"You mean you're leaving?" Potter asked, sounding at once soothing and apprehensive.

"You're damned right I'm leaving. I'm on the seven-forty-five Greyhound north."

"Is something wrong?" Potter inquired softly, in the saccharine tones of one who had dealt with such difficult situations countless times. "You *can't* leave. You're the official escort."

"I'll tell you why. These people think I got ten thousand dollars in cash in this fucking duffel bag."

"Ten thousand dollars?"

"You're damned right. The goddamned life insurance money. Some of his cousins just cornered me an hour ago in the backyard. 'We know the army give you ten thousand dollars,' they said. They wanted to know whether I planned to pay 'em off now, or tomorrow at the grave. They surrounded me like *Zulus*. I was the only white man there. I didn't like the looks on their faces. I ain't *got* no money, I said. They told me I was lying. The biggest one called me a damned lying *Yankee*. He said I wanted to keep the money for myself. Then about six others come up. 'Where's our money?' Then I *really* lied. I said I'd go back to the hotel and get the damned money. Then I got outta there." This febrile monologue had left him breathless, and he stood there now, looking grimly down at us.

I had never before seen Potter Ricks speechless. He glanced across at Woodrow. "I'll talk to them," he finally said. "I'll explain that the army won't send the insurance for weeks, and then it's a check to the next of kin."

"Uh-uh," the corporal said.

"I'll take care of it."

"Uh-uh. Oh, no. I got better sense than that. Mother of Jesus! I just spent eleven months surviving five fucking million Chinks on horseback blowing trumpets. I ain't about to die with a switchblade in my liver in *this* burg."

"Let me make a call," Potter whispered. "I'll get Luke to come over." He picked up the telephone. "Two-six-four-one, please, operator."

"No, thank you. I don't give a shit if you call General Ridgway. I'm on the seven-forty-five."

"No answer," Potter said, and gently replaced the receiver. He glanced imploringly at the incipient defector. "Come with me to their house. We can work this out."

"You gotta be kidding! I wouldn't go out there again with a goddamned rifle company." He glanced at his wristwatch, then picked up the duffel bag and tossed it over his shoulder. "So long, *paesanos. Arrivederci.*" He was already out the office door.

"Corporal Righetti . . ." Potter rose and pursued him. The farther door slammed. For a moment Woodrow and I sat looking at each other. "Come on, Swayze," Woodrow said. With swift dexterity he got up from his chair and hastened to the back entrance. I followed.

The night air was bracing. There was a pale fresco of stars, and dark willowy clouds drifted across the amber moon. Somewhere in the distance a car horn was stuck, and dogs howled down from the hills. The streets were all but deserted at this hour. The Greyhound station was two short blocks away, and a most exotic sight we must have made — Potter, Woodrow, and I — trailing the wrathful warrior as he strode purposefully down the sidewalk.

Potter's brisk, dutiful footsteps clicked on the pavement, his silver hair flying in the wind. "Corporal!" He was shouting now, the first and only time I ever heard him do so. "You can't do this!"

"The hell I can't!" the soldier retorted, just before disappearing into the swinging doors of the depot.

When Potter caught up with him he was standing at the ticket window. "One way on the seven-forty-five to Cleveland, Ohio," he said to the clerk. "Change in Memphis," the clerk replied. As the corporal headed for the platform with his ticket, he turned abruptly on his heels and faced us. "So long, motherfucking Dixie," he said, and for the only time that evening took notice of me. "Add *this* to your history of embalmers," he said, and strode onto the platform and boarded the bus. As the big Greyhound pulled away in a cloud of fumes, we saw him one last time, in profile at the window. He gave us a lofty, exaggerated salute, and then was gone forever. Potter stood there, stunned. Surely the human animal, even the mortician among us, needs time to digest experience. "Thirty-five years in this business," he finally said ruefully, "and now I've seen everything."

For days the town had been pervaded by its sorrows, and perhaps it needed this bizarre coda. Luke had me describe the stormy contretemps twice, once to him and again to Amanda, and made me repeat what Potter had said walking back to the funeral home: "That man should've been less *obstinate*." Arch deemed it merely a smart tactical retreat; in Crenshaw's, von Schulte declared it "un-American"; Sarge Jennings called it "desertion in the line of duty" and embossed the story's details to the extent that Righetti had drawn an army-issue .45 automatic on Potter Ricks in the Greyhound depot to keep him at bay. Mr. Leroy Godbold dispatched a letter to the Pentagon about Negro extortion. Potter himself never mentioned the episode again. The next day in the cemetery, despite protocol, Luke substituted as the official escort; it was he who presented the folded flag to Dorsey Kimbrell's mother, and told her that he represented the president.

Christmas was coming. The junior varsity basketball season had begun. I had played some the year before, about half of every game, but now I was a starter, and I began to suspect that Coach Asphalt Thomas had a case against me. I remember the stark winter sun on the windows of the old gymnasium during our games and practices with the varsity, the dancing strands of orange light on the polished floor, the American flag draped on the rafters, the prayers in the dressing room before the weekly matches. In the practices Coach Thomas would blow his whistle and stalk up to me and scornfully look at me with his withering saturnine eyes. "Can't you even *bounce* the ball?" he would shout, and then rip it from my hands and give a long, intricate demonstration of how best to dribble with the left hand, then the right. Another afternoon he ordered me and a youth named Comet, a tall, skinny cousin of Lank's and the only

Ruston Hill boy who had ever played organized basketball, to remain after practice until we had each made fifteen free throws in a row, our efforts monitored by the team manager, Leon, and it was well after dark when I departed the arena, leaving Comet there to continue. When I managed two jump shots in a row at home against Monroe City, I could hear Luke hooting energetically among the three dozen or so spectators; it was wasted valor, since we lost 49 to 43.

The town seemed a different place from how it was in the parched hot vistas of summer. Everywhere was the odor of pine needles and cedars, which never smelled quite so wonderful at other times of the year. Everything seemed *contained*. From the library to the bend in the river, the main street was magically transformed, twinkling with lights, its store windows with a filigree of frost on the panes and overflowing with the rewards of the season, more gay and felicitous to me than Fifth Avenue itself in later Christmases of my life would ever be. At the river's curve were lighted floats and trees, the lights making dappled images on the rippling waters. Jehovah's Witnesses of all generations strolled about selling their tracts and proselytizing passersby. Ablaze in its decorations, the courthouse was like a Victorian spinster dressed against all expectations for her betrothal. The Christmas trees on the lawns of the boulevard were a mosaic of incandescence, and the lighted cedars on Blackberry Hill and New Africa Road transformed the weary facades. With the radiant lights on its front gallery even the Ricks Funeral Home looked inviting; in Crenshaw's the Legionnaires put up a Santa Claus mannequin with a bottle of Pabst Blue Ribbon in one hand and a pint of Four Roses in the other. The flags of the Gold Star Mothers were in the windows of the Tidwell house, the Crosswait house, the Kimbrell house, and the others.

It was cold, about as cold as it ever got there. Everywhere people rushed to get indoors. At first the skies were a chilled, brittle blue but soon deepened to a lethal purple that pressed hard and sunless against the earth, mocking the momentary cheer. Dead leaves lay frozen on bone-hard ground. An ancient widow named Mrs. Ivy died of old age in the house four down from us on the boulevard, and as Dusty and I stood on our front lawn in the raw, gloomy afternoon hearing the staccato clicks of the tap dancing inside, I saw Potter and Woodrow ponderously carrying the covered stretcher from her house to the hearse at the curb. Several black children stood on the corner watching, the mist from their whispers curling upward like wisps of smoke, and the whistle from the 2:18 freight to New Orleans resonated down the garlanded boulevard. Inexplicably, I have never forgotten this simple little tapestry of sorrow.

Arch and I worked three days a week during the holidays. The Jitney too was festooned with ornaments, the flypaper of summer replaced by swirls of glittering tinsel and filaments of lights from front to rear. An interloper from some less fortunate of God's dominions could not easily have absorbed the prodigal bounty. Kinsey presided once again over the elongated meat counter. Rich people from the boulevard and the plantations and Tara Estates filled their carts high with their profligate hoard, hams and porks and fowls and sirloins and T-bones and sausages and oysters from the gulf, and black patrons counted their quarters and dollars for the smallest of turkeys.

Georgia descended like the acquisitive Angel of Christmas with her usual stock of $5 bills and accumulated a dozen cans of crabmeat and smoked oysters from the rarely frequented exotic delicatessen section, two jars of macadamia nuts, and a container each of Portuguese anchovies and French foie gras. Mrs. Leroy Godbold, thin and pale in her fur coat after her time in the rest home, filled five shopping carts at a cost of more than $150, and Silas Delaware, milky-eyed blind and all-seeing, departed mysteriously with $20 worth of sliced bologna, a case of RC Colas, five pounds of chicken livers, and two cans of salmon. Georgia's mother, wearing a fancy woolen skiing cap from Neiman Marcus in Dallas, gathered up nearly as much as Mrs. Godbold, then tarried before me at the checkout counter, handsome and inquisitive. "I hope you're getting Georgia something nice for Christmas, Swayze." I believed she had never once forgotten that I had not sent Georgia a corsage for the junior high homecoming prom those years before. "Yes, ma'am, I am." She looked me over, up and down, with her haughty, appraising glance, and despite the season, or perhaps because of it, I yearned to tell her the things she did not know about her daughter and me. Mrs. Idella King, who was having cousins from Atlanta, stacked two carts herself before pausing to chat with Georgia's mother. Isabella, attendant and companion to Mrs. Alabama Darnell, left with two inexpensive mesh stockings of hard candy, a supply of bacon and eggs, and two bottles of laxatives — a spartan holiday for that silent and venerable mansion. Amanda came in wearing *her* fur coat, her face flushed from the cold, a vision of wintry beauty, in noticeable contrast to the mother-in-law who had spurned her, and hugged Arch and me cheerily at the counter. Asphalt Thomas arrived in his familiar green peacoat and crimson "F.L." baseball cap. He had his girlfriend with him, the hairdresser from the capital city. "This is Thelma Pickett." They were both chewing gum, and I could barely make out his introduction. She still had on her white hairdresser's uniform like a nurse's.

The owners had a store Christmas party at closing time one afternoon, and only Kinsey was not invited.

Comet and I were shooting in the gym the next afternoon. (Comet had acquired his nickname from the town boys because of his unconditional lack of speed — "slow as pig turd in a jar of sorghum," Asphalt Thomas said.) Georgia had seen the lights in the gym and come inside. She took off her shoes and joined us in her stocking feet. She clapped her hands for a ball and began shooting. She was really pretty good; and every time she made a basket she enthusiastically applauded herself. When Comet departed to milk his mother's cows, she and I loitered in the gym. I tried to teach her the game called one-on-one. Since she mistook it approximately for a form of football, it did not work well. Eventually we collapsed in a tangle on the hardwood floor. She giggled and wrapped her legs around me in a wrestler's lock. She tried to tickle me on the ribs. "How does *this* feel? Are you a sissy? God, you smell bad." Suddenly a voice boomed across the deserted chamber. We sat up startled. "What the hell you think this is — a goddam *skin* parlor?" It was Asphalt Thomas with his girlfriend, Thelma. "You kids get outta here. This is a *sacred* place." We detached ourselves and sheepishly rose. "Throw me them balls." As we left, Asphalt and the hairdresser were already shooting baskets.

I had saved some money from the Jitney to buy Georgia's present. The next day I went across the street to the jewelry store with $17.75. I asked Mr. Levine's counsel.

"Who's it for, Swayze?"

"My girlfriend."

"*Georgia?*"

"Yes, sir."

"She's a pretty girl, Georgia."

There was no one in his place, and he showed me everything. We picked a small sterling silver cross and a silver chain and gift-wrapped them together. When I gave the necklace to her a few days before Christmas, she opened it right then and tried to put it on. Unfortunately it had been made for a baby's neck and was much too tight. She insisted on wearing it. But it scratched her skin and made a welt. I went back to Mr. Levine and got a longer chain.

The next day she and I drove to the big river city fifty miles away. In a mood of defiance and adventure we had plotted it all week. She had told her mother, and I mine, that we were going there for Christmas shopping.

The drive from Fisk's Landing to the river city was along the last and southernmost finger of our flatland. With the high bluffs to the east the great flatness would gradually diminish into a tiny reluctant sliver barely more than two miles wide. All about us the land lay dark and sluggish under the somber skies. The bayous rose level now with the little levees. The cotton stubble was gray and frozen, and the winter clouds were like snowbanks at the wet, misty horizon. The houses along the way were adorned in gay Christmas colors, ivy and holly and berries and sparkling tinsel. Thick spirals of smoke drifted from their chimneys, and in the front yards boys with socks on their hands against the cold shot baskets at homemade hoops nailed to the trees.

She was sitting close to me on the front seat. Even in her blue jeans and red woolen sweater she looked grown up and composed. "This is like . . . *eloping*," she said. She glanced at me with high color and flashing eyes, then took my hand and intertwined her fingers.

She had just seen Amanda that morning in the Sears store, buying a present for her father. "She's a sweet girl, Swayze. They really ought to get married. But how *can* they?"

They would someday, I thought.

"Oh, I know they're being careful — *cautious*. Like *us*. But what would Mr. Godbold do if he found out?"

A light frigid rain was falling as we reached the city of hills, this old Gibraltar, where they had dug caves, eaten rats and mules, fought to death and submission in the Civil War. There was an aura of honor to the place, and a residue of horror. The steep thoroughfares were lined with the grand dwellings that had outlasted the long bombardment those years ago, and were festooned now with holiday lights in the gloom. At the apex of a mighty hill stood the majestic gray courthouse, which too had survived, and farther on were the towers and crypts and obelisks of the battlefield where we had come as children, and the contours of the old trenches in the precipitous bluffs, and in the distance the big river itself in the icy rain.

The motor court was at the fringes of town near the bridge and was named the Alamo Plaza. It had been there a long time, a succession of detached wooden bungalows set under a grove of pines around a secluded circular gravel drive. There was not another car in sight.

"We're *really* going to?" she said. "I can't believe it. I guess I'd better duck down." And giggling ludicrously she hid herself under the dashboard as I parked and went into the office. I put on an Arch Kidd scowl and gave the clerk $7.50, signing the register "Tom Thompson, 108 Pecan St., Lutherville."

The bungalow was warm and cozy, with Norman Rockwell reproductions on the walls, a Gideon's Bible on the table, and a big bed with a navy blue quilt. Rain was falling heavily on the roof and a boat's horn echoed from the river as we stood inside and embraced. Then she sat in my lap in a large overstuffed chair, and we kissed for a long time.

"Merry Christmas, Swayze."

She lay nude on the bed, except for the necklace I had given her, the silver cross resting in the tiny familiar indenture in her neck that I had known since our childhood. I stood by the bed looking down at her. Her little breasts were arched upward, dark against her chest, and her nipples were crimson and taut and long. Her girlish beauty was set off by swirling tan-colored curls, surprisingly luxuriant, and her gleaming slit protruded from them like a sheath. Wordlessly she had propped herself on pillows, so that she was half sitting, half lying. Her arms were resting on each side of her on top of the pillows, as if in an attitude of supplication. She spread her thighs and lewdly touched her breasts. Her eyes glistened. She lightly undulated her hips as she gazed up at me. "Am I pretty, Swayze?" She touched herself. "You like this, don't you?" She had a funny smile. "This is where the feeling is. This is my heaven." Standing before her, I recalled the little girl who killed Japanese ants with me, the girl who did not want a typhoid shot, our first kiss in the spring-time dusk. And I have remembered forever her glowing cheeks that day, her bobbed blond hair, how young and beautiful she was. Yet spread-eagled before me she was not childlike, and my memory of her there is a terrible hurt in my heart, and makes me want to cry.

"What are you going to do now, Swayze? Come here to me. I love you. I love you so much."

The next evening was the traditional Christmas caroling at the courthouse. Georgia and Arch and I went together. The children's choir from the grammar school was assembled around the big decorated tree on the lawn. Two or three hundred people, heavily wrapped against the cold, were gathered; black people of all ages stood at the edges of the crowd. Few there perhaps recognized the irony when our Jewish mayor, Isaac J. Fink, wished his constituents a merry Christmas and formally introduced the choir, which forthwith broke into song. The mayor's nemesis, the lonely von Schulte, lurked under a nearby oak, and Potter Ricks walked by in a green overcoat, wishing everyone merry Christmas to the strains of "Silent Night." I felt Georgia put her hand in my coat pocket just as I saw Luke leaning against the Confederate monument, glancing innocuously at Amanda several yards away. My mother was in the middle of the crowd with a number of her tap dancers. The lights shone on the serene frozen Confederate soldier gazing eternally across the street at the Elks Lodge, and the men on the balcony there gazed down at us, holding their pool cues.

The children began singing "O Little Town of Bethlehem." I recall how its strains reminded me at every Christmas of my own town, as if the words had been written about it alone:

> O little town of Bethlehem
> How still we see thee lie,

Above thy deep and dreamless sleep
The silent stars go by.

Many years later, on a cold and frosty Christmas Eve, I would sit with my wife at the high mass in the cathedral of King's College in Cambridge, England, a thin skein of snow on the great sweeping seventeenth-century quadrangle outside. The magnificent stained glass and the elaborate flickering candle-light and the resounding organ and the grand processional in Henry VIII's vaulted chamber were among the most beautiful things I would ever see in my life, the assembled choirs of little English boys in their red ceremonial robes and high collars coming ever so slowly down the aisles with their flags and maces, their voices rising:

Once in royal David's city,
Stood a lowly cattle shed,
Where a mother laid her baby
In a manger for his bed. . . .

As their voices rang in celebration, I would remember Fisk's Landing — our own little Anglican chapel on the boulevard and Georgia and Arch and me in the cold that night under the statue at the courthouse — and long for it.

Charles Pennebaker's funeral was on the afternoon of Christmas Eve. The temperature was three degrees above zero, the skies opaque and oppressive, the ground so hard, Potter Ricks said, that they had to use drills to dig the grave; it took two hours to complete the job. From the cemetery I could see wood smoke spiraling upward from the shacks on Blackberry Hill. Here and there people in overcoats were placing Christmas wreaths on family plots, and as I wandered about awaiting the cortege, I noticed that someone had put a fresh holiday garland on the mossy, solitary grave of "Richard Melemore Purvis, 1862–1910." Who might have done this for him, I idly wondered, so remote and alone under the bare, gaunt oak at the farthest edge of the old section, and gone more than forty years? If, as they say, one does not really die until he is at last forgotten, until the last of those who knew and recalled him are themselves gone forever, then Mr. Purvis was still with us, hanging on for dear life, so to speak, because someone had just remembered him at Christmas.

Arch's parents had presented him that day with a brand-new $150 trumpet from the music store in the capital city, an Olds Ambassador from Elkhart, Indiana, with a mouthpiece like a vise and a two-toned case that could sit on its side like an odd-shaped suitcase, beige and a kind of washed-out rust, the interior a soft bluish velvet, and at the open grave people came to admire it, Luke and Woodrow and the Legionnaires, and to listen as he played the scales. I joined in as usual to loosen up; the cold made it difficult on the lips. Georgia had come with Lank Hemphill, who had known Charles Pennebaker from Ruston Hill, and the two of them and Luke sat on a high crypt a few yards away talking. Lank had gotten his artificial limb in time for Christmas. Having gained a little weight, he looked prosperous enough in a new coat and the American Legion cap, and when I came their way he pointed to the new limb, and said, "It's ugly, ain't it?" On the hill under my magnolia as the procession came in, I saw two old men placing flowers on a distant plot stand at attention with their hats on their hearts, and in the town below the wonderful holiday lights glistened in the icy afternoon's gloom. When it was over, Amanda, shivering in her fur coat, met me halfway down the hill. "We're going to New Orleans tonight," she whispered. "In separate cars. Merry Christmas." And she kissed me lightly on the cheek.

A strange thing happened. Almost as soon as the service was over, the temperature began to rise, an insane cataclysmic change, as elemental as the earth. In little more than two hours the numbing winds had turned into soft, warming breezes, and enormous threatening clouds descended, and soon a deep, heavy, impenetrable rain, accompanied by angry crests of lightning and low, growling thunder such as had never been seen within anyone's memory in the town at Christmas. It was horrendous, this sudden brooding storm, and it lasted a long time, shrouding the streets in early darkness, making small ponds in the low-lying places, the swift jets of lightning illuminating the houses and trees like phantoms.

Georgia disappeared for a while that night. I knew where she was, because I had seen her purchases that morning in the Jitney — groceries for the old blind man in the Bottoms and a box of Red Heart dog food for his scraggly yellow dog and gifts for a few other people and dogs down the road.

At the midnight mass in our church, Georgia and I heard the vicar pronounce the words of Herodotus: "No one is simple enough to choose war instead of peace. For in peace sons bury fathers, but war violates the order of nature, and fathers bury sons." Then Potter Ricks stood, and said, "This afternoon, Christmas Eve, we buried Charles Pennebaker. This prayer is for him, and for our country." He read from the prayer book in his high and magisterial voice:

> Almighty God, who hast given us this good land for our heritage; we humbly beseech thee that we may always prove ourselves a people mindful of thy favour and glad to do thy will. Save us from violence, discord, and confusion; from pride and arrogance, and from every evil way. Defend our liberties, and fashion into one united people the multitudes brought hither out of many kindreds and tongues. Endue with the spirit of wisdom those to whom in thy name we entrust the authority of government that there may be justice and peace at home, and that, through obedience to thy law, we may show forth thy praise among the nations of the earth.

The chimes from the courthouse counted midnight through the rumbling thunder. As I watched through the candles' glow the solemn ritual and heard the amens, I could smell yuletide whiskey on Anglican breaths.

9

WE BROUGHT in the new year at Luke's cabin — Amanda and Georgia and Luke and I and Shotgun. Luke brought out two bottles of New York champagne, which he had ordered specially from the bootlegger, and served it in regular water glasses. The bacchanalia at the country club, attended by my mother and Georgia's parents, where the previous year a drunken attorney had rolled headlong down the incline between the third and fourth greens and cracked his rib cage, and where an auto dealer and a planter with noted predispositions to mayhem had gotten into a fistfight over something pertaining to college football, could never have rivaled what turned out to be one of the brightest and most contented evenings of my life.

Only the day before, because of two or three lingering and unlucky injuries to his seniors, Coach Asphalt Thomas had promoted me to the varsity. "You're gonna get some *playin'* time," he had said, "whether you like it or not. Don't want to promote you but ain't got no choice. Wish you'd put on a little weight. How tall are you anyhow?"

On New Year's Eve when I told Luke this news, he got a tape measure and had me stand against the wall. "Five eleven," he said. "Eat right and you'll make six one."

Without much thought of it, all of us got a little intoxicated. Watching from his chair in the corner, with Luke's cat drowsing in his lap, Shotgun soon developed a fretful case of hiccoughs. Luke slapped him in several places on his back to resuscitate him. Amanda and Georgia giggled hysterically over some whispered confidence, and I was strangely light-headed and giddy, a most curious sensation. There was the sound of firecrackers from somewhere down the way, and Roman candles at the edge of the nighttime sky. The radio was reporting from Times Square in New York. To "Auld Lang Syne" I shared Georgia's long sweet kiss; Amanda and Luke were embracing on the sofa, rosy-cheeked and glowing with the warm light of love, the sunny-sly, mischievous look of love. Then Luke stood up and waved his glass in our direction. "A toast," he said. "To Georgia and Swayze. May they profit from the mistakes of their elders. And there are plenty of them." Suddenly, with no warning, I felt a momentary stab of foreboding, a bleak, tiny veil of apprehension and sadness. The next morning, the first dawn of that anguished year, as I drank my fifth glass of water, my mother said: "What is it — are you sick? What did you *do* last night?" We had a basketball practice that afternoon, and I learned then that hard exercise is the surest cure for dissipation; I ran off the first hangover of my life.

There was an unusual pause in the burials. Luke got a long letter from his cousin Lieutenant Billy Permenter, which he read aloud at his cabin.

> The fighting is still hard and the casualties still high. The place we are at now is Kumgong-Ni, N.K., but don't look for it on the map. Night patrols are worse than they ever were. I count the days when I collect my points to leave this hellhole. We're in reserve now, about three miles behind the MLR, but sometimes I'd really rather be up there. My hope is for this 8th Army to hold tight till Feb. The more we stay on line the more points since we're getting only 2 off line. Believe it or not but I'd rather be getting 3 on line. Also, in reserve it's almost as dangerous from the shells around the bunkers. A shell hit the mess one outfit over and killed 7, including an officer I knew

from Bolivar, Tennessee. The cold freezes the rifles. The snow outside tonite is knee deep and the temp. is supposed to be 15 below. One week from tonite Santa Claus comes. We'll even have turkey that day with good old artificial potatoes. I have indigestion after every meal so bad till I usually get rid of it. Yes, I'm afraid I am changing. Some of us already have the sneaking suspicion that all this won't prove very much. Look after Dorothy for me. How is Amanda? Have you seen her much since the bad news of Durley?

We had a false spring in mid-January, presage always of a hard, impious winter. The temperature reached the high seventies in the sunshine. Men, beasts, and the elements were confused. Sparrows and jays chattered in the naked oaks, frogs croaked in the twilight distance, and a solitary crocus burst expectantly through the earth on the schoolhouse lawn. The pollen was out in the pines, causing the people with hay fever to sneeze prematurely, and the Japanese magnolias came forth in deranged bloom; even the baffled huckleberries had put out white flowers. The sunsets were warm and golden, and disordered owls hooted dreamlike from the shadows. Dusty swam in Potter's Creek; the girls wore springtime dresses.

People responded oddly. A suspect movie called *The Outlaw* came to the town, and a number of the pastors demanded that the Rex Theater close it down, but unlikely adults furtively bought tickets and repaired to the most obscure rows in back, just as we had done as children in the courtroom gallery. My mother and Georgia's had lunch one noon in the restaurant of the Earl Van Dorn to confer on lineage for an article that a United Daughters of the Confederacy dowager was writing on prominent families, and afterward Luke actually saw them playing the pinball machine in the lobby — "Your mama *tilted* the damn thing," he said. Arch put two bananas and a pint of worm medicine for dogs in the gas tank of Mrs. King's Chevrolet and a dead pregnant rat in her glove compartment. When I entered Son Graham's grocery one afternoon, the rooster was in the rafters and the Legionnaires had the vinegar jugs on the butcher's block, and I was witness to a sudden fierce scuffle between the returning veteran Wayland Bunch and Herman von Schulte. More accurately, the drunken bootlegger Bunch attacked von Schulte for something he had said and shoved him into a stack of canned beans. Son Graham and Sarge Jennings held Bunch back. "You mean, crazy bastard," the Sarge said. "You got forty years on him." The rooster descended from the ceiling in his usual flurry of rusty red feathers, and Wayland Bunch staggered away into the warm, uncertain night.

Arch and I were working most Saturdays at the Jitney, and unusual things were transpiring there too. Kinsey had become the object of curious visitations by solitary white strangers and an occasional black one, all with northern accents, bulky and dapperly dressed men with rented cars. Trying to appear inconspicuous but hardly succeeding, each of them would amble into the store and ask Arch or me for Kinsey, and we observed them in sober conversation with him behind the stacked boxes in the storeroom and in the dark little alleyway behind the store. Four or five times that month we saw these outlanders' cars in front of Kinsey's house on Blackberry Hill. Once the visitors got into town, they apparently did not linger very long.

All of this was not lost on the manager of the Jitney. "What's goin' on with Kinsey?" he asked us.

"I think he's being recruited by the FBI," Arch said.

"FBI, hell. They might be Yankee agitators. Or N Double-A CP. I don't like the looks of it. I think I'll call the sheriff." It turned out, however, to be innocuous enough. The interlopers were assistant football coaches trying to persuade Kinsey to come to their universities the following fall.

"Where you want to go, Kinsey?" Arch asked one day in the storeroom.

"Illinois, maybe. Maybe Michigan or Minnesota."

"That's a long way off."

"Yeah?" He looked down at us with his watchful, heavy-lidded eyes. "Not long *enough*." In little time Kinsey had some spending money and was wearing new clothes around town, cashmere sweaters and khakis, his little sisters were riding new bicycles, and his father had a new set of teeth.

The Ricks Funeral Home suffered an imposing trauma. During a procession into the cemetery for an aged widower, the prewar hearse broke down with transmission failure fifty yards from the grave. Fortunately the pallbearers were sturdy, young nephews and grandnephews, who carried the coffin the rest of the way. Potter Ricks was as chagrined as I had ever seen him; he apologetically gave the family a 40 percent discount, and the establishment began hoarding its earnings to buy an expensive new conveyance direct from Detroit.

Asphalt Thomas's forestry class encountered similar trouble. We were on a field trip in the hills beyond Luke's property to bear witness to the disoriented ecology of the ersatz spring when the bus slid off the road and foundered in a sea of mud. No amount of brawn could salvage it. I trekked the three miles to Luke's cabin to telephone the wrecker, the whole class returned to school covered head to toe in mud, and the principal had the coach meet the $10 hauling fee from his own pocket. "How's that for *justice*?" the coach complained. "I take my men out to learn about trees in a jalopy with shitty brakes and it costs me half a day's wages." It was that kind of January.

Finally the false spring began to drift away. "Men is motivated by two things," Asphalt Thomas was known to say — "reward and fear." Late afternoons were for basketball practice, and two nights a week we had games.

He harangued us unmercifully in the practices. "Palms up! Palms down: left hand out, right hand down! Close that lane!

Close that paint! You're the puniest excuse I ever *seen* for ball-players," he would shout, after some especially impressive miscue. "Start hustlin' or I'll put somethin' on you Moses couldn't get off. You couldn't whup a little girls' team." Further into the scrimmage, morose and growling, his whistle hanging disconsolately from his bullish neck, he would say, "Noggin, what the hell's wrong with your scrawny ass?"

"Back hurts, Coach."

"That's from too much *trick*-fuckin'. You couldn't knock a sick whore off a piss pot. I don't appreciate them black circles under your eyes. What time you get in last night?"

"'Bout eleven, I think."

"Yeah? Hong Kong time? Get your pitiful tail off the court. I'm gonna play a little with these other turds." Using his long, thorny elbows as he played, he would smack skulls, noses, ears, and midriffs, making buffoons of his sullen charges with deft Southeastern Conference moves and fakes and shots, leaving us prone on the floor in his wake. After about his fifth straight basket he would say, "I'm hotter than a depot stove," and then he would have us circle the arena twenty-five times doing wind sprints and order Leon the manager to guard the water fountain in the locker room afterward.

During the games I sat at the end of the bench and, like a neglected and forgotten gosling, more or less languished there. Because of injuries there were only eight boys on the team, almost all of them seniors, but Asphalt Thomas would sometimes look down my way where I crouched like a fetus to avoid his attention. I was not at all unproud of the crimson knee guards and the heavy warmup suit with "F.L." in white over the number 18 on the back, but what indeed was I doing there? Arch did nothing but confirm my feelings of doubt. With little but contempt for athletics, considering them, like church and schoolwork, a folly and a waste of expectation, he made light of my impoverished efforts.

"You should be home practicing the horn," he said. "Your 'Taps' is shaky lately."

I let this slander go, as I usually did with him, just to save energy, and admitted I was not as good as he on the trumpet.

"Then what *are* you good at?" the ever-patronizing young sinner asked.

But then there was Luke. "You run fast," he said, "and you're gainin' weight. It's good for you. And it gets you out of town." Traveling to our away games on the feeble crimson and white sports bus with "The Choctaw" emblazoned on its sides, we would watch the nocturnal prospects drift past, the dark, expansive flatland with its row after row of seared cotton, and the precipitous piney woods ensnarled in sleeping gray kudzu vines, and the little secluded hamlets of the black prairies with their weak and trembling lights and bereft thoroughfares. As always when I was in prolonged masculine company — these long road trips, drives with the Legionnaires to a burial, forestry class explorations — I would think of Georgia, her tenderness and adventuresomeness and passion, the feeling of her, her warmth and beauty and love, and I would envision her and miss her. Asphalt Thomas would be at the wheel, as dead leaves swirled on the highway and insects splattered against the windows in the departing counterfeit spring, and the older players would be engaged in their mad and boisterous horseplay, which by his demeanor the coach himself seemed vaguely to elicit after a victory:

"Hey, Coach, can't we go no *faster*?"

From behind the steering wheel, looking straight ahead: "You don't deserve to go no faster. We only beat them fairies two points."

"Hey, Coach, let's stop for some *beer*!"

"The way *you* played, you'd vomit up Pet Milk."

"Hey, Coach, we won! We won away from home in the last minute!"

"And so you did, you jackass. I knew you was gonna say that. I just been sittin' here waitin' on it. Save it for Shu-qualak."

Their names were Thomas, Jerry, Calvin, John Ed, Clarence, Percy, Verner Ray, their nicknames being "Bouncer," "Nog-gin," "Steak Lips" (for reasons obvious to all), "Termite" (shortened to the more manageable "Term"), "White Boy" (his full name being Clarence White), "Nigger" (because of his dusky complexion), and "Blue" (he was Syrian, and the others claimed he *looked* blue). I will never forget the crackerbox gymnasiums of these poor little towns — the old hissing radia-tors, the narrow, forlorn locker rooms crawling with water bugs and roaches, the ponytailed cheerleaders in saddle ox-fords and pleated midcalf skirts, the white wooden backboards and cheap tacky paneling, the abandoned elevated stages where a few dozen spectators sat on portable green bleachers, the benches and scorers' table coming right up to the out-of-bounds lines, the ancient round clocks with the swooping sec-ond hands that tied you more truly to time than the later digital ones. When Term or Blue churlishly complained of the condi-tions, Asphalt would rejoin: "Fancier than what *I* played on at your age. You're spoiled as a shit house rat." The walls stood so close to the courts that White Boy once made a basket while running fast and sprinted right through a door into an empty classroom, where he knocked over several chairs and desks.

If Coach Thomas vilified *us* during practices, imagine his conduct with the referees. "They don't know whether I'm gonna kiss 'em on the mouth or kick their ass," he would say of his own shifting cajoleries and rages, his sly supplications and venomous ill tempers. Once during a time-out he accosted one of them and whispered, "Ain't it about time you get your damned cataracts took out, Randy?" and withdrew his big gray pocketknife, and on another tense occasion said to a hairless and vociferous Italian among their number, "You screamin' dago! You're bald as a goddam gorilla's nuts," which earned him not one but *two* technical fouls, because, Asphalt later philosophically explained, "a gorilla's got two nuts." In those tough little towns, adults and students in equal fervor cursed and defiled our team, considering us metropolitans, and in one of them an angry echelon threw rocks and empty bottles at us as we rushed from the gymnasium to the bus, Asphalt Thomas herding us aboard and then standing briefly at the driver's door, where he shook his fist at them and shouted: "You scraggly-ass, pointy-head peckerwoods! You don't know basketball from cuckoo squat!" but then wisely drove us out of there in a hurry.

Arch, Amanda, and I were practicing a trumpet number for the state competition, meeting at 6:45 two or three mornings a week in the school auditorium. It would still be dark outside, with frail threads of pink and gold on the drowsy horizon, and soft, indistinct stirrings, and from Blackberry Hill the raw cries of the roosters — the inexact divide between night and day, the time I would later forever associate with getting ready to travel to some strange and inviting place far away. One morning a puffy-eyed Amanda took off the silver bracelet that Georgia and I alone knew Luke had given her for Christmas, and sat down at the keyboard. As we ran through the intricate andante, our imperfect notes resounded up the aisle into deserted hallways. "Well," she said at one point, "I think we've got a long way to go."

"It's *him*," Arch said.

We didn't get home from Shuqualak till 2:00 A.M., I said — a blown gasket.

"That's the problem," he persisted. "What's throwin' a ball through a hole got to do with *music?*"

"Let's try again," Amanda said.

The speaker at our first assembly of the semester was Mr. Leroy Godbold. The principal was almost coyly deferential, describing him as a leading planter in the state, a public servant, and "one of the greatest Americans." Godbold's face looked worn and haggard, but he was dressed in an expensive dark suit and vest (in contrast to his indifferent seersuckers in the summer), and his hard humorless voice, terse, emphatic, and dour, had a vascular yet flowery force, a cursory authority that carried to the farthest reaches of the chamber and compelled people to listen attentively. One could not help but recognize that the older boys in particular who, like Arch, were difficult to engage on many matters, were absorbed and riveted by his presence, for he carried a harsh and deliberate aegis of infallibility. Our history teacher had assigned us a brief report on his remarks, and I am looking at my scrawled notes on them now, in an old spiral notebook from the box containing the other memorabilia of those days:

> Finest state in U.S.A. . . . Outside radicals wd. destroy it . . . Grave nat'l. encroachmts., wanton mental invasions . . . Colored inferiority, etc. . . . Don't take care of what they've got . . . Redistrib. to other areas of U.S. those dissatis. with their life here . . . Confeds. had best soldiers in history, only our machines failed us . . . States rts. vs. communists . . . Reds and coloreds . . . N.Y. urban scum. "I lived in monster 3 mths. and know its entrails" . . . Irresponsible newspaper ed. in upper flatland is *a moderate by his own admission* . . .

The rest of my notes on that day are a little clearer, and I will take the liberty here of giving them cohesion, for he was telling the students of their culture and birthright, and they were listening:

> Our great and sovereign state is an empire within itself, vast in its natural resources, unparalleled in the glory of its heroic deeds and chivalric history, unrivaled in the splendid progress and achievements of its brilliant past. The time has come to reconsecrate our lives as loyal and faithful citizens as grateful people should do. I urge each of you to exalt and extol the highest and the best cultural and spiritual values of your native soil. The high standards and lofty ideals, the sovereignty,

autonomy, and independent dignity of our untrammeled state cannot be dimmed by the traitorous calumny of brutal and alien critics who would seize and destroy all we hold precious and true.

When he had finished he invited questions. Marion Whittington stood up. He had been reading a book in the library, he said, which argued that the state constitution impeded progress. Didn't we need a new constitution? "Who wrote that book?" Mr. Godbold asked. He was surprised it was allowed in the library. This constitution protected our way of life. Marion Whittington sat down, surely aware of the hostile and amused glances of his contemporaries all around him. After two or three other desultory questions, Mr. Godbold was rewarded with thunderous applause. He remained for a while to shake hands with a number of the teachers and students, just as he had with the jury and the sheriff's deputies at the murder trial those months before, then departed through the stage door. From the auditorium windows I saw him alone, leaning briefly against his muddy Cadillac to light a thin cigar, a faint, cool smile on his face.

The next morning a winter storm descended. It arrived in Fisk's Landing with dull gray clouds and icy winds sprung up from Kansas by way of the upper flatland, then diffident snowflakes began to dance in demented little circles upon the vulnerable and expectant town. With the first flakes the students in their classrooms began to whoop and shout with an exuberance rarely known in those quarters; even the sternest of totalitarians would have had to acquiesce to the riotous celebration. The principal came on the loudspeaker and demanded order, but he was equivocal at best and promised to make an announcement soon about the school schedule. In half an hour we were closed down.

It was only a pulse at first, the early snow, then in the gloomy afternoon it thickened before my eyes into great swirling veils that began to enshroud the earth and the trees in a soft virginal whiteness. Dusty and the other dogs along the boulevard tried to catch the foreign flakes in their mouths, and so did the children, who moved about in gleeful hordes and rolled and tossed in the spotless drifts. It was Friday, and that evening Georgia and I walked to Arch's house. The fire in his fireplace, big hardwood logs, was so huge that the flames danced and crackled powerfully, making a shimmering light on the ceiling. "Isn't it strange — and *fun,* Arch?" Georgia said. Arch rolled his eyes in disgust, but we knew he was just as excited as we were. Later, Georgia and I walked down the back lawn toward the alley, her hand in mine, icy and chilled, her breath frosty in the cold, her lips and cheeks wintry, and I remember most the pine trees on this night with Georgia, silvery and absolute, and all about us the windless, embracing dark.

The snow continued far into the night, then gave way to a heavy impenetrable sleet that fell muffled on the pillowy rooftops. The next day, during a brief calm, we once more ventured out to see what God had wrought. The town was quiet. Georgia and Arch and I, trailed by Dusty, trudged down the boulevard. The children and dogs had this new world to themselves. At the bend in the river the cypresses stood somber and frozen in ice and snow. The main street was all but shut tight, only Crenshaw's in flourishing trade, and there was sparse movement on the thoroughfares, the occasional vehicle spinning and gyrating madly in the unaccustomed elements. Georgia and Arch and I stood at an intersection and watched the boulevard ladies in their skidding cars that looked much like the little electrically operated one-seat convertibles in the carnivals, one lady spinning completely around a half dozen times before crashing into a derelict school bus, which slid into a runaway pickup truck, which in its turn narrowly missed Mrs. Idella King, who jumped the curb into the Tidwell yard. We remained there a long time watching the collisions. It was better entertainment than the Rex Theater or the courthouse trials.

Potter and Woodrow were in the driveway of the funeral home attaching chains to the tires of the hearse and the ambulance. It was from Potter on this day that we heard of the death of Corporal Lamar Teaster. "A hero, we're told," he said, standing at the ambulance in an outrageous fur hat with purple earflaps, his eyeglasses flecked with tiny gleaming particles of ice. "He rescued his patrol from an ambush. You probably didn't know him. Just moved to town two years ago. Worked in the sawmill — a bachelor, thank God. Three younger sisters in Lutherville, though. I'm sure they'll have a hero's burial when the time comes."

The storm continued that night, unabated now for at least twenty-four hours. It was more than anyone had bargained for, this unaccountable Siberia. The *Sentinel* called it the heaviest snowfall since 1930, and Mayor Fink announced that Fisk's Landing was borrowing one of the capital city's two snowplows. The electricity had by now failed all over town, and along the streets and byways there was the flickering light of a thousand candles. Two ball games were canceled. The furnace broke down in the deserted school, Luke's hardware store ran out of oil lamps, and in the long, empty daytimes Arch and Georgia and I languished in Arch's front room playing poker and shooting marbles, and the mothers of the marooned children who had lost interest in the snow and ice went quietly mad, and school would not resume for another three days. When a frigid sun finally reappeared, the whole earth was bedazzled and shining, and along the boulevard the houses were crystal palaces. From the lawn of Georgia's house that evening we saw our first aurora borealis, so rare in the South, and a marvelous sight it was: the high night heavens suddenly a streaming amber, luminous transcendent arches of light appearing as in a mystic vision.

Amanda came to our house the day after the sun finally emerged, to confer with my mother about music. From the parlor I could hear them in earnest conversation. I went out to the backyard to shoot baskets. Some might judge this non compos mentis, but it was strange and gratifying to bounce the ball with a gloved hand against the hard even snow and to hear it crunch rather than whish as it passed through the frozen strings, making a bizarre melody. On the boulevard Luke's truck slid in the ice and bounced two or three feet over the curb onto the lawn. Hands in the pockets of his mackinaw, he stepped lightly across the snow. I saw him coming out of the corner of my eyes. "You're crazy," he said.

I reminded him how he had preached the value of practice.

"But in *this*? Why not the gym?"

It was closed. No heat. "Who is it?" I asked.

"Troy Hudspeth." He had arrived last night from Monroe City. "Funeral tomorrow at two."

It was still cold when he picked me up the next day. The road leading into the new section of the cemetery was glazed and treacherous, and Luke had to handle his truck gingerly to avoid the gullies and ravines on both sides. When we got out Arch demonstrated something he had learned at the Pennebaker burial in the even more bitter December cold. He lit a match and warmed his mouthpiece with it, and I did the same to mine. All around us was an unspoiled blanket of whiteness shining in the afternoon sun. The crosses on the tombs in the Catholic enclave were frosty white, and above these the familiar branches of my tall magnolia were so tautly frozen that they creaked and groaned in the wind. From the road to the new Hudspeth grave there were only three or four sets of footprints, of the gravediggers and Woodrow and the sexton no doubt, and someone had shoveled the snow from around the canopy and the funeral home chairs to reveal the hard, glassy blades of grass beneath. Two other sets of footprints led to a quartet of mimosas up the hill, where the gravediggers were half-hidden behind the limbs. Within an arc of no more than fifty yards we could ascertain the recent graves of Scuttles and Pine and Jetter and Crosswait and Huskey and Strong and the others, the round unsunken parapets of earth on each encrusted in snow like swollen, icy midriffs.

Soon the old Legionnaires and Lank Hemphill came up the hill in Roach Weems's sedan. Having won the toss, Arch left us to start the long climb into the rise of trees, cursing to himself as he labored upward through the drifts, his new trumpet reflecting the sunlight in tiny flashes of gold. Mr. Chase Bowie, the sexton, joined Luke and me near the canopy. "Ain't had many like this," he said as he surveyed the landscape. "Five, six, no more than that." When the procession finally appeared below, it was more than a quarter of an hour late, ascending so slowly and warily that it hardly seemed to move at all, the chains on the hearse tires making noisy thumps on the road not unlike the steady ceremonial beat of drums. After the longest time the people got out of their cars. Georgia was there with her parents — the dead boy, like Marshall Pine, had once worked for her father — and she separated herself from them and stood with Lank Hemphill behind the line of Legionnaires. The volley when it came was at most a perfunctory one, because Son Graham's and Fabian Tubbs's guns had failed to work in the cold. When the service was over I met Georgia down the way. "Have you noticed how Lank *shakes* during these funerals? And it's not from the weather. He just *shakes*, Swayze."

She sometimes wore a blue velvet dress that winter. Who could forget the touch and feel of velvet on the first girl you loved? On the evening of the Hudspeth "Taps," a wind rose, powdery with snow and deep and chilling to the bones. "Be careful on these roads!" her father admonished as we left the house. "And stay on the main streets." She had been inside by the furnace since before dark and was surprised by the wind: "Oh, it's cold! *Brrrr.*" In the car behind the cotton gin the heater was on full blast, and the windows fogged over, and a dance played on the radio from WWL in New Orleans:

> They try to tell us we're too young,
> Too young to really be in love. . . .

Our refuge was warm and secret and cozy like Luke's cabin. Outside, a waxing moon gave a luster to the snowy roofs of the gin, and long, tapering strands of ice like silver arrows dangled from the rough wooden beams. Georgia teasingly drew a diagram on the misty window and played a game of tic-tac-toe with herself. Then she slowly unbuttoned the top of the velvet dress and with her own fingers brought out her breasts to me, fondling them softly with her funny, familiar half smile, then turned to me, brushing her nipples so that they swelled against me. After a while the heater was not working so well, and we trembled together from our emotions and the cold.

Her sister, Cassidy, gave birth to twin girls in Kentucky, and when her parents went there for three or four days to visit their favorite daughter, she moved in with her eccentric grandmother next door. The grandmother reminded me of my mother. She wandered about the house at all hours, and with her flawed eyesight was sometimes engaged in private discourse with trees, brooms, garbage cans, and upright vacuum cleaners. She was addicted to watching wrestling on the television, less for the images, I think, which she could hardly see under the best of circumstances, than for the grunts and groans. She also had difficulty distinguishing day from night. One afternoon after basketball practice at about 5:00, Georgia and Arch and I were in the yard when the grandmother emerged on her back porch. "*Bedtime,* Georgia! Now come have a glass of milk and go to bed!" Under such inconstant chaperonage, Georgia stayed out as long as she pleased. In the guise of working on the funeral home assignment for Mrs. King, we drove as far away as Monroe City or Lutherville, merely for the novelty of it, or went to the drive-in movie at 10:00 P.M., or stayed at Luke's until midnight learning poker.

"You're a riverboat gambler," Luke said one night after she bluffed him out of a dollar with a pair of fours.

"I think she cheats," Arch said, and I suspected he was not far from the truth.

She merely tolerated, however, the sport of basketball. She would go to the home games, usually sitting alone, or with Amanda, or sometimes even with Mrs. Idella King, who was scarcely aware of the rules and regulations but attended out of fealty to her unlikely protégé, Asphalt Thomas. With the team roster now depleted to eight, I was finally getting into the games.

One day after practice Asphalt Thomas had pulled me aside. "I gotta use you a little tomorrow night. Don't drink no milk or Cokes or water. Don't drink nuthin'. Get a good night's rest. Pray to the Lord. My boys are droppin' like flies." I tossed and turned in my sleep, and all the next day my stomach churned with a million wavy butterflies. Sure enough, with four minutes to go and a nine-point lead, Asphalt Thomas looked down my way. "Get in there for Blue. He looks like he's about to throw up." I felt naked as I entered my first varsity game, glacial and cold in my joints. It turned out all right. "You just lost your cherry," the coach said to me afterward. "Didn't do much harm at all." In the next game three nights later I played a few minutes and was as self-satisfied as I had ever been in making six points against the lumbering and unfortunate team from Tuckaho. As moody and distracted as ever, my mother was frantic on the subject. "It's *dangerous*," she said. "You're going to get hurt, I know it. They're better than you. Wait and see. *You're going to get hurt!*" For once she was not entirely mistaken.

*　　　*　　　*

February arrived, and we had had only one snow burial since Charles Pennebaker's on Christmas Eve. But we had long since learned that such things sooner or later had a way of compensating. In recent months the town's mood had oscillated between sadness and high buoyancy, between baffled melancholy and the odd exhilaration of escape, surely the most human of extremes. Young, violent death was palpable, as insidious as our darkest January, but could one live on that?

It was no doubt fortunate, then, that this year it was Fisk's Landing's turn to host the conference high school basketball tournament. The other teams were from boroughs more or less the size of our own, summoned from the anxiety and ambiguity of the flatland to our place (it was a funny league, to tell the truth, not especially good in basketball, stepchild as this was to the football gridiron, but who would volunteer to admit it?), and the town sought to embellish itself for its incipient visitors. Why did little American towns in that time come so alive for outsiders? Was it from fear of seeming paltry in their own eyes? From assuaging their own day-to-day isolation? Or in this instance had death's specter spurred the urge of release? There were directional posters on the light posts — self-flattery indeed to think someone might get lost there — historical signs in front of the old houses, crimson and white bunting on the storefronts, and an enormous multicolored streamer on the courthouse: "Welcome, King Cotton Conference!" The yellow out-of-town school buses were everywhere, and dozens of cars with license plates bearing alien county names, and in the afternoons cheerleaders from the other towns strutted the narrow streets around our school. Asphalt Thomas was in his utmost element, and ubiquitous, offering directions to all comers, talking basketball with the rival coaches in agitated little clusters, exchanging high-flown felicities with visiting principals and superintendents — "I'm gonna be one of them *principals* when I hang up the jock," he said to Luke, "so I might as well get used to my future colleagues." The gymnasium was packed for the competition: Thursday and Friday matches, both boys and girls, then the semifinals and finals all Saturday. The festive containment of organized celebration reminded me a little of Christmas.

Early in our first game, Blue sprained his ankle and had to leave for the season. Then, toward the end of the third quarter it finally happened, as I had known with a dire inevitability that it would and must — White Boy crashed mightily to the floor near our bench with two adversaries on top of him, and his wail of distress rose up and over the crowded assembly, suddenly mute now as he grimaced in honest pain, heaving and sputtering on the hard wood like a fallen sparrow, his whole left arm protruding outward from his torso at a grotesque, unholy angle.

Asphalt Thomas bent over the stricken warrior. "Can you fix him?" he asked Leon, who was examining the injury.

"No, sir, Coach. This thing's broke."

"Hurts like hell," White Boy said. "Gimme a shot, Leon."

"I'm jinxed," the coach said after he had comforted the contorted victim, who was led away to the hospital. "What did I do to deserve this?" Then he dubiously turned to me.

This was the big time. I was consumed with the same churning irresolution I had known at the initial playing of "Taps," the dry-mouthed giddiness I had felt the first time I kissed Georgia. Please, I silently beseeched the entire Anglican hierarchy: No mistakes.

The prayer was in its fashion answered. Playing the entire final quarter I committed no blunders, but for that matter did not make a single contribution that to this day I can recall — an invisible entity, more or less, if ever there was one. Luckily our squad was leading by several points when the quarter began. The opponents were big but slow and cumbersome, and we won.

But the next morning, Friday, when Dusty woke me as usual,

my whole lower right foot was a terrible blood blister. From my toes down to the arch was a pool of blood, covered with bursting membrane. I had had two or three before, but nothing like this one. Given my almost Quaker-like distaste of blood, I greeted this sight with horror; to my own surprise, however, I did not faint, or even retch. I could barely walk; the massive blister mocked my efforts, indeed as I see now perhaps even my very youth itself. I stripped off my pajamas and looked myself over. I also had a charley horse from a blow I had received to the thigh. Asphalt Thomas once told the team that charley horses were inevitable for ballplayers, as if ordained by the Old Testament, and he also often surmised that blood blisters were the price one paid for being fast and bowlegged, as I was and am. Nonetheless it was humiliating to discover I had *both*, and this after playing one scant and obscure and lusterless quarter. Was I suddenly regressing to my eleventh year, with its warts, rashes, and insomnias?

I knew I had to get out of the house quickly, before my mother found me in harm's way, for her reaction would have been little shy of epileptic in its magnitude. Luckily she and her students were leaving that afternoon for a two-day recital in the capital city and would not return until Sunday. For the first time I was grateful for the sounds of the tap dancing in front. I was tempted to telephone Georgia to come get me in her car, but decided to make my own way. Ordering Dusty to stay, I limped out across the back porch and detoured through Mrs. Griffin's yard to the boulevard, hitchhiking a ride with a schoolmate's father to the schoolhouse. I hobbled toward Mrs. Idella King's homeroom. Great stabs of pain were shooting through my foot, and then the charley horse started to throb too; the sensations in my whole lower body were insufferable, and this made me feel both angry and vulnerable, but especially angry. I had never really been hurt before; it was a new experience in life. My thoughts went out to Lank Hemphill and his arm, and to Luke and his foot, and to the official military escorts who had converged on the town with their missing fingers and ears and toes.

Georgia was tarrying inside the main entrance under the Plato statue just before the bell. "Arch and I waited for you. Are you hurt?"

I probably should have acted proud of my wounds in front of Georgia, an honorable gladiator representing his school no matter how ineffectually, as in the Baptist preachers' oft-mentioned tale of the poor crippled lad who ran in the race because he was all his town had. But the thought of the pool of blood in the blister left no room for heroic pretensions.

I required support from both Georgia and Arch to get to Mrs. King's room. After roll call she took me to the back of the classroom and got me to take off my shoe and sock. Arch and Georgia and three or four others came over to watch. The sight of Mrs. King bending down in her black dress to examine my blood blister was unsettling, and the way Arch and Lank and the other students stared down at me as if I were little more than an experimental cadaver in a windowless morgue was no less discomfiting. "Asphalt should see this," Mrs. King said.

She wrote me out a hall pass. I made my way down the corridor to the coach's office under the gymnasium, but he was not there. "He's teachin' driver's ed first period," Leon told me as he tossed last night's uniforms into the washing machine. "You hurt, ain't you? You sure *look* hurt." I attended the first class, then went to the gym again. Asphalt Thomas was sitting in the little cubbyhole adjoining our locker room, a dip of snuff lodged in his lower lip. "Let's see." Again I removed the shoe and sock.

"*Whew!* Worst I ever saw," he said, spitting all the while into a cup and gazing philosophically at the foot. "We'll handle it. We don't play again till tomorrow anyhow. We're down to the bottom of the barrel." He reached into the drawer of a battered oak desk, rummaged around, and brought out a long needle. He also withdrew a box of Diamond matches and began to heat the end of the needle.

Do we have to do this? I remember asking.

"Turn your head, then," he said. "Prop up the foot."

I closed my eyes. There was a quick, sharp pain, accompanied by an audible *swoosh*. When I opened my eyes again, there were splashes of blood on the dingy walls.

"Have to wash that damned stuff off," he said. "Now *that* was a blood blister. Where's Leon? *Leon!*" Leon came in with a wet rag and cleaned up the mess.

"It's okay now," Asphalt said. "Don't even need wrappin'. I got twenty against Vandy on the road after a blood blister like that." The blister was indeed deflated, like a fire hose after the water had gone through, and it felt better. From a bottle on his desk Asphalt applied a copious amount of Toughskin, the cure-all of the era. He used half a bottle, and the smell was piquant.

"Got a little charley," Leon said. "How come you so beat up? You only played a *quarter*. Got to protect yourself better. Use elbows when the zebras ain't lookin'. And I don't mean chicken wings, I mean real *elbows*." Now he examined my thigh. Then he handed me a tube of analgesic, the hot kind — "Red Hot Kramer" the tube said, known to us colloquially as "Atomic Balm." I rubbed some of it into my skin. "Just go ahead and empty it," Coach suggested. "We got a year's supply." After that he and Leon wrapped the thigh in an Ace bandage, then put about five yards of adhesive around it. "Don't take this off till after the finals," he said, "*if* we get to the finals. You can take showers in it. It's waterproof. Just shake your leg and limber up every little while. Can't let it get stiff, like a dick. Maybe run some in the back this afternoon. Idella might let you out of class to run some. You're a rookie and damaged goods, but you're all I got. Got to play with pain. Pain never hurt a real player. The Lord's testin' you. Keep your brain off the foot and on the game. I always played best hurtin'. Sank twenty-four against Auburn with a busted-up nose and blood for snot."

His admonition rang hollow when I went out in a sweat suit behind the gymnasium that afternoon to loosen up my leg. It was cold and clear, not a cloud in the sky, and a flock of wood ducks flew in V-formation overhead, and on the nearby street Potter Ricks's hearse led a tiny procession toward a civilian burial in the cemetery, an infelicitous contrast to the military corteges of that year like Harvey Tidwell's and Arnold Cross-wait's. There was a girls' game in the gym, and the noises of the crowd drifted my way. Four or five of the cheerleaders from Monroe City, planters' daughters, were resting on the lawn; I recognized them from school dances. "What's wrong with *you*?" one of them inquired. "You smell like a drugstore." They drew back in mock sympathy, slouching in the pluto-cratic flatland manner they had learned from their mothers, hips arched high, hands angular on each side of them. "How's Georgia?" And they laughed inanely and chattered in timeless persiflage like a skittish cluster of parakeets as I circled the field again.

The ever-present Asphalt Thomas had observed this tableau from the back door of the locker room. I knew he was there be-cause of the sound of his jangling keys. "Showin' off to the lit-tle gals," he said as I came in, "them silly spoiled rich gals with tight pussies. Better go home and soak the leg and don't drink water and sleep twelve hours."

The team went into the semifinals the next afternoon, Satur-day, against Monroe City, people overflowing into the balcony and hallways, some propped on boxes and ladders and watch-ing through the high windows outside. Amanda was in the gal-lery several rows removed from Luke, who sat in a vociferous phalanx with a few of the Legionnaires — from their florid catcalls at the visitors it was obvious that the old veterans had recently made a pilgrimage to the vinegar jugs in Son Graham's grocery — and Potter Ricks was with them too, prim and abashed at their graphic language. Even Arch was in attendance, as a member of the pep band. Merely adequate as I was, playing most of the game and scoring a paltry four points, the remaining seniors, Nigger, Term, Noggin, and Bouncer, performed with such deft and unexpected nobility that Asphalt Thomas called it the best-played game of the season. In the closing minutes one of the opposition's Notreangelo boys (they had three) whacked me across the back of my neck with his clenched fist when the referees were somewhere else. *"Kick the bastard out!"* I heard the shout from the grandstand. It was unmistakably Georgia, and I learned later that several of the surrounding onlookers had stared at her coldly for long moments, and a preacher's wife complained to Idella King, who replied in words that ring down to me now: "Well, they *should* have kicked him out." Fisk's Landing prevailed by six points and would play in that night's championship.

Dizzied, throbbing, I soaked myself in the shower. My thigh under the elastic bandage was burning hot, my foot an enormous palpitation. I asked Asphalt Thomas for a bandage on the foot. Once more he looked it over. It was crimson at the bottom now, with shriveled skin at the edges, but yellow too from the medicine. It looked awful. "Naw," he said. "The blood has to circulate. It's healin' real nice." Leon gave me three aspirins and applied more Toughskin, so that I looked like a leper.

Having defeated Monroe City and the Notreangelos, we would play in the last match for the trophy, which Fisk's Landing had not won in more than a decade, at nine that evening, four hours away. Our adversary would be the only accomplished team in the conference, Lutherville, with the best and most adept player in that league, the all-state Number 8, who averaged twenty points a game. Our game would follow the girls' finals.

High school locker rooms have likely always had a distinctive smell. The mingling scents of ammonia, analgesic, Toughskin, iodine, and Chlorox bleach (which Leon used to do the wash), as we waited for Asphalt Thomas on that distant afternoon, linger with me now, and the odor of the place is still as real to me as any I have ever known.

When everyone was ready, Asphalt Thomas got us together for a talk. He dressed up for the games, as if paying a kind of pious sartorial obeisance to the sport itself, and on this day he wore a half-buttoned wool sweater vest over a shirt and tie. "You men sucked it up out there today. I'm proud of you. See what you can do when your mind's off the snatch?" He told us to go home and relax and not eat too much. "Don't even *think* about losin', for Chrissake. Tell your mamas to cook you a small hamburger steak or somethin' like that, but no *grease*." He wanted us back an hour before the game, he added, because he was working on a special defense against Lutherville. "We once tried this against LSU," he said, "when they had a big ol' center and damned tricky guard. We got to hold down Number 8 and Number 20. But don't worry your heads till you get back. Then we'll worry. Let's whip their maggot-ridden asses. What are we — men, or mice?" As the others filed out, he took me aside. "You're on Number 8. I ain't got no choice." Number 8!

I rode around with Arch for a while, thankful that in his aversion to all forms of athletics he was immersed in one of his scowling silences, punctuated by viperous frowns. In the dying afternoon, out-of-towners were milling about the courthouse and on the main street, spilling out of the Earl Van Dorn restaurant and Crenshaw's, cruising the boulevard in their cars, admiring the houses. The green and white crepe of Lutherville abounded, and near the Elks Lodge the impromptu cheers of their assembled students filled the twilight. On the next corner I even sighted the Notreangelo who had whacked me in the neck only two hours before. He was standing there with his tough upper-flatland chums and his snarling siblings, and when he saw me in Arch's car he stared in haughty disdain.

Arch dropped me at Georgia's, whose parents had promised us something to eat. Then she and I sat on the front porch. The air felt good. It was getting on to dark now and the blow on my neck was beginning to hurt for the first time since the game; shooting stars would appear before my eyes when I turned my head, and the blistered foot was all but numb. As with my playing those earliest "Taps," I wondered why I had ever voluntarily gotten into this, for in that moment it really did not make good sense. Was there an Anglican prayer against Number 8?

"I've worried about you all day. You look funny." Kneeling before me she took off my shoe — everyone seemed to want to take off my shoe — and gently massaged my foot.

From the school across the street the crowds were congregating for the girls' game. Georgia's mother and father came out the door on the way to the gym. At Georgia's caressing touch I had felt a surprising swell at my thighs, and I hid it quickly with my hands. "Kick a little tail, boy," her father said. Her mother tentatively assessed us as Georgia rubbed the foot. "Are you going to the midnight show after the game?" she asked. "Yes'm," Georgia said, and they departed toward the school.

A lucid yellow moon was rising when Luke wheeled his truck to the curb and got out. "It's me," he said as always, and pulled up one of the chairs.

A burial tomorrow afternoon. J. W. Renfroe. In the new section.

"The boy who worked at the gin?" Georgia asked.

"That's him."

We sat there for a while in silence, absorbing the gay shouts and laughter from the schoolyard. "Look," Luke finally said. "You're as quick as he is. He puts his pants on one leg at a time, just like you."

At first I actually believed he was talking about the returning soldier J. W. Renfroe, and I looked at him quizzically.

"Number 8," he said.

In the locker room toward the end of the girls' game, Asphalt Thomas had the big portable blackboard marked with his X's and O's, and he went over them meticulously — a floating zone around the basket against the tall Number 20, man-to-man on Number 8. Then he just stood there for a second summoning his words. He often dropped scriptural references into his terse pregame speeches, sometimes claiming a large regard for religion, although I suspected he did not believe any of it to be true — had he lost it on Okinawa? "Get out there and *fight,* men! Run out on that fuckin' court with your hand in the hand of the greatest coach of all times — not me, but the head coach from Nazareth." Just before we went out he approached me again. His eyes were glistening as he sat on his haunches and whispered, "If Number 8 bends down to tie his damned shoelace, you bend down and untie it. If he goes to the commode to take a shit, you follow him and lock him in. If he spits, you spit." I sat there before him on the locker room bench. "You scared? Nervous? When I was eighteen years old," he said, "I crawled on my belly halfway across every island in the damn Pacific, scared shitless. So did Luke down there in Europe. Think about that when you get out there." We put Toughskin on our hands before leaving. As the home team, Asphalt said, we would start off with a fairly old ball. If they brought in a new, slick ball, we had more Toughskin on the bench. In the warmups, the Toughskin with the old balls made the shooting easy, as all basketball boys of that time with Toughskin on their hands and old balls to shoot know and remember.

Number 8 was swift and smart, and also a gentleman. His fakes left you breathless. "Keep away, keep away!" he would shout nervously as he moved, but he would never have whacked me across the neck. He was only an inch or so taller than I, but heavier, and two years older, and I was no match for him; nothing in my previous experience — "Taps" or Luke or the goal in the backyard or Georgia's warm affections or Idella King's iambic pentameters or Potter Ricks's vivid confidences or the loyalties of a good dog — had prepared me for this public humiliation. Why had Asphalt Thomas allowed me to play the entire game? Our team was beaten badly.

Right at the final buzzer I ran into the wall after a loose ball and just sat there on the floor. The game was done, and the Lutherville people were rushing onto the court to cut down the nets, their cheerleaders performing one somersault after another. Blood was oozing a little from my shoe and my mouth felt full of cotton. Number 8 came over and sat down next to me. "I'm whipped," he said, and extended his hand. Three years later he would be all–Southeastern Conference at the state university, and honorable mention all-American. I clipped the *Sentinel* article about our game and saved it all these years: "Kent 'Lightning' Boult, all-state standout of Lutherville, scored 28 points Saturday night and wrecked Fisk's Landing's defenses as the Bobcats defeated the valiant but injury-riddled Choctaws, 56–33, for the conference crown."

Asphalt Thomas was a man streaked with raw violence; unlike Luke, he was rampant and ungentle. Yet he had too an odd begrudging tenderness in him, the ferocity and care existing in odd and unexpected tandem. In the locker room after the game he cuffed me gently on the head. "Don't worry, kid," he said. "You're young. You *learned*. Put on some weight. Use the elbows more. Work on the jumper. Listen to Luke."

Almost everyone was gone. I was the last to leave, except of course for Leon. Georgia was waiting under a young oak on the campus. In the pungent shadows was the promise of early spring. Across the street from where we met were the familiar shanties, quiet now except for a black woman on the front stoop of one tending to a bawling infant.

"Are you all right?"

I was okay.

"You played good."

"Oh, come on."

"Well, you did. *I* think you did. After all, it was only a game."

That is what they always said when you got whipped badly, but it was not true, not in that time and that place. For years, I had an ugly burn on my thigh from the analgesic under the bandage. There is still to this day, a slight remnant of it there, and sometimes I look at it and remember those days. But, as the years pass, I do not think much about losing to Lutherville before the packed house at home. Instead, I recall how I was hurting after the game and how gentle Georgia was with my wounds, her tender touch, and the mingling pleasure and pain.

"Don't look so damned hangdog," Luke said in the cemetery the next day as we stood at the grave awaiting the retinue. "You've got plenty of time. Always expect the worst, and then you'll be pleasantly surprised. Asphalt says you're a year away, if that helps. It wasn't like it was brain surgery — or *this*. Here we are again, and we'll be back."

10

L IEUTENANT Billy Permenter's wife showed Luke a letter he had written his son on the boy's third birthday. Luke had copied it and passed it on to me at the cabin:

Pack Sok-Tong, N.K.
8 Feb

Dear Franklin,

The first time I got a letter from my daddy, also named Franklin, was when he was thousands of miles away in WWI in a terrible place from every aspect that one could look at. Now, how befitting it is that you get a letter from me in the same way. If you never have to write your own son under similar circumstances I feel that I have accomplished something and am glad to have given what little I can to this fracas.

I guess by the time I get home I'll have missed some of the best and most important parts of your life. We'll try to make it up though. We'll go fishing and go to some ball games because when you get big I want you to play halfback for the Fisk's Landing Choctaws!

I was just about to forget to mention the fact that this will serve as a birthday card. Here's hoping I'm home for the rest of them and you too. I'll bring you a Chinese sword and some foreign money for a late present. You be a good boy for Mama cause you know she's really my other big baby too.

Love always,
Daddy

His letters to Luke were assuming an increasingly despairing drift. "Morgan and I was just sitting here talking about how different your attitude gets when your points get so high," he wrote in late February. "I use to never think anything about going on line before but now everything scares me. I don't feel like I'll make it some days. A Capt. Lally from Minnesota who was really a nice fellow was killed this morning. He had just come in last week — it seems it is always new men who get hurt. New ones don't last very long."

Later that month:

> I'm sitting here concerned over Morgan, he's out on arsenal outpost in charge of laying tactical wire, blundering around the damned mines. They are all of 150 yds. from the Chinese. They had 6 casualties last night. Tonite is supposed to be his last night out there. I guess no one knows how close people get in places like this especially when we have so many things in common like Morgan and I — Fisk's Landing, school, etc. He always lets me read his mail when I don't get a letter and vice-versa. We are getting a blow tomorrow. Our Company comm. is getting transferred. He is pretty hard, but that's normal to be rough here.
>
> On that other night Morgan was out laying the wire, three of the six men were killed, three were Guard men from town — Williamson, Craig, and Hammond. It's horrible, horrible and all in one night's action. It's too much to take. What do I write the families?

In the weeks that followed, these letters to Luke grew into what seemed to be anguished prayers for survival; with my memories of Billy Permenter from his seventh-grade science class, I wanted Luke to stop showing them to me.

> Tried to write Dorothy last night but did not have strength to pick up a pen . . . I am so homesick I can't hardly make it tonite, and am getting worse all the time. What can you do though? I am at a complete loss for words to express this terrible feeling. I pray a lot, but I know it don't do any good . . .

F Co. in nine days lost all but 2 officers and 62 men. A capt.
and I went back to the morgue later. Bodies everywhere, on lit-
ters, in bags. Blown out faces, disconnected arms and legs.
Bodies already decomposing. I've seen this shit before, but I
don't know how much more of it I can stand . . .

A sergeant had his dick blown off, never saw so much
blood. I've always heard of that but never saw it til now.

The other night I was sitting on my helmet eating, about
half asleep, when I noticed my hand covered with somebody's
dried blood. I remember how Mama used to say wash your
hands before you eat. But I went on eating because Mama
wasn't there and besides I figured I could wash them later.

As with the close string of casualties back in July, everyone
was stunned and saddened by the deaths of Williamson, Craig,
and Hammond on the same night. Amanda had graduated
from Marshall Consolidated High School with Williamson,
and Luke knew Craig and Hammond well — hill-country boys
— and for days he was disconsolate, even more so than he had
been in the summer. He kept talking about Billy Permenter.
"I'm really worried about Billy. I know how he feels. He thinks
his luck's run out. For God's sake, I hope not."

Later that week he asked, "How are you and Georgia?"

I wanted to talk with him about her — about how much I
loved her, about sex.

"Georgia told Amanda," he said, "but Amanda knew anyway. So did I."

How did *they* know?

"By the eyes. Amanda and Georgia talk about these things.
Just don't tell another soul, and be good to her, and be careful."

He fell silent. I knew him so well I could tell he too wanted to
talk some more. "I love Amanda," he said, "Like you do Georgia. She saved my life. I've never known anybody like Amanda.
Durley damned near destroyed her. We want to get married,
but we can't. We want to have a kid. It's a hard situation. You
understand, don't you?"

I understood. Georgia and I discussed them all the time. They had brought us purposefully into their trust — us and Doc Patterson and Shotgun. They were more cautious now than ever. In Fisk's Landing they were never alone together in public, and when they traveled somewhere they did so very circumspectly. I understood their relationship, how much they loved and needed each other. He had given me a key to his front gate so I could come out to his cabin any time I wished. Late one Saturday afternoon Georgia and Dusty and I had gone there. I unlocked the gate and drove up the long winding driveway. Luke's truck was parked there and, yards away, almost entirely obscured in a dense grove of trees, Amanda's Buick. When we walked around the cabin toward the front there were rustling sounds from the bedroom, a woman's cries, strange little implorings. Georgia looked at me knowingly, and we gathered up the dog and got away as discreetly as we could.

It was not easy for them, and Georgia and I prayed for some happy resolution to their terrible dilemma. But what would it be? Officially Durley was, of course, only missing. Although the several witnesses, and Billy Permenter also, had surmised that on that night no one except the two badly wounded men had survived the severe mortar and cannonade, there would be no official decree confirming this, no testament or scroll or declaration. And because of that, Luke and Amanda were illicit. Luke had even done some guarded research in New Orleans on the possibility of military precedent in such a complicated matter. At the least there could be no solution until the war ended, if indeed it ever did.

The snow and ice had long since vanished. There was the sudden fragrance of new grass, of fresh, chaste buds and the awakening vines, swift sweet odors that had outwitted the implacable winter.

The baseball team had begun its practices, and from the field behind the school rose the reassuring echoes of bat on ball, ball on glove, the birdlike chatter of the infielders. We had only two more basketball games; the crippled seniors had not yet healed, and in the next-to-last game of the year even I scored sixteen points in a return match at home against the Shuqualak Confederates. Arch and I were perfecting our duet for the state competition, still meeting Amanda in the early hours in the auditorium. On some mornings Lank Hemphill, who said he woke with the foot soldier's instinct at 5:00 A.M., would take the town bus to the schoolhouse and sit in the back row of the auditorium, where he would listen for a while to our music before nodding off to sleep again. Amanda was pallid and nervous, with a strange, haunted expression, much as she had been that night she gave me her cryptic message for Luke. Sometimes her fingers stumbled on the keys.

"Are you feeling all right, Amanda?" I asked one morning when Arch left for the band room to get some valve oil.

She looked up from the piano bench. Her fingers rested lightly on the keyboard. She was wearing her hair longer; a wisp of it had fallen over her eyes, and the fresh, early sun streamed through the windows and danced across her sweet, lovely face. I can close my eyes and see her there before her piano now, pale and splendid.

Her answer was a sigh, as palpable as the softest murmur. "Oh yes, Swayze. Yes, I'm fine. We're going to win a Superior."

Often our weekly school assemblies in the second semester consisted of variety acts, some leading toward hazard and calamity. Now, less than a week before the state band competition, our practice performance of the trumpet duet before the student body made a mockery of Amanda's sanguine prophecy. We were preceded by a veterinarian with two cocker spaniels performing tricks. "I can't believe it," Arch complained as we waited backstage. "We have to follow a damned smart *dog* act. And my valves ain't laying right." We went out and Amanda began the piano accompaniment; we were no more than a minute into the number when the trouble struck. Arch had indeed been having difficulty with the valves on his new trumpet, and the middle one suddenly became hopelessly stuck; while I played the tuneless supportive second part, he stood there feverishly trying to get the valve in working order again. The audience began to laugh and hoot. Never a well-received figure in that public institution of wisdom, Arch was now at the mercy of regimented derision. The more he pulled at the valve, the more flushed his features grew, and then sweat began to stream down his forehead. It was a fairly lengthy number, and this became a marathon of futility. "What's wrong, Arch?" the captain of the football team shouted from his appointed place in the front row. "We thought you were an *expert*!" I suppose Amanda and I could have stopped and tried again when his horn was working, but frankly I was secretly enjoying his chagrin, and Amanda was so embarrassed as she sat at the piano below that she continued to play her accompaniment, stiffly and perfunctorily as by rote. Finally, near the end of the composition, he was playing again. "Just in time, Arch!" another of the observers exclaimed, and we exited to a din of laughter and flamboyant catcalls. Backstage again, Arch unleashed a volley of thundering expletives and seemed about to smash his expensive instrument against a table before he came to his senses.

"*You!*" he said. "You weren't any help."

"Poor Arch," Amanda said when she joined us. "Please don't let that happen next week."

"I did it on purpose!" he peevishly replied, and packed his trumpet in the case and departed into the corridor.

"Butterfingers!" someone shouted as he regally made his way down the hall.

I am aware that my story reveals a sturdy trace of paranoia — the warts and rash and angst at the age of ten, an overwrought memory of the beating by Durley Godbold behind the Darnell house, the dread of the open grave and of the mother, the perverse predilection for the Ricks Funeral Home, the omens and presentiments and mystical sorrows at the playing of echo, the nervous delirium over getting into the ball games, the awful fear of blood — and along with all this a proclivity for the desolate, the insufferable, the troubling. The list is already lengthy, yet I must describe the worst and most blatant juncture of all, which was more or less of my own doing, although I was not nearly smart enough to know it then.

Georgia and I had always been so close, echoes of each other — sisterhood, brotherhood, friendship. Had we become *too* close, like siblings? In the crazy skittishness of love, especially at that age, we began to have arguments. Often they did not amount to much of anything, yet they had to be symptomatic of something more important than either of us could understand. What an odd pair we were! Our feelings, I could see in later years, were becoming too deep to manage, the touch of skin and the laughter and silences, the lingering moments together, the cresting pleasures and lapsing contentments and little mutual conceits. We were too young to marry, certainly to have a child, yet there had to be a more subtle affirmation. Where was it? It was destined that we would somehow test ourselves and arrive at a painful crossroads. Did love itself, no matter how deep, germinate its own destruction — in self-doubt and insecurity and fear? Would distance reveal to us who we were? It was our shared emotions, and the sunsets, the elements, the people, the funerals, the sensuality, the growing up, the friendship with Luke and Amanda, the flatland itself, which shaped and molded our love — a relationship, it is plain to me now, that was foreshadowed by death.

I had never seen her more beautiful. She began to obsess me, and I felt myself increasingly jealous of the older boys growing more and more attentive to her. Their brazen glances in the hallways, their whispered confidences, the sight of her casually bantering with them in the schoolyard or auditorium angered and repelled me. I fell to formless jealousy, gradual yet relentless, to the fruitless frustrations that accrue with love, and I did not for a moment comprehend it. "But I wasn't *doing* anything," she would say. "Just joking around. I can't be with you *all* the time, can I?" One night she did not want to make love. "I'm just not in the mood right now," she said. "Girls are that way sometimes. Let's just talk." Talk about what? "About where we're going to college. Or basketball. Or Leroy Godbold. Let's talk about the Civil War — what'd you say the causes were?" It was no longer all velvet dresses and love and rides with Dusty.

Her mother was giving her trouble about everything again — the way she dressed and talked, her grades, her sloppy bedroom. She plunged into vague little pouts and defiances. I was trying to get her to stop smoking. She smoked only about six or seven Kools a day, but for some reason it had started to bother me. "You want me to be perfect?" she asked. "Can't I at least have a *minor* vice?"

We had a frivolous spat over schoolwork, perhaps the paper on the funeral home, and she began talking about Amanda, how much she liked her. Something seized me, something mean and crass and demented.

"I saw her naked."

"You *what*?"

"I saw her naked. I saw her . . ." and pointed cruelly at my chest.

"I don't believe you."

"Want me to describe her?"

She looked straight at me in shame. "You love her, don't you?"

"I love her. I *fucked* her. She wanted me to."

"No you didn't! *When*?"

"After Durley left. Before Luke. She was lonesome."

Georgia was bitterly silent. She stared down at her hands folded in her lap. For the longest time she said nothing. "I want to go home," she finally said. "Take me home." Why, after all of it, did I want to hurt Georgia? And with such a vicious lie? The whole next day I avoided her.

This was the first week of March. We had had our final basketball practice of the year — the last game would be the following evening — and I had remained behind in the gymnasium after the others to shoot some baskets. I was monstrously ashamed of myself, and was trying to summon the nerve to apologize to her. As always since boyhood I was using the lonesome ritual, the swish of ball in net, the bounces and solitary silences, to ponder things. I had to go see her, and do so quickly. Outside, in a gentle orange twilight, were the shouts and curses of a group of the older boys, the seniors from the football team engaged in an aggressive and disorganized game of touch. I went into the boys' locker room to take a shower.

I was alone in one of the shower stalls. In the adjacent stall, divided from mine by a tall concrete wall with an open space just below the ceiling, I could hear three of the football players talking above the hiss of the water. One of them had been the captain of that year's team. (To this day I hold him in such contempt that I can hardly bear to write his name.) *Teddy Powers* was the son of the owner of the furniture store, a sturdy, handsome young man, dark-featured and of medium height and distinguished in the locker room for the size of his penis. He was destined to succeed as an outstanding player at the esteemed state university, where football was, if not a theology, then a sociological imperative. He was nicknamed "Snake." Although he made terrible grades, he was president of the senior class and an influence in the student government; he was rough and breezy, cheerful and self-assured.

Unlike at many other schools in our isolated region, our football players rarely played basketball or baseball. They were not aware that I was in the next stall, and I was not listening with great attention to their conversation, which would have been, at best, vacuous, but merely thoughtlessly absorbing it along with the hot water from the shower before I went, ashamed, to Georgia's.

The football captain was talking about a good-looking girl whom he had liked for a long time and was going to "start takin' out steady."

"I don't like her much," another one said. "She's a little funny. I'm a tit man myself. But I sure like her ass."

Zamma Bailey would have blushed.

"Boy, that's *pussy*," one boy said.

"I'd like some of that too."

"I been callin' her every night for a few days now," the captain was saying. "She likes it. Called her late last night and told her I'd take her to the senior dance, that it's a real honor."

"And what does *she* say?"

"That she don't care, but I think she does."

"What makes you think so, Ted?"

"Because she called *me* back last night, said she might want to go to the dance with me after all."

"That's pussy talkin'."

"Well, what're you gonna do, Ted?"

"What do you *think*? Take her out. She likes me. I can tell. And she knows it."

"What about Swayze?"

"What about him? You think *he's* any worry? He plays in the band and rides the pines in *basketball*? Plays the horn all the time with that mullet Arch Kidd? She don't belong in the same room with him."

"They been together a long time."

"Ten minutes by herself with me and she'll forget he ever lived. And she knows that too. All I got to do is slip this dick into her cunt and she'll forget everything she knew."

They had left the stall now and were dressing. I remained in my own shower so long that the tips of my fingers were shriveled. Finally, when the three of them departed, I came out, dry-mouthed, brutalized not so much by the words about me, although they stung, but by the ones about her, the obscene insinuations, the confidences of betrayal, such that to this day I recall them as in an awful hallucination.

The manager, Leon, came into the locker room. "What's wrong with *you*? Look like you been hit on the head with a skillet. How's the bad foot? Need some Toughskin? How about some Atomic Balm?"

I walked home, detouring an entire block off the boulevard to avoid her house. Fearful images flashed before me. It was like looking at my father in his coffin. The awakening trees along the boulevard taunted me, the houses, the moon and grass and clouds. I retreated to my room, locked the door, turned out the lights, and crept under the sheets as I had when I was ten. Dusty lay at my side and gazed at me, put his head on my naked shoulder. Only an hour before I had been casually tossing a round ball at a metal hole. It had happened so quickly. Was this sudden unforeseen wretchedness an invention of artless inexperience, I ask myself as a grown man now, of dumb righteousness before the heart's illusions, of indulgent conceit? No. There was nothing callow to this pain.

In the shadows of the room my thoughts ran wild, as if I were falling helplessly into the night — conjurings of the football captain in a parked sedan with her, his fingers on her, his lips touching hers. Why had I tried to hurt her? Where lay the sources of my cruelty? Had I taken her for granted? Was there something of the heart I was ignorant of? Was he lying to his friends? Or had I imagined all of it?

It was late when I slipped into the kitchen and called her number.

"Hello." The word itself was a threat.

"I have to see you."

"What's wrong? You sound sick, like the other night. Are you sick, Swayze?"

"Meet me in the alley behind your house."

"Now?"

Thin filmy clouds were in the sky and a light rain was falling when she came out the back door of the darkened porch. I waited for her.

"Swayze, what *is* it? I'm very mad at you."

Anyone who deemed the distresses of adolescence mere ancillaries to mature existence would have judged this midnight consultation an expression of the truculent mores of American youth in that time an eternity ago: football captains' conversations in locker rooms, senior dances, devious nocturnal calls, troth. Let him measure that moment as he may, for we were what we were.

"I lied about Amanda."

"Why did you lie?"

"I don't know."

"I don't think you lied."

"I did. It was a terrible lie."

"I love Amanda. You really hurt me. I don't understand you. What would Luke think?"

This was the worst blow. Luke. Stricken with guilt, I stood before her and gave release to the accumulated tensions and anxieties, my accusations pouring forth about the football captain and the other older boys in a nearly biblical torment, an embittered soliloquy that left me numb and breathless.

"Why didn't you tell me?" I was whispering.

For a moment she said nothing. I waited. "Well, what do you *want* me to do? Hang up?"

"And you've been calling *him*."

"I have not."

"Now you're lying."

"Then what if I am? He's nice to me. It's not my fault, Swayze. I don't understand *myself*. I'm sorry. I can't help it if I like him a little, too."

In that moment, as if someone foreign to me were doing it, I slapped her as hard as I could across the face.

She bowed her head, then lifted it and gazed at me with glazed eyes. Her hair, moist from the rain, had fallen over her forehead. The little scar at the corner of her mouth was livid from the blow. In the instant I was overcome with a disgrace and love so powerful I thought I would die.

She did not cringe or cry. In fact she slapped me back, and just as hard.

We faced each other in the darkness. "*Georgia*. What's happening?"

"Go to hell," she said, and turned and left me there alone.

I arrived at school early the next morning to ask Mrs. King if I could change places and sit in the rear of her class.

She glanced up from her desk and asked why.

"I'd feel better."

She had a strange, knowing smirk, as if she had dealt with such things countless times in the decades with her half-formed charges. "Very well, then." I withdrew among Arch Kidd and the other back-of-the-room renegades.

Dreadful things come quickly, I was learning: they merely happen and are dreamlike in the unfolding. I lay curled in bed late at night waiting for the telephone. It never rang. There was only silence. It was far worse than the precocious melancholia at age ten — that childhood's despair was nameless, but this one had a source. In the febrile nights I would get up a dozen times and go to the kitchen for a glass of water just to be *doing* something, for movement helped, and for the same reason I would shift to different positions dozens of times in my bed. I talked to myself, and to my dog. "It's not that bad, Dusty." In an effort to change my mood I would recite poems from Mrs.

King's class, or make up a basketball game in which I outscored Number 8, or think of the crazy things Arch Kidd had done, or try to conceive of myself as a ridiculous character in one of the radio soap operas for the lovelorn, and there would come a few moments of calm and security, an odd kind of lull, or truce, the anesthesia at last working on the ravaged patient. Then suddenly I would feel several mighty pumps in my deepest heart, not so much physical pain as an abstract palpitating awareness, the body's return to reality, as if the brain were sending a short-circuited reminder to the heart itself: "Yes, it *is* this bad."

The worst was having her close at hand during the rituals of school, the sight of her, the sound of her voice in class, and seeing the vistas and landmarks where we had been together — certain trees on the boulevard, the courthouse, the Rex Theater, the hills overlooking the flatland, street corners, front porches, the Sears store, the cemetery, the Indian mounds, the country club, the petrified forest, the library — and always on the radio were the strains of the popular tunes we knew. I was entrapped in pride and the cadences of youth.

Then it began. One day at the noon recess I looked across the school ground to the corner of the lawn where the older students gathered. She was sitting next to him on one of the wooden benches. I would see her walking with him in the hallways, and then riding alone with him in his car. I was sleepless with my images of them, ravaged by thoughts of them in the nights, her nude breasts and erect nipples before him, her kisses, her arched and trembling thighs, how he would hurt her as he split deeply into her. I went to the church and prayed in penance, as I had as a child. Lord, do not let him hurt her.

In the empty nighttimes the fantasies of retribution saved me. I would engage a physician, perhaps Luke's friend (or why not Potter Ricks?), and with hired roughnecks abduct the football captain in the night, whisking him to a secluded domicile with laboratory facilities out in the piney hills. He would be generously anesthetized. Then, one day at a time, the doctor, or

Potter, would proceed with the amputations — first the little toe of the left foot, then the other toes, then on to the fingers. Next the ears and the tongue, and a brass ring thrust in the nose. The left arm to the elbow, followed by the right. The right leg to the kneecap, then the left. We would leave him with one eye. Because by now he had no teeth, he would be fed intravenously. Then we would force down a gallon or so of castor oil before putting him in a small straw basket and returning him to the town one midnight. By now he would not be smelling very good. At the school ground we would attach the straw basket to the chain on the flagpole and lift it to the top. The next morning as the students began to gather, the janitor would spot the basket on the flagpole. A large crowd would congregate as he lowered the tiny receptacle. People would bend down and look. *"Eeeewh!"* someone would say. "It looks like Teddy Powers!"

Variations on this satisfying dismemberment would get me through the insomniac hours: we might deposit him instead on the altar of the Baptist church, the meat counter of the Jitney, or on his own front porch, or Georgia's. But what about *her?* When I saw them together from a back row at the Saturday-night show, I prayed too for her unhappiness.

"Nothing's worth the way *you're* acting," my mother said. *"She's* certainly not worth it."

Then I had an encounter with Georgia's mother. I was walking down the boulevard when her car pulled to the curb. She motioned to me, and I approached the opened window.

"I was just about to telephone you," she said.

What about?

"She told me you slapped her," she said sternly, looking out as always with her narrow, inquisitive eyes. In a curious way she reminded me in that instant of Mr. Leroy Godbold, questioning me about the dogs when I was twelve. She even *looked* a little like Mr. Godbold. "I got it out of her. Is it true?"

Yes, ma'am, it was true.

"You're no gentleman, then. I hope her daddy doesn't find out. I'd be afraid to tell him. I never want to lay eyes on you again, young man."

There were black circles under my eyes, and I was losing weight. "You look bad, bad," Arch said. "I ain't seen you look this bad. Maybe you need a *mental* farm." I spent long hours at his house watching the snowy television. Or I picked the lonely places, shooting hundreds of baskets in the backyard, walking with Dusty in the woods at Luke's. I began to see that everyone in the town seemed troubled — all you had to do was look around: Amanda and Luke, Potter Ricks, Georgia, Georgia's parents, my mother, the Godbolds, a warehouse of tormented souls. Only the boys we had buried were no longer unhappy.

And then I began to perceive that nothing *lasts*. From all the burials and now this, I slowly came to harbor a kind of dim and private vision of the town that I believed no one else had ever had in the whole world, apparent only to me at not quite seventeen, too callow to know that whatever in any instant one hopes or fears or suffers has been felt by someone else somewhere. It is a beautiful day of, shall we say, early springtime, the air is soft and serene, all the people seem happy in their myriad doings — conducting their businesses, going to church, entertaining their children, dressing for a wedding, watching a ball game, drinking coffee in the cafes, visiting their neighbors, and talking, talking — the human commerce! There is so much to do; everyone is so *active*. Who cares that time is so arrogantly passing? That the sweet, placid, lovely cancer of the days is gnawing away at time and the earth? They are busy also at the hospital and at the Ricks Funeral Home, and in front of the nursing home the old people are waiting and waiting in the sunshine, and it is a pretty day too at the Fisk's Landing cemetery, where the dead of the town outnumber the living.

> There pass the careless people
> That call their souls their own;

Here by the road I loiter,
How idle and alone.

"It's pride," Luke said, "both of you. You're stubborn, and it's both your faults. It's in your blood and probably can't be helped for a while." It was only American adolescence, I perceive now, circa 1950s, and of course Luke knew it then. Yet it was more than that too: it was complex love and sex at an innocent age, in an innocent time.

I was heartbroken, I said, and confused. It had happened so fast, like an *explosion*.

"Things like that always happen fast," he said.

I told him of the arguments, my jealousies. How did I let her down? What was I not giving her? Had I failed to consider her needs? What *were* her needs? Why did she suddenly want to be with the football captain?

"Oh, it's not really the ballplayer, I don't think. Sounds to me like she's *trying* herself. And you're trying yourself too. It ain't unhealthy. Arguments? They're symbols. I say give her a little room right now."

"But I lied to her about something. And then I hit her."

"Not with your *fist*?"

"I slapped her."

"That's something you don't do. You don't slap Georgia, or any girl. Knowing her, I bet she slapped you back." He was smiling a little, however, suppressing some tender emotion I could not in that moment understand. "Well, write her a letter. Apologize for hitting her. And don't do anything *irreversible*." The next morning I left a penitent little note on her school desk, but she never replied.

We had our first burial since the snow. It was a pale afternoon of high March winds. The last wood smoke of winter drifted from the chimneys on Blackberry Hill, lifted in wispy spirals into the tossing sky.

I was at my station in the trees at the summit of the new section looking down at the service. Suddenly a doe appeared, perhaps twenty yards from me in the woods, and stood gazing at me. Holding my breath so as not to frighten her away, I admired her smooth tawny coat, the musk of her, her gentle silhouette, her quivering muscles. We stared at each other, until all at once the volleys sounded from the grave below, and her whole body became momentarily taut before she swiftly leapt and disappeared into the underbrush. I heard the dead leaves rustling as she fled, then silence. She was as irretrievably gone from me now as Georgia was, and I turned to wait for Arch's notes.

The day arrived for our duet in the state competition. Amanda and Arch and I drove to the capital city. The performances were in the sprawling old school across from the capitol building, which loomed grandly before us on its high green terrace like a picture postcard.

After a long wait we played our number for the judges, then while Arch lingered, wanting to hear the decision, Amanda and I went outside to a verdant park nestled in some elms and hickories and sat on a stone bannister. She looked handsome in her white linen dress, her legs resting lightly above the grass, her shoes falling one by one onto the ground. She was contemplating the great gray capitol dome with the spreading golden eagle on top and the immense monolith memorializing the Women of the Confederacy on the greensward and the wisteria wrapping the walls and fences around us. Several brave sparrows darted nearby, and a pair of robins preened in a birdbath.

"You did well," she was saying. "I'm glad Arch's valve didn't stick."

As she glanced at me with her grave gray eyes, I remembered the days years ago when we sat in the wrought-iron chairs in my front lawn and assessed the new postwar cars on the boulevard, and talked about piano lessons, and the afternoon she told me she was getting married, and the wedding in the little church in Marshall, and the new house in Tara Estates. Sitting there with her now, I silently blushed to recall for the hundredth time my evil, impetuous slander to Georgia.

"We're thinking a little about leaving town," she said.

A vacation?

"No, I mean *leaving*."

I did not need to ask why.

"Maybe Atlanta. He can get a job. Sell his interest in the store. And I've got the piano. You can do anything with the piano, as I told you. I've always wanted to live in a wonderful big city like Atlanta. On the other hand" — she paused — "Mr. Godbold's gone to Washington again — to the Pentagon. I've been so nervous about our . . . situation."

We sat there contemplating this. She touched me warmly on the shoulder. "She'll come back to you."

I tried to reply.

"Girls that age have to, well, *try* themselves," she said in a rush. "I wish I had. I don't know what the problem is, and I don't *want* to know, unless you want to tell me. These things happen. In a curious way it doesn't have anything to do with you. It's just her. I know it doesn't help to say you're young, but you *are*, both of you. She'll come back someday when you least expect it. A year. Two years."

I don't want her back, I said, and meant it.

"Don't be silly. Just take care of yourself."

A flurry of young Catholic nuns carrying clarinet cases floated by, toward the school building, and from the distance a vehement phalanx of legislators emerged from the statehouse onto the sloping green grounds.

There were emphatic footsteps behind us. We turned to see Arch, oiled hair awry.

"Superior!" he shouted. "The judges said I'm the hottest trumpet there is. We did it again!"

Had I misunderstood? Had he actually said *we*? The three of us stood in a semicircle, like ballplayers in a huddle, and grasped hands in the airy sunshine.

Luke appeared during band practice the next afternoon to inform Arch and me of Corporal Lamar Teaster's funeral two days hence. Lamar Teaster was the one who had been killed the week of the snowstorm; he had arrived in Fisk's Landing via New Jersey and Monroe City the previous midnight. Because of his citation for heroism and his subsequent posthumous Silver Star, the military had decided to honor him with interment in the national cemetery in the Civil War battleground of our big river town fifty miles south. We would leave with Luke and the Legionnaires early that morning and miss the whole day of class.

I was happy to be away from the town, even if for a few hours. Since von Schulte's hybrid omnibus had long before split in two, Luke and the veterans had conscripted Coach Asphalt Thomas to drive them to the battleground in the school's crimson and white sports bus. I had never seen Asphalt in a suit and tie, and with these and his blue Veterans of Foreign Wars cap he looked remarkably respectable, as did Sarge and the others; their own shiny suits were more carefully pressed than usual for these special rites, and, except for Roach, who had no hair, they had applied even more greasy tonic than usual to their heads. As we rode through the dwindling flatland, the aromas of drugstore colognes rose en masse above them.

Lank Hemphill was sitting next to me on one of the rear seats. He touched me inquiringly with his artificial limb. "Say, how come Georgia's taken up with the *football* player?"

The drawled words penetrated like needles. Spasms of homicidal jealousy swirled once more in my midriff. I closed my eyes and blanched. When I opened them again the world was shadowy. "You don't look too good," he said. "Can I get you somethin'?" I shook my head. There was nothing to be gotten anyway, unless you counted the Legionnaires' fifths of hard spirits hidden in a cardboard box under one of the empty seats for later.

We were half an hour ahead of the funeral procession as Asphalt drove us into the outskirts of the river town. I darkly recalled these very thoroughfares twinkling happily with Christmas lights on that rainy afternoon with Georgia, and when we passed Alamo Plaza Motor Court and I saw bungalow number 7, I was wrenched with a bleak, throbbing desolation.

We drove on to the cemetery, where we unpacked our things. The whole earth was enraptured with springtime's promise, the rich bluffs in the bright, late morning's sun, the robins and cardinals and thrushes descending everywhere from the giant old trees, and since I had won the toss, I climbed to the top of the eminence and walked among the stones marking the graves of those boys who had died there ninety-odd years before. "In a civil war," a plaque bearing the words of a writer said, "the firing line is invisible; it passes through the hearts of men." Most of the stones were inscribed only with numbers, and on the highest ground I paused and read from another scroll: *Four score and seven years ago our fathers brought forth on this continent . . .* The Spanish moss shimmered like silken threads, and stretching away below as far as I could see were the rows of white crosses, thousands of them, and beyond them the great river itself, twisting and curving upon its own flagrant contours to the farthest horizon, brown and lonesome and seeming hardly to move at all. Standing there I remembered the official citation Potter Ricks had read Luke and me earlier that week for Lamar Teaster's valor under fire. It stated that Corporal Teaster had reflected "the highest credit upon himself, the infantry, and the United States Army."

And now, far below, his cortege was entering these magnificent grounds.

You could think what you wished about Arch Kidd. Given

his misanthropic cynicisms, his mulish scowls and phobias, his silly preoccupations with secreting time bombs and taunting Mrs. Idella King, his banal silences and rages and lassitudes, I pondered in later life why I with my own unfortunate paranoic despairs was ever in his company at all. Although I had known him since infancy, sometimes I would look at him in those days and wonder who on earth he really was, from what peculiar sources he had indeed evolved. Yet in those months his "Taps" had grown more and more proud and haunting and true. At the grave and in echo, his notes had become more beautiful and certain, and I understand now that this had little to do with the trumpeter himself (for at times any of the earth's sinners might be lyrical and exultant), but with the simple fact that with his trumpet he too was a hero — that, unlike me and most of the others, there was one thing he could do well, and he did this one thing with consummate grace and fulfillment, and in this way he, like Potter Ricks, somehow triumphed over God. His "Taps" in that long-ago March in the grand national cemetery was the finest I ever heard, seeming to rise full-blown like a song from the new earth, sweeping across the sea of white crosses, reaching out to caress the clouds at the edge of the sky, hovering sweetly over the immemorial river itself as it lingered and was lost.

I answered with mine, and when I had finished I tarried for a moment at the crest of the bluffs, just absorbing everything — recalling Lieutenant Commander Harvey Tidwell's burial in the distant summer back home, my venerable and trusted magnolia, the silvery navy jets in V-formation, Georgia in stocking feet and linen dress, the vicar's prayers tossed up to the two of us, alone there together in the sibilant world.

11

ALMOST OVERNIGHT the earth had come alive. The pears rushed out, the redbud, the azaleas and dogwoods, and with the warmer days, the trees and shrubs along the boulevard brought forth their supple leaves. The flatland too was cataclysmic with change. The fresh aroma of its fecund ground, newly broken, rose and mingled with the honeyed essence of grass. The very world around us was voluptuous and impassioned.

The day after the hero's burial, Arch and I were sitting on his front porch in the late afternoon watching the cars go by. The house was empty and Arch was chain-smoking his Camels, carefully depositing each butt into a large, long-necked urn. We were listening to one jazz record after another through the open door to the parlor. There had been a baseball game that afternoon, and the bus with the team from Shuqualak churned up the boulevard on its way out of town. Luke and Asphalt Thomas passed in Luke's pickup truck piled high with sacks of fertilizer. Seconds later an ominous gray sedan sped by. It was the football captain's car, and Georgia was close by his side. Where were they going?

"Let her have the son of a bitch," Arch said.

I had not spoken to her in a long time. When I first noticed the captain's senior ring on her finger, wrapped in layers of adhesive tape to make it fit, I closed my eyes and tried to obliterate her from my life. Lately she had tried to be friendly, in a bizarre but considered way. I avoided her. When I saw them again one night on their way to the senior dance, it did not seem to hurt as much as it once might have. I suppose it should have been funny. But it was very strange, like a death. The pain was slowly dwindling, day by day, like a healing wound, and with it something else was leaving me too, or so I told myself. The answer to this lie came in the recurrence of those strange palpitations of my heart, pumping dull grief and ache and hurt, reminding me all over again of my own rending desperation and shame. What, God, would I ever do without Georgia? In spite and loss, I was tempted to visit the eighteen-year-old prostitute near Lutherville whom I had heard the older boys talking about, but I never did.

That Monday I mustered my resolve and went to her desk in Mrs. King's classroom.

"Georgia?" The name itself sounded distant and contrived.

She looked up at me coolly. "Yes?"

I needed her notes on the funerals.

"Why?"

I was about to start writing the paper.

"Want any help?"

"I don't need it."

"Okay then."

The next morning she came back to my desk with two spiral notebooks. Without looking at me she thrust them out.

"Thank you," I said.

"You're very welcome."

For the first time there was talk of a military truce on the scorched peninsula across the world.

But at the funeral home Potter Ricks was expecting the arrival any day in Monroe City of Privates Craig, Hammond, and

Williamson, trapped and blasted in the same action in early February, the one Billy Permenter had written Luke about. Would they be shipped down together, or separately? If together, there were sure to be logistical problems.

One afternoon after school that week I went to the post office to mail a letter to the state university asking for its course catalogues. From the back drive of the funeral home next door, I saw Potter and Woodrow bending low over the engine of the hearse. I approached them through the tiny lawn.

"It's on its last legs, I'm afraid," Potter said. "We've gotten real service out of it. Since, what, '38? No telling how many miles it's given up. It ran out of numbers."

The hood was raised high and Woodrow's head was almost obscured in the vitals of the motor. "Transmission's shaky," he said, his words coming out metallic and indistinct as if from a distant chamber.

"It's the last thing we need. And I just bought a new set of tires. Do you think it's terminal?"

"Probably another month in it, maybe six weeks."

"Well, that's that. We'll have to order a new one."

"No choice in the matter," Woodrow said, as he withdrew his head and closed the hood, then wiped the grease from his hands with a towel. "I think we got the money."

We stood there in the warm hazy sunlight. Amanda was walking up the steps of the post office and waved toward us. The 4:30 Greyhound to Memphis moved clumsily up the main street, and I thought of the swarthy corporal from Ohio that night last autumn, hastening resolutely toward the bus station with Potter Ricks on his heels. As Amanda emerged from the P.O. and drove away, Mr. Leroy Godbold parked and entered. They had barely missed each other.

They were still awaiting the telegram on the shipments from the east, Potter was saying. You know the *army*, he complained. And it could not come at a less propitious time. Luke, Lank

Hemphill, Sarge Jennings, and the other old veterans were attending the state American Legion convention on the coast. Nor did the weather seem promising. He gestured westward, to the far horizon of the flatland, where an ugly bank of cumulus was forming, dark and massy and piled high like a range of mountains.

A vaguely familiar figure was walking down the drive in our direction, a slight woman with graying hair, wearing a frayed gingham dress and bright new tennis shoes. There were two paper sacks in her arms. I recognized her as the mother of Oscar Goodloe, the first boy we had buried nearly eleven months before.

"Hello, Mrs. Goodloe," Potter said.

"Hello." Her voice was as wan as I remembered it, but not nearly so dolorous, and there was a new glow in her cheeks.

"I see you've been shopping again."

"Yes, sir."

"What do you have today?"

She set one of the sacks on the concrete drive and reached into the other, happily withdrawing a gleaming new apparatus.

"An electric can opener?"

"Yes, sir. Ain't it nice?"

"And what else?"

She reached deftly into the second sack. Out came another impressive gadget.

"It's nice too," Potter said. "What is it?"

"Electric eggbeater," she said, and held it forth in the sunlight. It might have been the Hope diamond.

"You'll have the finest kitchen on Ruston Hill, Mrs. Goodloe." She stood there, gray and fragile and proud as she absorbed the accolade. "May we drive you home?"

No, thank you, she said. She needed to get to Sears before it closed for the day.

"Well, well," Potter said as we watched her drift away toward the main street again. There had been no record of her son's birth date, he explained to me, and she herself could not remember. "She's illiterate, you know." He had helped her get the $10,000 from the army on a sleeper clause. She had finally received the money ten days ago. "Since then, heaven knows what she's bought — a television, an electric carving knife, a sewing machine, a refrigerator, a washer and dryer, a bird dog, tennis shoes, dentures for her husband."

"And half of Woolworth's," Woodrow said.

"And half of Woolworth's," Potter repeated.

You can find it in the records at the Fisk County Courthouse. Beginning that midnight, the fifth-heaviest rainfall in the state's history descended on the town. For more than an hour there was only the lightning, deep swift yellow throbs across the whole sweep of the horizon. When the raindrops finally came they were as round as bullets. By early evening the flooded river had crept up to the gin, the railroad tracks, and the old train depot. At the shacks on stilts in the Bottoms and on New Africa Road, the water rose above the porches and into the rooms, and water moccasins were discovered in the low-lying places as far away as the library and the boulevard. The highway to the west was temporarily closed; so were the schools.

The following afternoon Arch and I were watching a movie in the Rex Theater when suddenly all the lights went out and there was a heavy rattling on the roof as if thousands of jagged rocks were falling from the heavens. We rushed to the front entrance to see hailstones as big as hens' eggs plummeting onto the main street, and winds so high that riderless bicycles and several frightened rats from the sewers were blowing down the sidewalk. And then the rain began again.

Not long after this came a warm, eerie dark. In the windless hush there was not so much as the chatter of birds or the barking of dogs. We were lucky, they said later. When the tornado struck it avoided the town, except for the outskirts toward the river. With violent lightning and a low roar like a freight train, its crazy, twisted path, narrow but treacherous, reached six or eight miles into the flatland. Leaping up and down in its lunatic dance, it swept away several houses and establishments, including Lena's Lizard Den and the hot tamale stand and the Holy Ghost Revival Center, ripping through cypresses at the river's edge, bringing down huge tree limbs, carrying farm tractors and cotton wagons and trucks from one plantation to the next. Pieces of straw were seen imbedded like miniature spears in automobile tires; the roof of a secondhand clothing store was torn away and about three hundred dresses and suits were sucked out. "Most of which I ain't seen since," the proprietor mourned, and a woman who was stark naked in her bathtub found herself solitary and exposed in an empty field after her entire house except for the bathroom floor had blown into her neighbor's vegetable garden. Four people were killed, and more than a dozen injured, but as they said, it could have been worse; a sibling to this very twister had struck the big river city to the south that same afternoon and claimed more than fifty unfortunate souls.

I went to see Potter early the next evening to check some facts in the funeral home paper before submitting it to Mrs. King. How I wish now I had never set foot there!

The storm's aftermath had left the skies dark and spiritless, its legacy a nasty little drizzle and a mist that rose in phantom swirls two or three feet above the earth. The dampened town was dreary and bare in that hour, and, to tell the truth, a little spooky, with fallen branches and baleful puddles shimmering under the streetlamps, but it was the merest and most coincident augury of what was to come.

I found the two of them in the office off the drab narrow corridor. Potter was talking on the telephone, his tie crooked and his silver hair disarranged; Woodrow was also speaking to someone in agitated tones on the other line. When Potter saw me in the doorway, he pointed to the telegram on top of his desk.

PLEASE BE ADVISED REMAINS OF PFCS LOREN R HAM-
MOND BEASLEY L CRAIG PERCY A WILLIAMSON ARRIV-
ING WITH ESCORT MONROE CITY VIA IC TR3 915 PM
CST THURS 18 APR STOP TRANSPORTATION COST TO
FISKS LANDING TO BE PAID FROM GOVERNMENT FUNDS
STOP REIMBURSEMENT BASED ON 52 MILES ONE WAY 20
CENTS PER MILE PER CARRIER STOP INSTRUCTIONS RE-
GARDING PAYMENT WILL FOLLOW STOP
                    MAJOR BURNETT S KRAMER CHIEF
                    AMERICAN GRAVES REGISTRATION
                    BRANCH NY PORT OF EMBARKATION

Woodrow put down his telephone and hastened without comment toward the back door. I could hear his footsteps among the outbuildings. Potter was talking to the stationmaster at the train depot in Monroe City. Would IC TR3 be on time tonight? Yes, it would.

When he finished, he turned to me. "The *army*!" He angrily waved the telegram. "We just got this thirty minutes ago — can you imagine?" He glanced at his watch. "The train arrives in just over two hours. Inexcusable! We've barely had time to notify the families and preachers." He too disappeared through the back door. I heard him and Woodrow conversing outside.

On the desk next to the telegram was a chart entitled "Checklist for Military Remains, Casket, Case." I caught part of its contents:

Face shaven (for male personnel).
Features arranged to present a natural appearance.
Fingernails cleaned and trimmed.
Abrasions, wounds, or incisions treated to prevent leakage.
Remains adequately preserved.
Entire uniform clean, pressed, and satisfactory in appearance
    and fit — decorations and ribbons in proper position.

Proper underclothing on the remains.
Restorative work appears lifelike.
Remains present an appearance of repose in the casket.
Clearance between head and end of casket adequate.

Phrases leapt madly out from the paragraphs:

Remains will be thoroughly preserved through arterial, cavity, hyperdermic injections, or chemical packs . . . Maggots and other parasites will be destroyed and removed, and their breeding media immunized . . . All orifices will be packed and lacerations, abrasions, and incisions will be tightly sutured and sealed to prevent leakage . . . Swollen or distorted features will be reduced to a normal likeness of the deceased . . . On thoracic or abdominal autopsies the viscera shall be removed, placed in a receptacle and covered with chemicals, and intestinal and abdominal gases shall be relieved . . . These organs shall be treated liberally with hardening compound and replaced within the cavities in the normal anatomical location . . . Cases of extreme mutilation, advanced stages of putrefaction, or severe burning or charring shall be treated, utilizing the arterial injection technique where possible . . .

I read as if hypnotized — shuddered, then turned away. Over the murmur of the reluctant rain, I heard the sleek, gentle purr of a motor coming off the main street into the driveway. Through the office window I saw Potter and Woodrow still conferring in the rear premises. There were lights on in one of the secret detached chambers. Suddenly from its closed doors appeared the blind ebony ghost, Silas Delaware, in shirtsleeves but with his familiar blue felt hat in place, as if he were dressing in reverse stages for some bizarre cotillion.

I was about to slip away from this turbulent and unpromising scene when Potter burst again into the office.

"We've got a problem. I have to ask you a favor." They were unable to locate Woodrow's son; he was likely on an errand somewhere with the Chinese grocer. Luke and the others were still at the Legion convention. The off-duty policemen and highway patrolmen and firemen were busy with the wreckage of the tornado. The roving bootlegger and returned veteran Wayland Bunch had promised to help in an emergency, but he was, well . . . drunk. Centennial Burial was preparing for four services and could not spare a single man, although they had lent him one of their hearses, which had just come in. "Will you drive one of the vehicles with us to Monroe City? I'll pay you ten dollars."

Well, uh . . .

"It's getting late and I have nowhere else to turn." By way of additional inducement, he added, "I'll read your school paper for you." That is how I was conscripted into action on that gloom-filled night. I was all the way into it before I could so much as politely demur; it was too late from the very start.

The three vehicles were lined up in a row in the back drive: first the modern postwar hearse from Centennial Burial, then the venerable Ricks hearse, and at the end the creamy white ambulance used for emergency calls. Silas Delaware briefly joined us, looking at us one by one with his opaque eyes. "When will you be back?" he asked.

Probably around 10:30 or a little later, Woodrow said.

"Got enough gas?"

"Uh-huh."

Potter guided me to his own hearse. He would drive the Centennial one in front, Woodrow the ambulance behind. "It's not difficult," he said, "much easier than the new ones." He explained the long dashboard, the gearshift, the windshield wipers, the light switches, the brights and dims. "Just like a car, only don't forget it's much longer."

He settled me into the driver's seat. I sat there examining uncomfortably the various controls. Potter and Woodrow got into their vehicles. Then, soon, with a simultaneous roar of engines we departed and were on our way, past the Elks Lodge and the courthouse and the Baptist church, toward the state highway north. On a sharp right turn at an intersection, the back wheels of my conveyance struck a curb and bounced off with a loud rattle. It was indeed longer than a car.

The state highway to Monroe City more or less straddled that emphatic divide between the flatland and the ragged hills to the east. In minutes the lights of the town were behind us. We skirted the country club, then the high eminent bluff where Georgia and I had first kissed on a matchless spring day that now seemed centuries ago, then the sharp gravel turnoff to the Godbold holdings. The highway was the same one we had often taken in our ancient bus to the out-of-town basketball games, and the terrain all around was not unfamiliar to me, yet on this dubious night was all too remote and foreboding, and it seemed that every other car flashing by us going south had only one eye, a circumstance for which the state was well known. The lights on the dashboard of the hearse cast an unwholesome bluish luminance inside, and the slow rhythmic thump of wiper against windshield was eerie, like the heavy beating of an old heart. Everywhere the fog clung to the watery land and spreading marshes, and under the bright forward lights the grass and overhanging foliage after the last days' rains were of a green so deep and impenetrable as to turn emerald in the afterglow.

Potter in the Centennial hearse was fifty yards or so in front, Woodrow at least that many behind, and as I gazed at him through the rear window, the sight of the silent empty chasm directly behind me, with its black silken drapes, served to remind me, if indeed I needed it, exactly what I was driving, and the precise purpose of this surrealistic mission. How many of the town's dead had gone to their graves in that grim interior compartment? Hundreds? Thousands? It was certainly not the first time in those months that I asked myself what on earth I was doing somewhere. It is tempting to impose shape on the events of one's past, yet likewise hazardous, and that nocturnal drive to Monroe City those many years ago really comes back to me now in a kind of preternatural yet all-too-vivid dream, as if the young man behind that driver's wheel were not truly me at all, but some shadowy young imposter, some traceless voyeur of adversity and of the night. According to my memory, as the obsidian prewar hearse whipped solemnly down that moist finger of asphalt, I was whistling to myself: "Dixie," "God Bless America," the Fisk's Landing fight song, and, yes, "Georgia."

And on this dark journey I was awash in swirling recollections of that important year, so that somehow the events of it and its people gradually began to *connect* for me as they never had before, and as I sit now at my desk, I remember with surging clarity how passionately I was trying to give a little sense and design to the things I had felt and learned and experienced. I thought of Luke, of how much I cared for him, of all he had taught me of this native ground. Of Amanda, her sweet kindness and dignity and her love for Luke. Of the scowling Arch and his heroic "Taps." Of Potter and his locked files of death. Of General Miles Featherstone and the town boys in France. Of the fierce perfectionist Asphalt Thomas and of Lutherville's Number 8. Of Mrs. Idella King and the wasted moments of youth. Of my mother and her ravaged discontent. Of Mr. Godbold and his summons to honor in the assembly. Of Lank Hemphill and his sudden tears under the tree. Of Billy Permenter's letters and Locust Grove and Blackjack Baptist. Of Dusty. Again of Luke and Amanda, their proud and secret love. Should they leave Fisk's Landing? Vanish somewhere forever into the vast and sweeping continent? And what of Durley?

And Georgia — her look and touch.

After a while the small hamlet of Dilsburg loomed before me, and for the first time since leaving Fisk's Landing, the three of us in our separate vehicles had to slow our pace. The highway turned at a right angle here, through the three or four meager

streets and crossings, before turning north again, and Potter
was only a few feet in front of me now and Woodrow a few behind. As we crept along the road, several black children were
standing in their front yard and watched our unique convoy.
They remained motionless there for an instant, like characters
frozen in a drama, then shrieked in unison and raced together
to the rear of their house. Black men and women sitting on
their porches rose slowly from their chairs when they saw the
cortege, then withdrew wordlessly indoors. As we waited in a
row at the lone traffic light, a handful of white men emerged
from an unprepossessing red-fronted establishment with their
beer bottles and pool cues in hand and quietly stared; then I
heard one of them yell, "Somethin' *bad's* happened!" and another, "One of 'em drivin' is just a *kid*! And the other's a
nigger!"

None of this was especially comforting, and as we left Dilsburg to its speculations, the empty highway stretching north
was a momentary relief. We were only twenty miles or so from
Monroe City now. Caught in the headlights, an elderly black
man by the side of the road was in the act of relieving himself
when he sighted the lead carriage, then mine. Eyes wide, he
backed quickly up a hilly incline, urinating all the while.

The outskirts of Monroe City lay ahead, half flat and half
hills like Fisk's Landing, a railroad junction town, more substantial than Dilsburg. I could see the cotton gin, the compress,
the water tower, the schoolhouse. Not far beyond the courthouse square, in a precinct of neglected stores and warehouses,
was the train depot. We parked the vehicles near one of the
tracks and, as the stationmaster approached, retreated under
the platform to avoid the rain.

"Hey, Potter."

"Hello, Burgess."

"Eight minutes to spare."

"Yes. We had problems."

"I guess you know the road pretty good by now."

"I'm afraid I do."

"You got *three*?"

"That's right. Three."

"Terrible, ain't it? No end to it. If it was me, I'd drop the damn *Adam* bomb in a damn second."

A car slowed to a stop on the street in front of the depot, and the people inside gazed curiously at our funereal armada. Across the way a man in a greasy apron in front of a cafe stood wiping his hands and looking in our direction. An amiable village dog wandered up, and I bent down and rubbed him on the ears. Why hadn't I had the wits to insist on bringing Dusty with me? Suddenly, with a lengthy whistle and a mighty axis of sound, the sleek modern streamliner from Chicago to New Orleans rushed by southward, as splendid as a whippet, a lovely and solitary ship in the morbid night. I caught a glimpse of elegant passengers in the club car peering out at the hearses and the ambulance before they disappeared once more into the enveloping dark. I gazed after it yearningly. I was not at all looking forward to the return trip home.

A family of passengers emerged from the sparsely lit waiting room — a mother and father and three scruffy children. The smallest of the children began to cry, until all five of them withdrew to the farthest edge of the platform.

"Here she comes!" the stationmaster said.

With a rumbling clatter and a giant hiss of steam, the engine rolled slowly past us. The IC TR3 was a humble medley of freight and baggage cars, with three or four rusty red passenger cars attached in modest compromise. In a collective tremble the entire long row of conveyances ground to a halt before us. The conductor jumped off, as did three or four passengers, and from the opposite direction the engineer strode toward us in grimy blue dungarees and thick cotton gloves. Then the conductor appeared before us. "Mr. Ricks?"

Potter stepped forward. They shook hands. "We've met before," the conductor said.

As the engineer looked over their shoulders, the conductor unfolded a large yellow sheet of paper and showed it to Potter. He examined it and nodded his head.

"Where's the escort?" he asked.

"He's been fast asleep since Memphis. Here he is now."

A tall, drowsy-eyed young soldier in tousled uniform, with a beaked nose and a dull, sallow complexion nearly the color of sand stepped down from the car facing us. The conductor introduced him: Private Sterling Autry. Potter welcomed him with a shake of the hand and a swift, appropriate bow of the head.

"Where are you from, Private?"

"Burlington, Iowa," he replied, lifting his duffel bag and dropping it with a thud on the planked flooring.

"Sorry to have to meet you under such circumstances," Potter said, which must have been his customary salutation in these situations.

"Me too."

"Why didn't they send *three* escorts, do you know?"

"Well, they thought this was special, I believe," the soldier replied. "I was in their outfit. We were all buddies." He added, "I had to switch three times from Jersey City. I'm beat."

"Well, then," Potter said.

The conductor gestured toward the rear of the train.

"I'll pull it up," the engineer said. Woodrow drove the three vehicles one by one up a concrete incline onto the platform, then backed each of them close to the tracks. In seconds a baggage car with a closed sliding door came to rest beside them. The conductor withdrew a set of keys, unlocked the door, and slid it open. Everyone climbed inside.

Three huge wooden boxes sat in a row in the middle of the shadowy compartment, surrounded by the appurtenances and clutter of less extraordinary travel: trunks, suitcases, crates, canvas bags. The boxes were painted steel gray, had dovetail joints and cement-coated nails and drop handles on the sides and ends. On the top of each was a name and serial number, the notation "Flag Inside," and a brown notice bearing the seal of the United States, the profiled eagle with the national insignia on his breast and arched wings and arrows in one claw and an olive branch in the other, and the words beneath:

The Use Of The Seal Of The United States Government Signifies Compliance With All Applicable Health And Sanitary Laws And Regulations Of The Federal And State Governments. The Above Health Permit Number Is Issued In Lieu Of An In-Transit Permit And Is Authority For Issuance Of A Local Burial Permit.

We stood there in the interior gloom. Strangely there was something imposing, one might even say *ordered,* about the three great stolid containers sitting there in the alphabetical sequence of their names. Potter Ricks withdrew a checklist, consulting it as he examined the boxes. "Everything seems fine," he finally declared.

As the receptacles were being loaded into the ambulance and the hearses with the help of several strong men from the railway junction, four or five high school boys in purple letter jackets got out of a car in the nearby parking lot and stood gawking at the spectacle. I recognized two of them as Monroe City basketball players from the tournament. In the train's adjoining passenger car, a man had lowered his window to look out. The escort from Iowa was standing below.

"What is it?" the man shouted. "Some kind of accident?"

"Yeah," the escort from Iowa replied. "You're right. Some kind of accident."

When the wieldy transfer was accomplished, the conductor had Potter sign his documents. With its noisy hiss and roar, IC

TR3 lurched and jerked from front to back, then churned sluggishly out of the depot and was gone. The back door of the Ricks hearse was still open, and I glanced apprehensively inside. I had Williamson.

We gathered there by the vehicles. Potter said he wished the escort to accompany him, since they needed to discuss the funeral arrangements. He would go first as before and drop the private at the Hammond household. "We'll see you back home," he said. "Let's not tarry now," and he glided the Centennial carriage down the ramp, gunned the accelerator, and quickly disappeared around the bend in the access road. Woodrow too cranked his motor and followed in quick pursuit. "Hey!" I shouted after him. "Wait!" But he also had hopelessly vanished.

I climbed angrily into the driver's seat. How had they dared leave the reluctant volunteer to bring up the rear? Were they so preoccupied by the night's unprecedented shipment that they simply forgot? Too anxious to reach home? Why hadn't they left the army private from Iowa with *me*? I started the ignition and sped into the adjacent thoroughfare, hoping to overtake them in the streets of the town. I took a wrong turn and had to go around an entire block. A traffic light slowed me on a corner of the courthouse square, a second in front of the school, a third at the city limits. By the time I reached the highway my companions must have been miles in front.

The rain was falling harder now, accompanied by spidery strands of lightning and faint rumbling thunder. There was practically no movement this time on the highway; it was dark and empty as far as I could see. The bluffs to the left were obscured by the mist, the flatness to the right a sea of profound blackness. How I wished Dusty were curled up next to me on the seat!

My thoughts turned to the cargo in back. I glanced around at the enormous silent container. With chilling resignation I remembered something Luke had once told us, having fun at Arch's and my expense in the days of those early funerals. A pilot he had known during the war in England was flying a six-seater with a corpse on a stretcher heading to Graves Registration, and as the plane descended the expiring air in the dead man's lungs made loud, gasping moans! Not here, not now, please God. I tried then to picture Williamson on those distant Saturday evenings at the farther end of the main street, clustered with the other uniformed guardsmen trying to impress the country girls. Had not he married one of those girls?

It was almost 10:30 when Dilsburg came into view, its streetlights feeble and uncertain in the rainy dark. As I crept past the same red-fronted establishment, the paunchy white men with their pool cues and beer bottles were once more congregating under the awning. "There he is *again!*" one of them exclaimed.

I was four or five miles south of Dilsburg in open, deserted country, on a lengthy stretch of risky serpentine road, when it began to happen. Imperceptibly at first, the engine of the old vehicle started to make a waggish noise, a kind of vague and girlish, almost whimsical, sigh — a tender, whispered exhortation as if prideful in its soul of its long and honorable years of toil. I cocked a horrified ear to it, and pushed down on the accelerator. The blue speedometer reached sixty when the hearse's first breath of complaint descended by subtle timbres into a malicious groan, and after that a sequence of rhythmic churlish growls.

Someday, the thought rushed through me, I'll remember this and laugh. But from the bowels of the motor rose now a veritable symphony of competing sounds: whirs, hisses, thumps, murmurs, whistles, singing consonances, and clucks. I kept as even a course as possible on the wet, murky asphalt, trying hard not to contemplate being stranded alone on this inclement and unpopulated night with the steel gray container in the back. Something must be done to mute the gathering interior fugue. I switched on the dashboard radio, turning the dial in search of dance music from New Orleans. A dreadful sound came out of the speaker — the slow creaking of a door, followed by a low, ghoulish laugh. It was a popular horror show called "Inner Sanctum," and I switched away from it fast. I found the music station, which was actually playing a song of the day called "Ghost Rider in the Sky," but that soon gave way to a soothing tune of young fifties love.

Clank! No amount of music could stifle the cacophony now. After a dozen or more vibrating shakes and rattles, the entire front of the carriage began to shimmy, as if it were enveloped in the crosscurrents of a sort of wind tunnel; the steering wheel too was bouncing back and forth, and I had to grasp it tightly to keep from running off the road. In that instant I peered through the windshield and saw large puffs of steam escaping from under the hood. That was when I heard the steel box in the rear slide with a thud against the partition.

What choice did I have? The stricken hearse plainly needed a respite. I pulled onto the shoulder of the road and got out. I seemed to be in the depths of nowhere, near a miasmic glade of oaks and vines. Not a single light was in view. I stood there uncertainly; the top of the hood was hot to the touch. Should I abandon it and hitchhike to the nearest telephone? I could see in the distance four or five shacks laid out in a row, long since abandoned, with caved-in roofs and collapsed porches, and a chinaberry tree blown down from the storm. On each side the highway stretched away, mute and deserted. After a time I suddenly discerned a faint swish, coming closer and closer, and from around the bend headlights appeared, reflecting in a dancing yellow path on the pavement. It was a decrepit blue pickup truck, and when I waved for assistance it began to slow down. Two men were inside, and when they came abreast of the crippled conveyance, they looked out, poised there for a second, and then abruptly speeded up and soon were out of sight.

By now the hood had cooled. Fisk's Landing was still about fifteen miles away, and I prayerfully cranked the engine and listened, as a solicitous surgeon might to a heart murmur; the only sound was the original querulous sigh. Regaining the road, I kept the speedometer at thirty, and for at least ten miles the motor was more or less unprotesting. Just short of the city limits, however, the hisses and growls ascended as before; by the time I reached the northern tip of town the entire front end was trembling and shaking again and steam pouring forth in thickening gusts. In my frightful descent from the hills into downtown, I was like a rodeo cowboy holding the reins of an addled stallion. Yet the streetlights and benign landmarks of the drowsing old town had never been so reassuring — how I loved it now! — the Victorian courthouse welcoming me as the most benevolent paterfamilias might, and when I turned right onto the main street and approached the driveway of the Ricks Funeral Home, I remembered with thanksgiving the song of the earlier war: "Coming in on a Wing and a Prayer."

The headlights caught Woodrow hurrying from the windowless outbuilding toward the main establishment. He stopped and looked impassively at me. "Where *you* been?" he asked.

The ambulance and the Centennial carriage were parked in back near the doorway to the separate private structure. Next to the building were the two steel gray containers. Their tops had been stripped open, and they lay there empty and neglected. As Woodrow backed the geriatric Ricks vehicle toward the rear building, Potter emerged from inside and carefully shut the big black door behind him. He was wearing an unfamiliar gray-green smock, which reached from his shoulders to his knees, and his eyeglasses glistened with the night's moisture, and in that moment, he looked spurious and forbidding, like a sorcerer or a backstairs alchemist. It gave me an uncomfortable feeling.

I described the litany of troubles. "I don't know why we gave you the old one," he responded apologetically. "We weren't thinking. We were worried about you. I can't thank you enough." Lifting the back of the smock, he brought out a wallet and handed me a $10 bill. They were very busy, he said. He knew it was late, but could he impose one last time? Would I go to the all-night place by the bus station and get them some sandwiches? "Just knock on this door when you get back," he said, and gave me another $5. "Six ham and cheese, and whatever you want for yourself." As I turned to leave, he disappeared inside, carefully closing the door again.

The rain had nearly stopped now, and the main street was hushed and lifeless, but the cafe was busy with the nocturnal truck drivers from the highway, and it was half an hour before I returned with the provisions.

The Centennial hearse was no longer there; someone must have taken it away in my absence. The main building was dark, and under the reticent moonlight the rear driveway was oddly menacing and still. I stood there by the windowless outbuilding, bag of sandwiches in hand. The imposing black door with its sign "Private — Absolutely No Admittance" was still tightly shut. I followed Potter Ricks's advice and knocked on it loudly. There was no answer. I knocked again. Silence.

I turned the handle and the door opened. I entered and closed it behind me. I found myself in a deserted, dimly lit antechamber, a neutral enough place, with a Formica table, three or four straight-backed chairs, checkered linoleum flooring, a red Coca-Cola machine, a portrait of Jesus Christ pointing to his own bosom, a plain wooden counter with a coffee percolator and several cups. The door to an adjoining room was ajar, revealing a large bathroom with an enormous bathtub, a shower stall, and shelves with dozens of bars of medicinal soap. At the far side of the main room stood the three big lidless boxes.

My eye flew to a pair of white floor-length swinging doors set in a drab purplish wall, behind which I could make out a strange whirring sound, not unlike the buzzing of bees. There was another sign, written on poster paper in bold elaborate script, on one of the swinging doors:

This Preparation Room is the Sanctuary of Faith. The Body that is entrusted to our care represents the most unbounded Faith of the Family in our skill and sympathy. All Employees shall exercise this FAITH by maintaining the most strict Discipline while in this room. "Do Unto Others as Thou Wouldst Have Them Do Unto You."

I paused before the doors. Then, against my own will, I pushed them open.

The whirring sound was more pervasive now. I could see Potter, Woodrow, and Silas Delaware bending over something in the farthest corner of the room. Their backs were turned and they did not notice me. I do not know how long I stood there, but what I saw seemed to swim before me in a fixed and cunning eternity, all of it bright and inert and suspended, as if stricken of the mandates of substance and contour and motion.

The place had the appearance of a grim and gruesome surgery, with a tiled white floor and sterile white walls and glaring fluorescent lights in an antiseptic ceiling, and grotesque instruments of all shapes and sizes on porcelain tables and in tall white glassed-in cabinets — spatulas and injectors and scalpels and pumps and syringes and trocars and scissors and clamps and needles and curved steel tubes and razors — and on long porcelain shelves sprays and paints and rubbing alcohol and Johnson's baby oil and perfection eye caps and derma surgery wax and cosmetic powders marked brunette, ivory, pink, white, suntan, buff, and tall plastic containers labeled anticoagulant fluid and tissue-filler solvent and hardening compound and big tin drums of embalming fluid, arterial and cavity. Then, in one quick glance to the side, I saw on the tiled floor next to a wall the three opened aluminum coffins, and the three kraft paper shrouds which had been tossed to the side of each of them.

I suddenly became aware of a dread, hovering presence, something monstrous and malign, a quivering green odor, gaseous and indefinable, the likes of which I had never known or even imagined. My gaze became fastened to the inside of the first coffin. And it was in that moment, oddly, that I believe I saw life as it truly was for the first time.

The thing inside was a putrescent sunken mass. The vague contours of a human form lay under rotted khaki; what had been a face was collapsed, like sponge, with hideous liquid eyes, and covering this horrid detritus was a thick spiderweb-like growth of mold, long repugnant strands of it faintly resembling Spanish moss. Around this fallen infested hulk the silken lining was stained with big dried pools of ghastly liquid, dark crimson seepage.

I stood there in a giddy fog. It resembled nothing I had ever seen. I could not take my eyes from it.

"What are you doing here?"

Potter had sighted me from across the chamber. He was wearing the gray-green smock and rubber gloves, and his shout was muffled by a large white surgical mask covering his face. Woodrow and Silas Delaware were similarly clad, and they too turned abruptly in my direction.

They were standing before two long enameled porcelain tables with headrests and loops; drains and buckets were set on the floor underneath. Then, in one swift terrible glance, I beheld the objects of their application. On the first table lay a moldy legless wreck — a gruesome torso with half an arm, a formless face like putty, the shattered silhouette of a human head. On the other was a second putrid pile, an abhorrent dismembered approximation of a man, swirling with the same thick whiskers of humus, riven in sunken decay.

I turned away, fought back the mounting crests of sickness. Quickly, sternly, Potter strode across the room. He reached out toward me with his gloved palm, with the hand that had touched — the things. I shoved him back, spun around, opened the swinging doors, and went through the first exit to the driveway outside. He followed on my heels.

The cool night air with its wet leafy fragrance was a deliverance.

"I'm sorry," Potter apologized, for the second time within that hour. He had pulled the mask below his chin; his features were faint and flaccid, his eyes opaque and vexed, his nostrils smeared with a slick, full ointment like Vaseline. "It's been a horrible night for all of us. Woodrow forgot the lock on the door. He's never done that." He paused momentarily. He looked very old. "We should never have gotten you into any of this. It was none of your affair." His gloved hands were clasped tightly before him in monkish distress. "Will you ever forgive us? And please . . . don't tell *anyone!*"

Which one was Williamson?

"I won't tell you. And you don't need to know."

I wanted to walk the way home. I passed the darkened library, the high school, Georgia's house and Arch's, the Darnell house. Crippled hearses and steel gray boxes. Porcelain tables with drains and buckets. The slain heroes had come home, and I had seen them in their glory. Is that all it comes to, extinction and death and rotting away? The earthworm mulch? Only when I reached my own front lawn did I realize I was still carrying the sandwiches. Dusty was on the porch waiting.

If everything except that ruthless surgery were hoax and fraud and worm in the rose, then how to explain the precious majesty of those dwindling April days? In the mornings the tuneful mockingbirds chattered, and the whippoorwills called at dusk. Those were verdant iridescent days, the shades of light and shadow, the imbuing pinks and purples and crimsons and yellows, the soft, nearly sexual, indigo. I felt I had grown much older.

The three separate burials, for the objects that had been Craig, Hammond, and Williamson, took place in a cemetery lush with crimson clover laid out like a carpet, with bluebells and buttercups, with lilacs. Arch had won two of the three tosses, but at the third ceremony, the one for Williamson, I was again under the magnolia, now with virgin buds, and Luke climbed up there as he always did to talk, and sat back against the trunk, a blade of grass in his lips. I really think he had come to cheer me.

Before they had left for the Legion meeting, he and I had taken turns teaching Lank Hemphill how to drive a car. During the convention on the coast, he told me, the one-armed foot soldier had come within a hairbreadth of running over a drunken female sailor in the United States Navy.

We laughed a bit over that.

"I heard about your hearse trouble. We call that special duty."

"It did not seem so special at the time," I replied.

"Well, I guess we've come a long way since that time when I first asked you about playing 'Taps.' You were barefoot and lying in the grass. Looking at the stars, I believe."

From below, in the familiar street leading to the cemetery gate, we caught sight of that very hearse, which had been patched up for $150. The arrival of the replacement was imminent.

He got up and dusted off his trousers. "Amanda's down there. Did you know she's Williamson's second cousin?"

He tarried now before ambling to his duties down the hill. "I also heard about the embalming room, or whatever they call it. Was it pretty bad?"

Yes. Pretty bad.

"There are some things you just have to try and blot out. Do you think you can?"

12

FOR SOME REASON I was not particularly surprised at the resurrection of Durley Godbold. There was a bizarre inevitability to it, a mad destiny: a phantom risen from the dead in that unheroic time of dying.

American and Australian platoons, miles out of position, unexpectedly broke the line and suddenly overran a small temporary POW compound not far from the Yalu, just before the hundred or so prisoners were about to be transferred into Manchuria. Among them were the two men who had disappeared in that bloody night's action in August: the private from South Dakota and Durley.

The word arrived circuitously at noon one day in the first week of May, inexplicably nearly a fortnight after the capture of the POW camp, through a wire-service reporter in San Francisco who telephoned Mayor Fink. Mr. Godbold's friends in the Pentagon reached him minutes later. Shortly after that, the official communication came by military telegram to Amanda, the next of kin. Western Union found her in the music room of the school as she was returning from lunch. When she read the message, she sat at the piano with her head slumped on the keyboard. Mrs. Idella King and Coach Asphalt Thomas took her home and got a doctor. "Her face was *bloodless,* poor thing," Mrs. King said. "She was drained white."

I heard the news from Mrs. King herself, in the corridor between afternoon classes. I went outside and sat on the steps by the Plato statue in the soft, warm sunshine. The birds were singing and the sounds of baseball lifted from the diamond behind the school and the chimes of the Baptist church down the thoroughfare resounded in thanksgiving. I was supposed to be in band practice, but all I could do was think about Luke and Amanda. What would they do now?

In all the wartimes everywhere, how many times had it happened, the wife taken a new lover? Not likely to be a preserved statistic in the official archives of the U.S. Army. "Coming back from missing is not an *everyday* occurrence," Potter Ricks said, "but of course it's certainly happened." The Quinn boy in the last war. *Two* boys from Lutherville in World War I, Sarge Jennings said.

In Mrs. King's classroom the next morning, Georgia took her seat and immediately turned toward the back to catch my attention. She opened her eyes wide and lifted her head toward the ceiling in an exaggerated gesture of uncertainty. It was the first real communication between us in a long time. Amanda did not return that day to the school. As it happened, Luke, having just been elected to succeed Sarge Jennings as commander of the Legion post, was away at the national convention in Washington, where he had driven in his truck to spare the Legion the expenses of airfare.

We learned that Durley had been flown to Tokyo for medical treatment and was now at a military hospital in California. He was reported to be in reasonably good condition. After the physical and psychological tests and debriefings, he would have three weeks of leave before he had to return to the West Coast.

The end of school was approaching and with it graduation. In the hallways I heard the girls discussing the evening dress Georgia's mother had bought her to wear to the traditional midnight-to-dawn commencement dance (her maid had told the other maids through the usual grapevine), a strapless sequined thing, if I heard correctly; the girls were scarcely able to contain their envy. As consort to the football captain and senior class president, Georgia was a fairer target than ever for the town girls; the corridors rippled with the kind of skittish prattle they had learned from their mothers. "Won't she be the *princess*!" one of them said, then, noticing me, smiled coyly, as if to affirm an unspoken fraternity of jealousy and contempt.

I summoned the will to telephone Amanda. Standing in the hallway by my kitchen, I let the phone ring for a long time. There was no answer.

I drove out to Tara Estates, among the latter-day manors that lined the circling drives and culs-de-sac and stood like arrogant bastions against the ripe green earth. There were no sidewalks here, no signs of age, no mystery, as if the whole vicinage had risen up en masse at an hour in time so designated and precise that history itself had been obliterated. It was not the boulevard.

Her Buick was in the driveway. I looked about to make sure no one was watching; the nearest domiciles appeared empty. I parked my car behind hers, and as I rang the bell the dizzying memory of that day when I was twelve rushed back to me. I saw a light beyond the drawn curtains, but there was no sound or movement. Then I heard footsteps, and the door opened.

She was barefoot in a light cotton dress. Her eyes were swollen red and her hair disarranged. Still she was as lovely as a faded lilac.

"Oh, Swayze," she whispered, "I'm so glad it's you."

Her home was luxuriant with carpet and paneling and gadgetry, a paean to modern convenience. I followed her to a large sofa, and we sat down. Her hands were on each side of her, her fingers squeezed so hard at the edges of the cushion that her knuckles turned white. Her features as she faced me were pale and listless. "I don't have anyone to talk to." Luke had hurriedly left Washington and was driving home, she said. "Thank God he's coming back."

The telephone rang from time to time, but she ignored it. "I haven't even been out of the house. Asphalt and Mrs. King came by. Georgia was here. I'm really okay. Don't worry about me."

A deep tremulous sigh belied this faltering certitude. Her eyes were sad. "I'm frightened, Swayze." She turned to me and put her head on my shoulder, and instinctually I put my arm around her. What could I do? I asked her. "Just be our friend. It'll be all right. Just stay with me a minute."

At that instant there was the powerful whir of a vehicle from the street outside. She rose and hastened to the front of the room. I trailed behind her. She peered through the curtains. "There he is. It's the third time he's driven by today." Leroy Godbold in his Cadillac, which glided slowly past, then gathered speed and disappeared down the hill.

"You can go, Swayze. Luke will be here soon."

The next morning before school Arch and I drove by her house. In the driveway, next to her car, was the Cadillac. When I telephoned her, there was no answer.

On a balmy day of drifting peach-colored clouds Durley came home. His mother and father and brothers had gone to the airport in the capital city to meet him. Amanda was still at home, ill. When he first came back some of the townspeople viewed him with a barely concealed distaste, even horror — no measure of hail-fellow welcome could disguise it — as if among them was the very specter of death itself. They needed time.

I first saw him on the courthouse lawn from Arch's Plymouth on the afternoon of his return. He was standing there in uniform with his father, his two brothers, the sheriff and a deputy, and the Baptist pastor. Arch parked down the way; we got out and watched from behind a protective azalea. On the street other cars slowed almost to a standstill, their occupants also inspecting the scene, and at the second-story windows of the Elks Lodge four or five men stood staring down. On the surface it was a casual enough gathering. Mr. Leroy Godbold, in seersucker and Panama, was saying something to the others, tilting his head back and forth as he talked. We could not make out his words, but even though he was smiling, they carried his heavy, hard authority. The pastor and the sheriff were frowning, then broke into broad, strained grins.

But the singular aspect of the scene was Durley Godbold himself. He was the person I remembered, and then again he was not; he seemed to have lost one dimension and acquired another, to have partly dissolved and then become embodied again, a subtle and elusive approximation both of the boy who had chased us down the boulevard with his contemporaries on long-past nights, and of the man who had roughly caressed his wife in the shadows of the country club those months ago.

I was looking at a dim and horrendous memory, an umbra of the past. He must have lost forty or fifty pounds. He had always been a large man, but now seemed a kind of dark, taut membrane, as if the vital juices had been squeezed out of him. His eyes were like dull ashen coals as he listened to the others. The very atmosphere around him seemed to smolder with . . . what? Bitterness? Revulsion? Malice? And there was something else. In the past he had possessed an arrogance, a swagger, a surly and reckless pride that some had found attractive. Standing there now on the courthouse lawn, he seemed to have discarded these just as he had his muscular brawn.

"He *looks* dead," Arch said.

Yet he really did not. He did not seem unhealthy. His color was unexpectedly strong, owing no doubt to the military cures, and he had come back all in one piece, unlike Lank Hemphill and some of the others. Had one not known him before, he could have passed for an approximately normal-looking American male.

Leroy Godbold lit a thin cigar, appraising the surroundings with his vehement, all-knowing gaze. The pastor was talking now, and as he did so, Mr. Godbold glanced secretly at his son, an expression of fleeting and acid unease, of troubled and fugitive displeasure. Handshakes were exchanged all around. Then the four Godbolds withdrew down the sidewalk to Mr. Godbold's Cadillac, which had been washed and waxed and polished to a silver gleam.

I did not learn until later where Amanda was those next two days, or what she was doing, or whether she was with her husband. Durley himself was seen around the town three or four times, in the Cadillac with Mr. Godbold, in the coffee shop of the Earl Van Dorn with his brothers, in the pool hall. His father and Sarge Jennings drove him on the second of those afternoons to the veterans hospital in the capital city for an examination, and later Sarge Jennings told the others that Durley was all right medically and mainly needed the right diet and vitamins. "But that boy won't say much of nothin'," he said. "Not much of nothin' to nobody."

The afternoon Luke returned, I saw him in his truck speeding down the boulevard, but when I went to the store he was not there, nor was he at his cabin. Neither Potter Ricks nor Sarge Jennings knew where he was.

I retreated to the town library to complete a modest last assignment for Mrs. King and to think. Lank Hemphill accompanied me there, after we had another driving lesson, and as Miss Lydia Fortenberry fluttered about in her soundless slippers, he settled at the opposite end of the table perusing musty copies of *Open Road for Boys*. I did not like the feel of things. It was as though we were caught in an awful riddle without a clue or solution. I felt powerless and could only wait.

Arch told me that he bumped into Durley in Arch's father's store. "How're you and that Swayze brat?" he had asked. "He looked at me with those twitchy, beady eyes," Arch said, "and I got out of there. How come the army let him come home? He's meaner than ever, I tell you."

And then at Tara Estates we saw Durley's old familiar sedan in the driveway. He was home to stay. And what was happening with Amanda?

Late the next afternoon I found Luke alone at the cabin. The front gate was locked, and I used my own key. He was on the telephone when I came in talking with Doc Patterson.

When he finished, he shook my hand as if he had not seen me in months. He seemed cheerful enough, although he was plainly forcing it. He looked at Dusty and me with his amiable, quizzical face. "Saw some of the guys I fought with," he said. "You'd like Washington. It's a pretty town."

I reminded him that I had never been north of Memphis.

"Plenty of time for that."

We went out and stood in the converging dusk. Dusty and the black cat sprawled in a cluster of wild violets. "Dusty thinks this place is his," Luke said, "and I guess it is. Look! The first lightning bug of the year." How much I needed his funny, valuable brotherhood, his confidences, his fealties. I tried to find the wit to express it, but I could not. Some things remain unspoken.

Images of Amanda with Durley hovered before us like ghosts. "I know what you're thinking," he said. "Don't worry. It's got to work out."

But I *was* worried for them, I said.

He sat down on the familiar front steps. I joined him there. In our time together I had long since learned when he wanted to talk. "I'll tell you about it. You deserve to know." Amanda was in the capital city at that moment consulting a lawyer about a divorce, he said. She would return here shortly. "She just intends to tell Durley she can't love him anymore. She'll tell him she's moving out of the house. She wants to take the same place she had before, the one down by the school."

He told me these things with a dispatch uncharacteristic of

him. He was briefly silent then, gazing blankly out into the tall
solemn pines. "The day the son of a bitch got back, he just sat
around saying nothing to her and then got on the telephone for
about an hour. Then he made her go to bed with him. She told
him that she was sick, but he forced her anyway. I was on my
way from Washington. It damn near killed me." His fists were
clenched hard. I shuddered at the thought of it, and the unmer-
ciful incubus of Georgia and the football captain rose before
me for the thousandth time. "I'm going to give them about two
or three days to agree on things, and that's it. Then I have to do
something."

What would he do?

"I'm not sure. But it's time to get this settled."

Just then there was the sound of a motor on the drive. It was
Amanda. Luke walked out to meet her. When she got out of the
Buick, they reached for each other in a long, unhurried embrace. She wore a white dress with polka dots, and her ash
blond hair flowed to her shoulders. The glimpse of them in that
long-ago twilight, the air soft with pine and springtime and the
new fireflies ashimmer, the two of them joined in their deep and
troubled love, would last in my heart.

Arm in arm they walked down the sloping lawn, and I left.

Those next days are attenuated in memory, elusive and unreal.
They seemed dominated by Durley.

He was officially awarded his Bronze Star. The governor
hosted a small reception for him in the mansion during which
Mr. Godbold proposed a rhetorical toast to returning warriors;
the ranking general in the state pinned on the medal. Georgia
told Arch that she and Zamma Bailey had overheard him and
his father in the drugstore discussing his future — after some
rest perhaps he would go to law school. Durley said he wanted
to make money, to branch from farming into development and
property. When they got up and Mr. Godbold was paying the

check in front, Durley noticed the two girls. "You're Georgia, right?" he said. "Hot little thing, ain't you?" And he reached down and pulled on a strand of her hair.

Arch and I began surreptitiously following him about, trailing his sedan here and there at a distance. Our perverse fascination with the Godbolds had endured and flowered beyond delinquency; it was an obsession. Although Durley was still in the military, and technically on leave, he was not in uniform, and that Saturday afternoon we tailed him and his brothers all the way to the expensive capital city men's store, where he bought some clothes. He had taken up smoking, and on the return drive to Fisk's Landing he tossed one cigarette after another from the car onto the highway. Back home he dropped off his brothers and drove to the funeral home. Potter Ricks told Luke that he came in to look over some documents on army disability, the ones kept on file there, and said to Potter that the army owed him a lot of money.

Amanda left him.

We discovered it on a Sunday when we spotted her Buick in front of the old house near the school. She was nowhere in sight, but two men were taking clothes and crates inside.

"She's moved out on the son of a bitch!" Arch exclaimed. "What's going on?" I could not tell him, of course.

He turned the car at the next intersection. "Let's go see her," he said. "We can carry things."

"Not now. Let's leave her alone."

As I would soon learn from Luke, she had her confrontation with Durley in the kitchen at Tara Estates, having carefully considered what she would say. She told him she had been thinking about things in his absence, that they were dissimilar people and each of them deserved a fresh start. She could not help it, she said, that she no longer loved him. She had tried. His family had never liked her, she reminded him, and surely he would be happier with someone else, someone of the same background and interests. They were both young; they could start again. He had a career, a prominent family; he could divorce *her* if he wanted. After all he had been through, the last thing she wanted was to hurt him. She would ask for nothing, she said, only her clothes, her piano, and a few other items. She would pay him in installments for the Buick. Life was not meant for unhappiness.

I could imagine her there, lovely and dignified and gentle, pleading for a chance for her own hard-earned fulfillment. He said nothing. She implored him to respond. For a moment she was afraid he might hit her. "Then good riddance!" he finally said. It was obvious she had married him for his money. He had made the biggest mistake of his life marrying a peckerwood from the hills. She had never been any good — just white trash. "I want your butt out of here in two hours," he said.

The next day after school we picked up his scent again at the Earl Van Dorn, trailing him and his father to the capital city once more, this time to the military hospital. They remained inside for half an hour, then stood briefly on the front lawn conversing with an army doctor. Mr. Godbold drove back to the Earl Van Dorn, where the two of them sat in the Cadillac, talking at length. When his father departed, Durley drove himself down the main street to the pool hall and went inside carrying a bottle in a sack. We went into Crenshaw's across the way. Soon there were sounds of mayhem from the pool establishment. "For Chrissake," Sarge Jennings said, "is it *war*?" He rushed out, returning a few minutes later: "Durley Godbold just beat up Wayland Bunch."

Late the following afternoon, in our compelling dementia, we were following him again. He was alone, driving west on the state highway into the flatland. "Where's he going now?" Arch scowled. "He's doing eighty."

We reached the outskirts of Lutherville. Far ahead our prey turned onto a drab little serpentine road leading north. After two miles he turned again at a private dirty byway with a rural mailbox at its crossing. He parked in front of a white frame dwelling near a sharp curve in the river. "It's that girl — the whore!" Arch said. We sat there a long time, brazen voyeurs of the early night. Arch glanced at his watch. "What's he *doing* in there?" We finally went home.

The next morning at school I was on an errand for Mrs. King. Amanda approached in the deserted corridor and motioned me into the empty auditorium. "I'm free, Swayze. Luke's in Atlanta. I'm joining him for the weekend. We're looking for a place to live." I congratulated her.

Her gray eyes sparkled, caught the morning light. "It's been a long time coming. I'm so very happy."

After classes Arch and I went down to the baseball diamond behind the schoolhouse to watch part of the game with Monroe City. We stood beyond the third-base bleachers. The Notreangelo boy who had struck me across the neck in the basketball game was pitching for Monroe City, and his younger brother was the catcher. "I hate baseball," Arch said.

I heard the sound of brassy jangling keys, and Asphalt Thomas strolled by us toward the bleachers. "Why ain't you out shootin' hoops?" he challenged me. "Ain't you serious? Season starts in six months." And he jangled away in the sunshine.

"Look who *I* see," Arch said. He gestured toward the bleachers, where Durley and his brothers were sitting with a sheriff's deputy and a town policeman.

I closed my eyes to absorb the sun. Soon I heard steps on the walk, and Arch stirred apprehensively beside me. Suddenly standing before us was Durley. His acid eyes were fixed on Arch, his finger planted on Arch's Adam's apple. "Didn't I see your Plymouth behind me in Lutherville?"

"Not mine," Arch said.

"Yeah. Yours. If I catch you and this tap dancer's boy again, you'll know it."

"My car's broke down," Arch lied.

"Why ain't you in the war?"

"Not old enough," Arch replied.

"Not *old* enough. I shot up my share of teenage Chinks." And he thumped poor Arch on the throat before striding away. Back in the bleachers, he and his brothers whispered among themselves.

"I hate his guts," Arch said. "A *hero*!" And he spat petulantly on the ground. But we never tailed him again.

There was a succession of hot, balmy days. The foliage was subtly changing, assembling the keener colors of the coming summer. On the afternoon of our final school examinations, the temperature fell and a heavy rain came — how I loved the deep cool rains of spring! — which gave way to an unseasonable late mist, then fog.

The smell of wet earth hung heavy that day.

Luke spotted me on the boulevard from his truck. Bring Arch and come out to his place that night for some hands of poker, he said. I knew Amanda was at a tap-dancing competition out of town and would not return until late. I had seen her earlier that afternoon talking with my mother. Luke said he needed a little company.

It was dark and still and the misty trees dripped with moisture as he greeted Arch and Dusty and me on the porch. When Arch disappeared into the cabin on his usual investigations, Luke took me aside.

Atlanta was fine, he said. They had their eyes on a house. "I guess we'll move over there this summer sometime, as soon as I sell my share in the store."

I would miss them.

"You'll come over. It's a big town, Atlanta. You can take the train."

The poker was desultory. When we finished, Arch decided to try some night fishing at the beaver pond. He wanted me to go with him, but I needed to talk with Luke. I heard him scavenging among the cane poles and bait cans outside, then he headed down the winding path.

Luke was on the telephone talking to Amanda in the capital city. I made a sandwich in the kitchen and returned to the front room. Dusty lay there next to me. Giving him part of the sandwich, I looked down at his gleaming golden coat, his warm black eyes, his floppy ears. He had been with me since I was nine, had seen me through the maze of childhood, walked down the boulevard to school with me every day, had lain at my side on all the insomniac nights. I touched his head. After a while he got up and licked my hand, then vanished through the open door outside. I could hear him rollicking with the cat.

Luke put down the telephone. "They won second place."

I would remember the next moments for a long time, the imponderable silence, and then the eerie cry of a swampbird, followed by the sudden mad screeching of the guinea hens. And then from the drive came the low, almost indistinct pitch of a heavy vehicle. Doors opened. Dusty barked. Luke rose tensely from his chair. Then a sudden deafening explosion, a quick blinding light. I heard a horrible, all-suffering whine.

I rose. Luke had picked up a butcher knife. For an instant we looked at each other.

"Get out of here! Get out the back! *Now!*"

I needed no encouragement. Insane fear welled in me. My heart pounded frantically, and I was limp with panic. My legs felt inert, like putty, and for one desperate moment I was afraid I could not move. But I did. I bolted in terror across the room, through the kitchen, out the rear door onto the porch. I took the steps in one cowardly bound, stumbled momentarily in the mud, lifted myself, and ran as fast as I ever had, racing headlong down the path toward the foggy pines. I heard my own helpless footsteps as I churned into the night. I felt the wretched spasms of my breathing, and I ran and ran. I leapt into the underbrush beneath a copse of hickories and lay there on my belly trying to stifle my gasps. I hid my face in the weeds and dug my hands into the soil.

Suddenly from the cabin came another nightmarish blast. The roar reverberated through the trees. Cowed in the protecting woods like a stalked beast, I could feel my body trembling next to the wet earth. I longed to burrow myself into the ground. But I raised my head and strained to listen. There were no sounds from the cabin. Then I heard quick, heavy footsteps behind me on the path. I crouched even lower and peered through the leaves.

It was Arch. I gathered myself, emerged onto the path, and whispered to him. Startled, he stopped and turned. In the low-clinging fog his eyes were bright and fevered. "I heard a shotgun," he said. "What is it? What's happened? What're you doing way out here?"

"I . . ." For the first time I confronted my own insensate shame. I had run away from Luke.

The two of us stood frozen in the moonless gloom. A breeze swept the pines. Arch turned his head toward the cabin and listened hard, as I had done. "Let's take off our shoes," I finally said.

We walked stealthily toward the cabin, halting often to listen again. I was seized with wrenching dread, as if a curtain were lifting on some unimaginable horror. The lights were on in the cabin. We paused uncertainly on the rear lawn. The door I had burst through in my retreat was still wide open.

We went inside, into the awful enveloping hush, and crossed the kitchen. Then we entered the front room.

Luke was lying on the floor, his shoulders and head resting at an angle on the edge of the sofa. Blood ran from the sofa to the fireplace, gathered in pools on the floor and rugs.

I was hardly conscious of my own movements. It was as though I were not myself, but someone else, and this was not

Luke, and I was gazing at two strangers from some faraway place. A voice that must have been mine said, *"No, please God."*

I went to him, and knelt before him. A gaping wound in his chest flowed with blood. His eyes were open. The knife was still in his hand.

I touched his forehead. It was warm and moist.

"Luke?"

Arch was standing behind me. His words reached me from an unreal distance. "He's dead."

But I knew.

Arch went to the front door and glanced cautiously outside. I stayed with Luke, looking into his face and holding his hand. I heard Arch in the kitchen calling Potter Ricks.

Kneeling there with Luke, I lost all sense of the passage of time. I rose after a while, dizzy and hot, and went onto the front porch to breathe the air. The acrid smell of powder was heavy in the wet, dark night. And then I saw Dusty.

I walked toward him. He was sprawled in a little sea of blood, one paw extended upward. His whole side had been destroyed, and the blood ran from it in rivulets down the hill. His ribs were shattered like splinters.

Again I knelt, bowed my face to his, felt his stricken eyes, touched his ears. I put my fingers on the great open wound, lay his head in my lap, hugged him closely to me as I had when he was a puppy. I held him for a long time. When would the grief come?

"Swayze." Arch was there again. "They're here." A pulsing red light reflected on the trees. It was Potter's ambulance.

Potter and Woodrow were there, and soon the sheriff and deputies, the doctor and coroner, then Sarge Jennings and Roach Weems. I could barely make out their shouts and whisperings; the world was a blur. Arch and I sat hunched on the steps of the porch. Sarge and Roach stood on the lawn. One of them pointed to a pair of white pillowcases, with slits for the eyes and mouth, which had been tossed to the ground.

"Why?" I heard Sarge Jennings ask. "It's something you could do yourself or pay somebody else to do. But why?"

The sheriff and a deputy questioned Arch and me. I do not remember what I told them, except that I had run away, down the path into the woods.

"Do you want a ride home?" Potter asked.

"No," Arch said. "We have my car."

Arch and I wrapped Dusty in a blanket. As we lifted him into the back seat of the car, Potter and Woodrow carried Luke to the ambulance. He lay on the stretcher under sheets.

The two of us went out the gate with the shattered lock, then drove in silence through the town. Lights were on in the houses. People already knew.

When we reached my house, we carried Dusty around the yard to the back porch. It must have been close to midnight, and all about us was the gray shifting fog; everything seemed insubstantial. We were both still barefoot. My shirt and trousers were covered in blood, Luke's and Dusty's, crusty patches of it on my arms and hands. Arch's eyes had the wide glassy look of one in shock, as mine must also have had. We were standing unsteadily and wordlessly, on the lawn, when the porch door swung open. My mother lurched down the steps in her nightgown. She was drunk.

"They could've killed you!" she shrieked, her voice carrying through the neighborhood. "I told you to stop going out there!" Coming closer, she pointed her sharp finger at my face. As Arch and I moved away from her, she began to wail, hysterical moans of anguish such as I had never heard. "When will you ever listen to me?" She cried in great forlorn sobs. Within seconds, it seemed, Mrs. Griffin had appeared from next door. "Now, Ella," she said, "please calm yourself down. Come with me." She took my mother by the arm. "She'll spend the night

with me," she said to me, leading her away. "Are you boys all right? Swayze, call me if you need me."

I followed Arch to his Plymouth. When he left, his headlights caught the outline of a police car parked across the way. I learned later that it would remain there through the night.

I retreated into the house to my room, turned off the light, lay on the bed in my clothes. I was at the final disorienting shore of emptiness and depletion; I felt dead. I heard the inner whispers of death. The pain and confusion and guilt mingled and ascended in a chimera of hideous blurred images and sounds: Luke and Dusty on a piney hill, a swift exploding stab of light. Then sometime later, out of my delirium, I became aware of a benign distant sound, a knocking. It began in a dull reverie, fine and indistinct, as a door opens and closes in the ageless wind.

"*Swayze.*"

I opened my eyes and listened.

"*Swayze.*"

In my daze I got to my feet and approached the screened window. Below, on the lawn, was a dubious silhouette. I could barely see outside, but I knew who it was.

I made my way through the kitchen, down the steps onto the cool, dewy grass. She stepped out of the fog and stood before me. There she was, the lost girl.

"Oh, look at you!"

She came to me and embraced me. "I love you," she whispered. "I've always loved you."

She began to cry, little rippling pulsations wracking her. I felt them on my chest, and her tears on my tearless cheek. "I've missed you so. Come back to me." She lifted her face and kissed me, and I could feel the beating of her heart on mine, and I smelled again the scent of her.

In suffering and uncertainty the truth is often revealed. Suddenly, out of all of it, all the fear and dishonor and love, all that had been irretrievably lost on this night that would dwell with me forever, I too began to cry, in dizzying spasms like the gushing of a wound, and I held her closely to me. "Georgia, I ran. I'm so ashamed."

In our embrace we fell awkwardly to the ground, our backs against the elm my father and I had planted when I was five, and cried ourselves out in each other's arms. We lay there together a long time.

"Where's Amanda, Swayze?" she finally whispered.

"I don't know."

"Poor Amanda. Oh, *Luke*!" She took my hand, put her fingers in mine. "Swayze . . ."

"Don't talk."

In exhaustion and grief I heard my own selfish voice. "Did you do it with him?"

She touched my forehead, brushed her hand through my hair, looked into my eyes.

"No, Swayze."

Then we drifted together in a dreamless sleep. She woke me sometime later. "Swayze. It's getting cold. Let's go inside."

We went into the house, to my darkened room. I got into bed and felt her taking off my clothes. She threw them on the floor, then went out. When she returned, she locked the door behind her and turned on the lamp by the bed. She had a pan of hot water and a towel.

There was so much blood that it had dripped inside my shirt and trousers. It covered my chest and stomach, had seeped down to my legs, was clinging to the soles of my feet. She bowed before me and began gently cleaning it away. Her hair fell below her shoulders, and I could feel it on my chest, could hear her light breathing. The movements of the towel made me warm and drowsy. When she finished, she rose and switched off the light. She was once again beside me in the dark. She wrapped herself tenderly around me, and we slept.

I awoke to the stirring of the light and the sound of roosters from the Quarters. She opened her eyes and kissed me. Suddenly a key was being angrily turned in the lock, and the door to the room burst open. My mother and Georgia's stood there before us. *"Good God!"* her mother exclaimed. *"Look at them!"* Georgia leapt out of the bed, shouting, "Get out of here! Leave us alone! Don't you know *anything*?"

We buried Dusty that afternoon, Arch and Georgia and I, under the elm in back. I wrapped him in the crimson and white letter jacket that I had won for basketball and put him in the grave. The yellow-eyed cat Dusty and I had never liked wandered over from the Quarters. As I started to read from the Book of Common Prayer, my mother appeared on the back porch. She walked unsteadily toward me and grasped my shoulder tightly, her face full of anguish. Then she began sobbing and dropped to her knees. Looking up at me, she pleaded, *"Swayze, don't let me down."*

Arch and Georgia and I helped her to her feet. As she turned to go inside, I was seized with the recognition that my mourning on this terrible day was for her also and for my father, that feelings of regret and sadness for them were intertwined with the grief I felt for the loss of the beloved companion of my childhood and for the man whose life and death had moved me out of myself and into the world beyond.

After a while Georgia and Arch left me alone there in the languid breezes of May. I stood the last time before my dog and told him goodbye. Then I shoveled dirt into his grave as I had watched gravediggers do so many times that year, for Goodloe and Pine and Crosswait, for Tidwell and Williamson and Strong, and as I would see them do again soon, this time for Luke.

13

A S IT TURNED OUT, the "Taps" for Luke would be our last.

It was an overcast afternoon, much like the one nearly a year before when Luke had found the spot for my echo, with a hot breeze and muffled thunder and intermittent rain. The creamy white blossoms of my magnolia were warm to the touch and deeply scented. Luke had been such a part of these graveside rituals that I could hardly imagine not seeing him today.

In my dull, throbbing sorrow, as I waited alone under the tree with my trumpet, I withdrew the jackknife Georgia had given me on my birthday and carved Luke's initials, then mine, into the bark, just as Miles Featherstone had done on the elm near the boulevard in 1901. You can visit the Fisk's Landing cemetery today and find this small gesture to immutability; long after the last mansion in Tara Estates has crumbled to ruin, it will surely remain. Gazing out at the familiar terrain and the old town there before me, I felt a haunted sense of endless earth, of inexhaustible and unremitting skies, of the heavens infinite and far away.

I grieved for Luke, and I knew in my inmost heart that I would live forever with my disgrace.

It began to rain harder. Soon the cortege came, led by Potter in the new hearse. Luke's C.O. from New England was there; Georgia and Idella King and Asphalt Thomas had brought Amanda. The pageantry of the grave unfolded and was followed by Arch's "Taps."

As I started my echo, it came to me that what we really had been playing all that year was a song to everyone resting in this graveyard, to everyone I had ever cared for, to my own distant progeny, as if in all those months here and at Locust Grove and Blackjack and the river town on the bluffs, Arch and I had been carrying on a secret conversation, just between ourselves, and that I had been giving answer to his question, over the grave and beyond it, about death in life, about the passing generations in their own solicitudes, about flawed people and all their dark inheritance:

> Day is done,
> Gone the sun,
> From the lake,
> From the hills,
> From the sky.
> Rest in peace,
> Soldier brave,
> God is nigh.

The notes from my trumpet rose in the unresisting air, and I closed my eyes against the tears.

A man who had crawled on his belly all the way across Europe was gunned down in his own home. And the murderers got away with it. That is the way it was then. But it turned out to be the last time such a thing happened in Fisk's Landing.

Luke's cousin Lieutenant Billy Permenter acquired his points and came home unharmed. There were no parades for Permenter or for the others who followed.

Amanda and Durley went through with their divorce. Amanda had conquered adversity before, and she found the strength and courage to do so again. She moved to Atlanta, as she and Luke had planned. She taught piano there and several years later married a music professor at Emory. She never returned to Fisk's Landing.

Durley inherited his father's plantation and invested much of his money in shopping malls and suburban developments. Although he amassed a small fortune, the coming of depressed cotton prices, political change, and civil rights irrevocably altered plantation ways, and the Godbold hegemony was never the same.

Arch now owns his father's store and still plays the trumpet in the dance band called the Merry Makers. Asphalt Thomas is the superintendent of the public schools. Most of the others are gone: my mother, Potter, Woodrow, Idella King, Lank.

Georgia's parents forced her that fall to attend a private girls' school in Virginia. She begged them not to make her go. But she had no choice in the matter. It was what they wanted.

At first we wrote to each other constantly. She deplored the school, its airs and pretensions. "We'll have to go to college together, Swayze. Let's pick one a thousand miles from home. That time's not too far away."

But it turned out that it was. Georgia and I didn't go to college together, and our lives outside of Fisk's Landing went separate ways. I now understand that in the course of an existence, friends and loves move in and out of one's life. Often we will not know the whereabouts of those once as close to us as anything on earth, or what they are feeling or remembering. Close relationships oscillate so between tranquility and destruction, between heat and ice, between storms of affection and deserts of fear and alienation. Under the guise of friendship and love, words can be exploding bullets. Old fidelities wither, and love dies as the lovers go on living, in the terrible fluidity of life on this planet. In our aching and restless hearts we are burdened by an elemental isolation. Surely we are basically alone; we go into the darkness alone, as we came into the light alone. We all want someone to save us from ourselves, neglecting that the savior too needs saving.

Yet love is all — moments come, and people, to assuage the loneliness, and even help us forget it for a time, or deny it, a few small islands of warmth and belonging to sustain us if we are lucky, and so it was then with Georgia and me, with Amanda and Luke, with all of us.

But for years I thought that what was most precious and dear led only to suffering, and that love was something I could not have. In school at Sewanee, I felt as though I were indelibly marked with sorrow and memory and shame, yet the place salvaged my soul, sharing with me its serene beauty and isolation, its love of poetry and the past, its sustaining peace and grace. I spent many hours in the ancient Anglican chapel there, lost in reverie.

Set beside the slow, dalliant days of youth, why must time dwindle so swiftly as one ages? Just as we begin to perceive the complexity of the puzzle, to ponder its disparate pieces, we must rush before the hour grows too late. "Happiness leaves such slender records," it has been written. "It is the dark days that are so voluminously recorded." And so I wander desolately now to that time in my life. I have now and again since that year in Fisk's Landing yielded to a fatalism about the terrible confusions of life, believing that there is little order or reason to it, that the eternal experience is all we ever have.

I have a vivid recurring dream of an echo. I am standing alone under the magnolia tree as the mourners disperse below. The old veterans have stacked their rifles. Potter and Woodrow are folding the chairs. The gravediggers have reappeared from their hidden places. Soon four figures gradually approach me from the lower sweep of the hill. At first they are dim and indistinct. Through a diaphanous mist I try to make them out. They come closer, and then they find me and stand lovingly before me: Georgia and Luke and Amanda and Dusty! I am with them again, and the accumulated past rises before me, and, beyond, the town itself, in all its sad and wonderful seasons, and the consuming earth where we briefly lived. And now I see that the earth — this restless, powerful land — is gentle too in its eternal promise of a place where all our troubled kind can rest when day is done.

Acknowledgments

Taps had special meaning for Willie. He conceived this novel very early in his writing life, probably even before he wrote his first book, *North Toward Home*. He worked on it intermittently for most of his life and completed a draft in the late 1980s. Throughout the 1990s during our marriage, he talked to me often about *Taps,* his love for it and the deletions and refinements he planned to make. Sometimes he even read sections aloud, and we discussed them. Now and again, he worked on the manuscript, making explicit notations in the margins. Unfortunately he died before he was able to carry them out, and I was left to finish the process. Although I had some hesitation about becoming immersed in the work so soon after his death, this experience was ultimately a uniquely fulfilling one — a sweet and lovely conversation with Willie. As always, I learned much from him about words and life, and even more about his tender, sorrowful, loving, full heart.

I wish to thank many persons, known and unknown to me, who provided Willie with valuable reminiscences and discussed the broader truths of the book, including Charles and Cornelia Henry, David Sansing, Dean Faulkner and Larry Wells, Ed Perry, and the Verner Holmes family, especially Vern Holmes, Jr., who allowed Willie the use of his cabin on the Bogue Chitto

River to complete much of the writing of *Taps*. Shaye Areheart was also a longtime admirer and supporter of this book.

In my own work, I shall be forever indebted to my friends Carol Cox and Ruth Williams, who read the manuscript and gave me thoughtful and important editorial advice. Hunter Cole graciously answered my many questions about natural and cultural phenomena of Mississippi. Jill Conner Browne, Carol Daily, Susanne Dietzel, David Rae Morris, Peyton Prospere, Seetha Srinivasan, and Anne Stascavage provided unwavering support and encouragement whenever I needed it. I would have been lost without my dedicated and cheerful assistant, Cristie Watts. The wise counsel and friendship of Willie's agent, Theron Raines, were indispensable to me.

Finally, I am grateful to Janet Silver, editor in chief of adult trade books at Houghton Mifflin, who was committed to this story from the beginning, and to the many other wonderful and talented people there — especially editor Susan Canavan, for her invaluable insights about the book and expert management of the editorial process; Jayne Yaffe Kemp, senior manuscript editor, for her keen eye and meticulous work; Bridget Marmion, director of marketing; Lori Glazer, director of publicity; Christina Smith, marketing manager; and designers Michaela Sullivan and Robert Overholtzer. Houghton Mifflin published Willie's first book. I know how very happy he would be that Houghton Mifflin is also the publisher of *Taps,* his last.

— JoAnne Prichard Morris

Willie Morris is the author of *North Toward Home,
New York Days, My Dog Skip, My Cat Spit McGee,*
and numerous other works of fiction and nonfiction.
As the imaginative and creative editor of *Harper's
Magazine* in the 1960s, he published such writers as
William Styron, Gay Talese, David Halberstam, and
Norman Mailer and was a major influence in chang-
ing our postwar literary and journalistic history. He
died in August 1999 at the age of sixty-four.